Long Peace Street

Manchester University Press

Long Peace Street

A walk in modern China

Jonathan Chatwin

Manchester University Press

The right of Jonathan Chatwin to be identified as the author of this work has been asserted by him in accordance with the Copyright, Designs and Patents Act 1988.

Published by Manchester University Press
Altrincham Street, Manchester M1 7JA

www.manchesteruniversitypress.co.uk

British Library Cataloguing-in-Publication Data
A catalogue record for this book is available from the British Library

ISBN 978 1 5261 3157 7   hardback
ISBN 978 1 5261 5173 5   paperback

First published 2019

The publisher has no responsibility for the persistence or accuracy of URLs for any external or third-party internet websites referred to in this book, and does not guarantee that any content on such websites is, or will remain, accurate or appropriate.

Typeset by Servis Filmsetting Ltd, Stockport, Cheshire

For Kate

The history of Peking is the history of China in miniature, for the town, like the country, has shown the same power of taking fresh masters and absorbing them. Both have passed through dark hours of anarchy and bloodshed. Happily both possess the vitality to survive them. (Juliet Bredon, *Peking: A Historical and Intimate Description of Its Chief Places of Interest*, 1920)

Good times, bustling activity, and color and sound were everywhere. The abrupt early summer heat was like a magical charm that bewitched the old city. Disregarding death, disaster, and hardships, it would flex its muscles, when the time was right, and mesmerize the vast populace, who would, dreamlike, sing its praises. Filthy, beautiful, decrepit, lively, chaotic, peaceful, and charming, that was the magnificent early summer city of Beijing. (Lao She, *Camel Xiangzi*, 1937)

To see what is in front of one's nose needs a constant struggle. (George Orwell, 'In Front of Your Nose', 1946)

Contents

Contents

Plates

List of plates

Unless specified, all images are the author's own. Images at chapter openings courtesy of Kate Chatwin-Ridout.

Preface

Long Peace Street is empty. Boots marching in lockstep and the distant echo of cannon fire are the only noises which disturb the artificial peace reigning here in the heart of China's capital. At the head of a procession of 96 soldiers, three officers march northward along a line bisecting Tiananmen Square, carrying the red and gold flag of the People's Republic of China. As the cannon fire ceases, and with flourishing trumpets, the flag is raised and thousands of voices singing China's national anthem ring out.

It is 1 October 2019, and the People's Republic of China is celebrating the 70th anniversary of its founding. These decadal celebrations on 'National Day' are always lavish affairs, but this one has especial symbolic power for China's leadership: in reaching its 70th anniversary, the People's Republic of China has managed one more year than the USSR. As President Xi Jinping says in his opening speech:

> Seventy years are but a fleeting moment in human history. But for the Chinese people, for our nation, these have been 70 years of epoch-making changes. The Chinese nation has realised a tremendous transformation: it has stood up, grown rich and is becoming stronger; it has come to embrace the brilliant prospects of national renewal.

Having delivered his speech, Xi emerges from the central gate of Tiananmen – the Gate of Heavenly Peace – in a customised black 'Red Flag' L5 limousine, head and torso sticking out of an opening in the roof, an array of microphones in front of him. He is driven east along Long Peace Street, past ranks of military personnel and hardware. Periodically, he addresses them, alternating between 'Tongzhimen Hao!' – 'Greetings Comrades!' – and 'Tongzhimen Xinkule' – 'Comrades, you have worked so hard!'. By the time he reaches the end of the line, Xi, somberly attired in a black Mao suit, has covered two miles of Long Peace Street, Beijing's main west-east thoroughfare and the so-called 'Number One Street of China'. The parade can now properly begin: it will take two hours for the 15000 military personnel, 580 pieces of military equipment, and tens of thousands of civilians to pass east to west along Long Peace Street, in front of Tiananmen. One float features an enormous portrait of a smiling, waving Xi Jinping. It smiles and waves in the direction of the enormous portrait of Mao Zedong hanging below the balcony of the Gate of Heavenly Peace. The real life Xi Jinping, standing on that balcony above, smiles and waves back at his portrait.

The parade is a grand piece of political theatre, aimed at imbuing a domestic audience, subjected to live three-hour coverage on state television, with a sense of national pride. It also has a message for the wider world, emphasising the military self-sufficiency and technological advancement of the People's Republic of China. For all watching, however, there is one key message implicit in the parade's symbolism, articulated by Xi Jinping in his speech, and reiterated by Chinese media in the days after the parade: that of China's strength and global significance on this, its seventieth 'birthday'. 'No force can ever undermine China's status, or stop the Chinese people and nation from marching forward,' he tells the thousands watching from Tiananmen Square.

These parades along Long Peace Street have become a reliable part of the nation's self-celebration, and, as with any anniversary, provide useful waymarkers by which to plot change in the way China regards itself. All look back to 1 October 1949, when Mao Zedong stood on the balcony of the Gate of Heavenly Peace and announced the founding of the People's Republic of China. Significantly, on that day, the foreign attendees were drawn primarily from the Soviet bloc and included the numerous advisors who would have significant influence over the style and substance of the nation-building, and reshaping of Beijing, that would soon ensue. Indeed, Long Peace Street itself, and the landmark buildings built along it over the course of the next decade, were inspired by Soviet ideas of what a modern socialist capital should look like. These radical alterations to the imperial pattern of Beijing were completed in advance of the first ten year anniversary parade, in October of 1959.

The 1959 parade occurred against the unmentioned backdrop of the Great Leap Forward, Mao's plan to speed up production in industry and agriculture, which led to millions of deaths in the resulting famine. By 1969, the Great Leap Forward was a distant memory, for China was now gripped by a new fervour: the Cultural Revolution. The October parade that year heavily featured ranks of fervent Red Guards in militaristic garb, waving their 'little red books' of Chairman Mao's sayings. Floats bore the ubiquitous slogans of the era: 'Long live Chairman Mao!' 'Long live Mao Zedong thought!'.

Some years have been notable for the lack of an anniversary parade. In 1979, three years after Mao's death, the 1 October celebration was cancelled as the country continued its rehabilitation after the long decade of the Cultural Revolution: China's new leader, Deng Xiaoping, would hold a parade in 1984 instead, marking the 35th anniversary of CCP rule and foregrounding the modernisations so fundamental to China's 'Reform and Opening.'

In 1989, the asphalt of Long Peace Street still bore the marks of the tanks which had rolled down in on the night of 3 June to clear the street and Tiananmen Square. The parade was cancelled, and amid tight security, leaders including the then 85-year-old Deng Xiaoping watched a display of dancing and fireworks instead.

September 2020 should have seen another military parade along Long Peace Street to mark the 75th anniversary of China's 'victory' in the War of Resistance against Japanese Aggression – known in the west as the Second World War. The previous anniversary, held on 3 September 2015 to mark seventy years since the end of the war, had seen the same grandiose celebrations as the National Day parades, though with a more international feel to the audience, with leaders including President Vladimir Putin, Park Geun-hye of South Korea, and UN Secretary-General Ban Ki-moon in attendance (the latter's presence drawing the ire of the Japanese government). The cancellation of this year's parade tells, of course, of a dramatic historical moment experienced not just in China, but globally.

The COVID-19 pandemic has reshaped the world, but more pertinently to this preface, has distorted and hardened global attitudes to China. Those of us who write on the country now face the prospect that travel and research has become even more profoundly difficult than it used to be. This is not only the result of COVID-19 travel restrictions; global and national politics have also had an influence. In March 2020, the Chinese government kicked out American journalists working for *The New York Times*, *The Wall Street Journal* and *The Washington Post*, in response to restrictions imposed by the Trump administration in the United States. To be properly understood, the shifting nature of the People's Republic requires its stenographers: those who watch, observe and note. Not since the end of the Mao era has that task been so challenging.

When I walked across Beijing along Long Peace Street in 2016, the prospect of such a momentous shift never occurred to me, of course, despite the increasingly restrictive nature of life in Xi Jinping's China. My walk, and this account of it, was never an attempt to offer a totalising account of the country at the time, but drew on what I had found valuable in my wide readings on China: the sense of a place as it is in that particular moment, free of awareness of the future. Those who attempt to look prescient when writing about China more often than not end up looking like fools – there is a slew of Western writing from the 1930s and 40s which confidently predicts the imminent de-

Preface

mise of the Chinese Communist Party – and I wanted to write a book which dealt with the immediacy of travelling through a place. I had pinned above my desk an aphorism of George Orwell's; it came from an essay of his, and asserted that: "to see what is in front of one's nose needs a constant struggle".

By the time I next return to Beijing, the city will doubtless have changed again, and the symbolic power of Long Peace Street will have subtly shifted once more. Here, though, is how it felt to walk along it on two sweltering days in August 2016.

Jonathan Chatwin
Birmingham, England
November 2020

Acknowledgements

My thanks go to Tom Dark at Manchester University Press for his unfailing support and editorial guidance. A number of people read early drafts or helped to shape my thinking on how best to approach the project: thanks to Sebastian Hesse-Kastein, Jeff Wasserstrom, Michael Meyer, Alec Ash, Jeremiah Jenne, Shuishan Yu and Paul French. Particular thanks to Michael Aldrich who drew on his exhaustive knowledge of Beijing and its history in offering advice on the manuscript. Any mistakes which remain are, of course, my own.

Thanks also to Peter Gordon, Christopher Cullen, Chris Lipinksi, Li Shan Shan, Ed Pemberton, David Cotter and Chen Xi. Early extracts from chapters 4 and 18 were published in the *Los Angeles Review of Books: China Channel*: my thanks to Alec and Jeff once again for publishing them.

This book owes numerous debts of inspiration: the writings of Roger Deakin, Robert Macfarlane, Bruce Chatwin, Rebecca West, William Dalrymple, V.S. Naipaul and Peter Matthiessen pushed me to think about place and travel in subtler, deeper ways.

The comedian Peter Cook used to tell the story of a man he met at a party who began their conversation by declaring that he was writing a book: 'Oh really?', Cook replied. 'Neither am I.' That this book *is* now finally written is down in no small part to the support of my

Acknowledgements

wife, Kate Chatwin-Ridout: for her patience during those hours and days when I was working away on this manuscript; for her enthusiasm for the project from inception to completion; for her wonderful artwork; and for accompanying me as I sought out yet another historical site in Beijing and beyond, I can only offer my insufficient but heartfelt thanks.

Timeline

Summer 1900	Anti-Christian rebels, known as the Boxers, hold the foreigners of the Legation Quarter hostage for fifty-five days. As an international coalition arrives to relieve those besieged, the Empress Dowager flees the capital.
October 1911	Anti-imperial revolution spreads from China's south.
February 1912	The last Qing Emperor, Puyi, abdicates, bringing to an end imperial rule in China. Yuan Shikai becomes President of the Republic.
1915	Yuan declares himself Emperor of China.
1916	Yuan dies. The warlord era begins, with control of the country divided amongst military cliques. It will last until 1927.
4 May 1919	Thousands of Beijing students protest the Treaty of Versailles at Tiananmen. The resulting intellectual crusade becomes known as the May Fourth Movement.
1921	The Chinese Communist Party (CCP) is founded.
1924	The last Emperor is evicted from the Forbidden City by an invading warlord.

Timeline

1927–37   The Nationalist Party (Guomindang) take charge of the country. The capital is moved from Beijing to Nanjing.

1934–35   The Red Army undertakes the 'Long March' from southern to northern China.

1937   Under Japanese attack, the Guomindang move their capital from Nanjing to Wuhan, and then to Chongqing.

1945   Japan surrenders. The Civil War between the Guomindang and CCP erupts once more.

1 October 1949   Mao Zedong declares the founding of the People's Republic of China from Tiananmen. The Guomindang retreat to Taiwan.

1958–62   The policies of the Great Leap Forward cause widespread famine.

1966   The Cultural Revolution begins; its stated aim is to destroy the 'Four Olds': Old Customs, Old Culture, Old Habits and Old Ideas.

1972   US President Richard Nixon visits Beijing.

1976   Mao Zedong dies.

1978   'Reform and opening-up' begins: economic restrictions begin to be gradually relaxed. In Beijing, 'Democracy Wall' becomes a focal point for political protest.

1989   Protests occur in Beijing and other cities across China. Military action brings these to a violent end in early June.

1997   Hong Kong returns to Chinese rule.

2001   China's bid to host the Olympics is successful.

2008   Beijing hosts the Summer Olympic Games.

2013   Xi Jinping becomes President of the People's Republic.

Timeline

2018   China removes the two-term limit on the presidency, allowing President Xi to remain in charge indefinitely.

Introduction

On a sultry August day, I set out to walk a straight line across Beijing.

A taxi had brought me that morning through the city's western suburbs to the literal end of the road. At a makeshift barrier, a young police officer waved us to a standstill. 'You can't go any further', he told the taxi driver, glancing pointedly at the foreigner in the back-seat, 'It's a building site beyond here: residents only'. Behind him and the barrier he tended, an almost empty stretch of gloss-black tarmac ran west.

I told the driver I would get out. 'Here?' he asked, raising an eyebrow in the rear-view mirror. Here was the very western limit of Beijing, where the frayed edge of the city rubbed against the rough dun stone of the Western Hills. Besides the checkpoint, there was nothing here but a few brick buildings, the forbidden road ahead and the construction site which bordered it, fenced off with blue corrugated iron panels. 'Here', I repeated, proffering my money.

I stepped out onto the roadside. The sky was uncharacteristically clear for Beijing, and the heat reflected back from the tarmac. As the taxi drove away, the same police officer, unsmiling but not unfriendly, asked me why I had come out here. 'I'm walking across the city, to Sihui East', I told him, naming the subway station on the opposite side of the city which was my destination. He paused. 'That's a long way!', he said, with the up-down intonation reserved in Chinese for the expression of incredulity.

It was: about nineteen miles, all told, from west to east along Chang'an Jie – the road which his barrier so abruptly abridged. Beijing, though now diffuse and massive, still roughly adheres to the symmetrical system imposed by its imperial founders, with most roads running either north to south, or east to west. The horizontal axis of this system is Chang'an Jie, which runs, arrow-straight and ten lanes wide in places, through the heart of the city. At its mid-point, Chang'an Jie splices the very centre of the Middle Kingdom, separating the Forbidden City, the expansive residence of generations of Chinese emperors, from Tiananmen Square, the shadowless public space built by the Communists to reinforce the glory of New China.

My aim was to cover the distance from this westerly point to the eastern suburbs over two days – enough time to allow for pauses and diversions – reaching the centre-point of Tiananmen Square by the close of my first afternoon.

'Why don't you just take the subway?' the officer asked me: Line One ran directly below Chang'an Jie, terminating at the station which was my destination. 'It'll be cooler, and from all the way out here, you'd be sure to get a seat.' He wiped his brow, an acknowledgement of the heat, which was already into the thirties despite the early hour. It was an observation I could not refute, and I pictured the scene from

Introduction

his point of view: a foreigner, out in the industrial wasteland of west Beijing on a searing August morning, talking about walking nearly twenty miles across the city. Mumbling something bland in reply, I shuffled away.

Chang'an Jie had been my first point of orientation when I came to Beijing. Despite – or perhaps because of – the apparent logic of its geographical system, Beijing can be a confounding city to navigate. Cardinal points often seem to move around at will, whilst the constant physical reimagining of the city means that even when navigation does not fail you, your destination may very well not conform to map or to memory. The broad unambiguous straightness of Chang'an Jie, with the landmarks of the Forbidden City and Tiananmen Square at its centre point, quickly became a comforting and familiar sight as I began to explore the city.

I had lived out in the remote western suburbs, and the road – along with the subway line beneath it – conveyed me east towards those parts of the city where I could access some of the comforts of home, or become once again an anonymous foreigner. As I travelled, I would listen to Chinese language recordings on my headphones; one early lesson taught to ask for directions: '*Chang'an Jie ne? Shi zai zher ma?*', it would posit, repeating in English: 'Where is Long Peace Street? Is it here?'

Long Peace Street is a poor translation in many ways. The character *chang* (长), though derived from one meaning 'to stretch or make long', in this context signifies 'eternal' or 'perpetual', and alludes to the name of another ancient capital of China, home to the illustrious Han and Tang dynasties: Chang'an (长安), or the City of Eternal Peace – known today as Xi'an (or Western Peace). The character *an* (安) indicates the 'peace' of this place name. It places the radical for roof above that for a woman, and suggests both security and tranquillity. A more poetic interpretation of the name would thus be 'Street of Eternal Peace', whilst, to a literalist, it could well be simply

Chang'an Street – just as London has its Oxford Street and Shanghai its Nanjing Road.[1]

Yet, irrespective of the nuances of translation, the inclusion of the characters 长 and 安 in the street's name cannot seem anything other than jarringly inappropriate to anyone with a cursory knowledge of China's past. In historical terms, this street has rarely been peaceful for very long. Many are the conflicts – large and small, physical and intellectual, public and private – that have played out on or very near to Long Peace Street. This is a storied stretch of the Middle Kingdom, littered with numerous reminders of the tumultuous and unrelenting drama of the country's history.

In particular, Chang'an Jie has, over the last century or so, stood witness to a seismic shift in the political and cultural terrain of China. With a whimper, an imperial system that had endured for millennia abruptly ended in 1912, and over thirty years passed in the chaotic attempt to impose a sustainable new administration in its place. As it so often does, conflict and uncertainty engendered autocracy and the imposition of order by a cruel hand. And even this did not last, for – unsatisfied with simply ruling its people – the Communist government of the People's Republic of China, installed as rulers in the last year of the 1940s, decided it was necessary to forcibly change them, and implemented catastrophic social engineering projects to modify their behaviour and reshape the nation.

If the twenty-first century will be looked back on, as some have said, as the 'Chinese Century', the twentieth was something very nearly the opposite of that: a period in which the country was brought to the precipice, and forced to contemplate the nature of its existence. A walk along Long Peace Street – punctuated as it is by the relics and reminders of this traumatic period – offers an opportunity to stroll through the country's modern history; a history ordered not chronologically, but rather physically. The street came to seem to me the equivalent of a geological core sample, in which, just as each layer of the cylindrical rock relates the story of a physical era, so each intersection, each building, each sign and statue seemed to have something to say about the decades of turbulence which begot modern China, and which continue to crucially influence the way the country views itself and its future.

Even the existence of Chang'an Jie in its present form is the result of violent assaults on the principles which guided those who originally designed the city. Imperial tradition had long dictated that it was the north to south axis of a city which should be accorded greatest importance in siting ceremonial buildings. Due to this abiding notion, many of Beijing's most well-known historical sites – the Drum Tower, the Bell Tower, the Forbidden City and the Emperor's throne within it, Tiananmen and the square to its south – run along the vertical centre line of the city: its so-called 'Dragon's Vein'.

The transformation of east-west Chang'an Jie to become Beijing's pre-eminent thoroughfare resulted first from the Japanese refashioning of the city during their occupation of Northern China from 1937 to 1945 – and thence from Mao Zedong's brutal assault on Beijing's architectural heritage. From the rubble of the old world, Long Peace Street would emerge as the 'Number One Street of China'.

In 1949, when the Chinese Communist Party (CCP) finally prevailed in an interminable Civil War against the Nationalist Party, or *Guomindang*, which had rumbled on since the late 1920s, they chose Beijing as their capital.

When the Nationalists had been in charge of the country, the capital was at Nanjing, not far from China's eastern coast. China's shape is often compared to that of a cockerel; if one visualises this, Nanjing is on its puffed-out chest, whereas Beijing is further up on the curve of its neck. Nanjing officially became the capital in 1928, and remained so for almost a decade. However, as the Japanese chased the Nationalists inland in the late 1930s, the capital would be moved to two increasingly withdrawn cities along the Yangtze River, ending up deep in the belly of the cockerel.[2]

Mao Zedong, China's new leader, was ambivalent towards Beijing; he was himself a southerner and something of a provincial, having grown up in rural Hunan, a mountainous region nearly a thousand miles to the south of the capital. His first experience of the city was in 1918–19 at its eponymous university – the finest in China – though he attended not as a student, but rather worked in the university library as an assistant librarian. Mao later told the journalist Edgar Snow that: 'My office was so low that people avoided me. One of my tasks was to register the names of people who came to read newspapers, but to most of them I didn't exist as a human being'.[3]

The notion of Beijing as somewhat superior – a place of equal parts intellectualism and bureaucracy, set distinctly apart from the working masses – would bother Mao when he became China's leader three decades later. The city had been the spiritual and political centre of the nation and home to China's imperial rulers for most of the last seven centuries, and was thus a monument in glazed tile and red ochre wall to all that the Communists had seemingly fought to overthrow: an antiquated feudal system in which those inhabiting the broad hushed courtyards of Beijing dictated the nature of existence for the Chinese masses. They had come to power to rid China of the inequities of its past, fierce critics of the passivity and profligacy of the Qing dynasty: were they now really to adopt its capital?

Mao set about addressing these concerns through the radical alteration – and in many cases the destruction – of the city's architectural design, and the culture and history it represented. The city's long past, at least as embodied by its bricks and mortar, would largely become something that existed only in the memories of those old enough to have seen it for themselves.

It was along Chang'an Jie that much of this change was most evident. The city walls and gates were razed, and the street joined up, widened, straightened and lengthened, partly to allow the military parades which still process along it each 1 October to mark

Introduction

'China's birthday' – the anniversary of the founding of the People's Republic of China in 1949. Along the street, old thoroughfares and houses were cleared, and a series of elaborate Sino-Soviet buildings were constructed, designed to glorify New China, including the city's Military Museum, its main train station, and the Great Hall of the People – China's equivalent of Capitol Hill or the Palace of Westminster. Tiananmen Square was refashioned into the sterile granite rectangle it remains today. In a conscious subversion of imperial tradition, Chang'an Jie thus became the central axis of Beijing, along which the Communists controversially oriented their new capital. The north–south axis was China's past – and the broad avenue of Chang'an Jie came to represent its future.[4]

However, partly because of the symbolic weight attached to Beijing's new east–west axis and the various offices of the government which line it, Long Peace Street also became a niggling source of anxiety for the Party leadership, offering a focal point for those frustrated by the strictures of life in the People's Republic of China.

Most prominent amongst these protests are those which took place in 1989 on and around Tiananmen Square. The paranoia generated by the events of early June that year ensures that both the square and the stretch of Chang'an Jie which runs between it and the Forbidden City, stretching west to Zhongnanhai – the sprawling compound which houses China's President – remains one of the most heavily policed public spaces in the world.

When, in the aftermath of the death of the popular leader Hu Yaobang, students occupied the square, demanding greater freedoms from the government, and building a papier-mâché statue christened the 'Goddess of Democracy', the Chinese Communist Party initially hesitated in their response, before fatefully calling in the troops. Along the streets to the west and east of Tiananmen – and along Chang'an Jie in particular – pitched battles took place between the People's Liberation Army (PLA) and the people, who had built roadblocks

7

at key intersections. Even now, no one is quite sure how many died, but the memory of the massacre came to haunt this section of Long Peace Street – almost literally for a time, as one of the city's historical chroniclers has noted:

> In the months after June 4th, the government erased all traces of damage save for one. Western journalists spoke of hearing an eerie rumbling rising from the tires of their cars whenever they passed over a certain section of Chang An East Avenue where scars from tank tracks proved to be intractable against efforts to erase them. The cries of wandering ghosts, or so said some elderly folks.[5]

June 1989 was just one occasion when this road heard the cries and shouts of protest and public demonstration. 1919; 1976; 1978: they had all seen moments of popular protest which concisely vocalised swirling feelings of discontent in the nation, and which led, in some way, to a moment which still refuses to be entirely erased from the collective memory, despite the best efforts of China's leaders. And, despite the state response that June, Long Peace Street continues to draw those who chafe against the constraints of the state, pulled by the memories of predecessors who have trodden its pavements before in search of justice or freedom, and the centralised power embodied by the imposing buildings which line it.

A walk along Long Peace Street prompts thoughts not only of the story of China's recent past, but also conjures a lingering sense of uncertainty regarding the city's present and its future. Over the centuries, Beijing has demonstrated an impressive capacity to adapt to the challenges of geography, climate and economics, as well as the demands of new leaders, retaining its status as China's first city somewhat against the odds. The city is currently being reimagined once more.

Skyscrapers now define the eastern skyline of a city once notorious for its lack of verticality, whilst accretions of uniform apartment blocks push at its periphery, belted by an ever-expanding series of ring roads. The residential districts of the old city, defined by the narrow, labyrinthine alleys known as *hutong*, remain in a state of permanent revolution: for many years helpless victims of the developer's wrecking ball, those that are left are now being reformed, tarted up to discourage the small-scale commerce which has come to define everyday life along them, or replaced entirely with expensive parodies of their former selves.

Meanwhile, in recent years, government officials have been refining an ambitious scheme to incorporate the city into a 130 million person megalopolis, which will spread across the North China Plain. The plan, intended to limit the population of Beijing proper, would see some of its bureaucracy shipped out to nearby satellite towns, leaving it to perform so-called 'capital functions', whilst also discouraging the low-paid out-of-towners who have built and serviced the city for many years from staying there.

If what defines a city, or indeed a country, is not its pure physical being, but rather the accumulation of ephemeral qualities – cultural, historical and social – specific to that place and people, perhaps the radical reconfiguration underway does not matter. This, after all, is a city which has demonstrated its ability to adapt and sustain over centuries. But though the emotion can be chalked up to the naivety or nostalgia of the outsider, it is hard not to worry, when surrounded by all this newness and change, that something more intangible, beyond simple bricks and mortar, is also being lost.

In his account of the life of the legendary Theseus, the Greek historian Plutarch presented a paradox relating to the preservation of the king's ship. It had been kept by the Athenians, Plutarch writes, for many centuries, and those tasked with its preservation had replaced the ship's timber as it rotted. Philosophers have since debated the logical problem presented by this restoration; namely whether, if one replaces every part of something, it remains the same thing. The story became, and has remained 'a standing example among the philosophers, for the logical question of things that grow; one side holding that the ship remained the same, and the other contending that it was not the same'.

The writer Juliet Bredon, reflecting on the affection of Beijingers for the life of the street, compared them to the citizens of Paris: both were born boulevardiers, she felt. Certainly, the streets and pavements of Beijing, particularly in older sections of the city, are commonly refashioned into zones for recreation and daily living. Makeshift card tables are erected on a hutong corner: a crowd of dispassionate men gathers to observe the vacillations of fortune. Toddlers play in a sand pile left behind by building workers, watched by squatting grandmothers fanning themselves. Young men sit on their haunches on the pavement of a busy street playing smartphone games, separate and alone for a moment in the midst of a chaotic city. At night, the pavement outside a hole-in-the-wall becomes a makeshift restaurant, the scent of charcoal and cumin carried on the hot air, locals squatting on pastel-coloured plastic stools with a bottle of beer and a tray of skewered mutton.

This spilling over of private life into public space is perhaps most noticeable in Beijing's parks. A day which begins with the slow-moving tai chi practitioners first thing in the morning continues with Beijing grandmothers on childminding duty in late morning and early afternoon, and synchronised groups of dancing middle-aged women in the early evening. Primary-colour collections of exercise equipment, resembling some sort of avant-garde street-art installation, draw pensioners keen to keep limber. People practise musical instruments, throw a diablo, play chess. Joggers plod the footpaths. Such casual adoption of public spaces is less evident, of course, during the hard frosts of the winter months, but even then many of the city's more venerable residents do still embark on their morning perambulations, and Beijing's lakes are given over to ice-skating.

However, walking is, and has long been, low on the city's hierarchy of transportation. In imperial times, anyone of import moved around the city in a curtained sedan chair, shouldered by servants. The narrow dirt roads of the city were scarred with deep ditches and ruts, which became quagmires during the sudden summer rains; when the weather was dry, as it most commonly is in Beijing, dust would rise from the streets. The Jesuit missionary Matteo Ricci complained of the uncivilised state of Beijing's thoroughfares some four hundred years ago, observing that 'very few streets are covered with brick or stone and those are always filthy with dust or mud. And because it rains so infrequently, the whole place is usually dust ridden'.[6] In the 1860s, Alexander Michie wrote that Beijing was celebrated for three things: its carts, its heat and its dust, adding that 'if it rained much the streets would be a sea of mud'.[7]

By the early decades of the twentieth century, rickshaws – a Japanese invention consisting of a wheeled chair with two forward-stretching arms by which it was pulled – were ubiquitous in the city. It has been estimated that, by the 1920s, rickshaw pullers and their dependants made up twenty per cent of Beijing's entire population.[8] In 1949, hand-pulled rickshaws were outlawed by the Communists, who viewed the vehicles as symbolic of the oppression of the working class; they were replaced in short order, however, by that emblem of Maoist China – the bicycle. Today, of course, Beijing's shape and feel is defined by the motor car, with the city quartered and sub-divided by the broad highways which run in a grid across it, and ringed by congested orbitals.

Though the city's streets are now smooth and paved, the weather continues to be problematic for those on foot; the clammy heat of the summer and the endless dry cold of the winter both present their own particular challenges, whilst the dust from the deserts to the north-west continues to return reliably each spring and early summer, combining with Beijing's notorious pollution to turn the city's air into a noxious stew.

Thoroughfares also indisputably continue to favour the wheeled vehicle. Pavements are generally narrow, uneven and strewn with unexpected obstacles – loudspeakers, blocks of concrete, crouching workmen brandishing acetylene torches, plastic crates of empty beer bottles – whilst crossing even relatively minor roads requires a strong constitution and the ability to accurately evaluate the willingness of oncoming drivers to cause you physical harm. These challenges are nothing new: the American nurse and writer Ellen La Motte noted in 1916 that the streets of Beijing were full of excitement, and that navigating them on foot was 'a matter of shoving oneself through the throng, dodging under camels' noses, avoiding wheelbarrows, bumping against donkeys, standing aside to let officials' carriages go by'.[9]

The perversity of my notion of walking across the city – particularly in the August heat – was met with reactions ranging from benign confusion to utter incredulity by most of the Beijingers to whom I told my plans. I took heart, though, from Simone de Beauvoir's observation, made after her 1955 visit to China, that in walking the streets of a city, one secures an 'immediate, irrecusable experience for which no hypothesis about a city, however ingenious, can be a substitute or as instructive'.[10]

And in writing down my two-day journey across the city, it seemed somehow that I might be able to preserve this singular experience, heavy with the weight of individual and limited understanding, which I could then hold and examine, turning it slowly in the glow of history and memory to see how it caught the light.

It was an odd notion, but it was why I was here at the western edge of the city on this overheated August morning, staring hard down the broad, straight, empty lanes of Chang'an Jie. I was here in search of an encounter with China's history, with its present and with its future – but one in which I had to keep moving.

Day one

Shougang Iron and Steel to Tiananmen

1

Capital Iron and Steel – origins – the Great Leap Forward – a bad neighbour – future plans

It had been four years since my last visit to this part of town. In place of the dusty traffic barrier which obstructed my progress this morning, a traditional carved archway or *pailou* had then marked the end of Chang'an Jie and the entrance to a rambling industrial site, which covered nearly three and a half square miles and housed, at its peak, around 200,000 workers. Where now was a fenced-off construction site across which bulldozers meandered, there had once stood the largest iron and steel works in the country: *Shoudu Gang Tie Chang*, or Capital Iron and Steel Works – *Shougang* for short. Within its walls the company had provided everything required for the quotidian needs of its workforce, including canteens, schools, dormitories, clinics and shops: a necessity given its distance twelve miles from Beijing's centre.

Day one: Shougang Iron and Steel to Tiananmen

The *Shougang Daily* was the newspaper of record, with all the news that was fit to print in what essentially constituted a large industrial town.

On the occasion of my last visit in 2012, the main production line at the plant had already been closed for over a year, but all the buildings – furnaces, conveyors, cooling towers, offices – had still been intact. Cathedrals of rusted steel loomed above and all around, pacifically awaiting their fate. Faded barber-pole striped chimneys dotted the skyline. Weeds grew up between the sleepers of train tracks which had once rumbled with cargoes of coal and ore. The rusting metalwork ticked and banged in the breeze: it felt as though the workers had one day gone on their lunchbreak and simply never returned.

This was heavy industry with Chinese characteristics, with traditional architectural styles mixed in amongst the generic machinery. Adjacent to the entrance archway were offices with sweeping Chinese roof lines of glazed tile and upturned corners, whilst looming over the site on an outcrop stood a three-tiered pagoda. Motivational slogans were still emblazoned on banners around the place: *Be happy at work, and return home safely* exhorted one reassuring example. Where once had been fire and collective industry, however, silence reigned. The whole place had a melancholy feel, like a seaside resort out of season – an impression compounded by the concrete reservoirs of dark coolant water, where solitary middle-aged men tended to fishing rods cast, it seemed to me, more in hope than expectation.

Many of those manning the rods were former Shougang employees, for most of the jobs of those who had once fed the relentless machines around them had by then been shipped out to Caofeidian, a reclaimed island which juts out into Bohai Bay two hundred-odd kilometres to the south-east of Beijing. In a 2007 piece on the impending move, published on the official government website, little discontent had been reported amongst the workers about moving to Caofeidian: 'Though the employees feel sad about leaving Beijing, they are absolutely willing to relocate and are now making preparations to do just that',[1] the article asserted.

In reality, the plant's departure in 2011 hollowed out the centre of a community which had built itself around Shougang, separated as it was from the capital's main commercial areas. One retired worker told me at the time of the closure that some of those employed by the plant had continued to keep their home and family in Shijingshan, the suburb which abuts the Shougang site, and took a three-hour company bus to the new facility. Workers would spend ten days working at the plant in Hebei, and return to their families for four days off. Increasingly, however, employees were either moving, trying to find work elsewhere in the city, or taking advantage of the compensation offered for early retirement, for which the company was willing to pay between 15,000 and 30,000 yuan (between about £1,750 and £3,500) at age forty for women, and fifty for men. The promise of the site's regeneration offered the potential of jobs in the years to come, but the factory had been the beating heart of Shijingshan, and for those who cast their lines into Shougang's murky water back in 2012, there was little to be optimistic about.

Shougang was established in 1919, during the tumultuous warlord era which followed the end of China's last imperial dynasty in 1912 and a subsequent experiment with republicanism. In keeping with the Chinese Communist Party's tendency to play down the success of any endeavour dating from this period, the official history of the company emphasises that before 'liberation' in 1949, Shougang was an insubstantial plant, unable to produce steel at all, and producing cumulatively just 286,000 tons of iron in that 30 year period (in 2007 alone it produced four million tons of crude steel).[2]

In the years after 1949, however, the Communist leadership invested heavily in the plant. Shougang's location close to Beijing also chimed with Mao's desire to transform the capital from a city of intellectuals to one of the working man. Shortly after the CCP had taken control of the country, Mao had looked out from Tiananmen – the Gate of Heavenly Peace which gives its name to the square directly to its south and marks the entrance to the Forbidden City – and commented that he wanted to see a forest of chimneys as he surveyed Beijing. A few years later, still dissatisfied by the character of the city, he had asked his fellow leaders of New China whether they needed to consider moving the capital elsewhere – there were still, he felt, too few industrial workers parading in the National Day procession.[3] Between 1958 and 1960 alone, 800 factories would open in Beijing; the suburbs of the city would come to reverberate with the sound of industry.[4]

Industry – and steel in particular – became an increasing preoccupation for Mao in the first decade of Communist rule. By the late 1950s, the Chairman was concerned with providing tangible evidence of China's progress since the 1949 takeover, and steel production figures seemed to offer a way to 'magically [distill] all the complex dimensions of human activity into a single, precise figure that indicated where a country stood on the scale of evolution', as the historian Frank Dikötter has observed.[5] Mao's insecurity about China's position in the global league table meant that, beginning in 1958, he began to push to drastically increase the amount of steel produced in China, setting unfeasible national targets. By September 1958, the Chairman expected a doubling of annual production, from 5.35 million tons in 1957 to 12 million tons in 1958, whilst by 1962, around 100 million tons were somehow to be produced as part of the planned 'Great Leap Forward'. 'By that time', Mao asserted, 'it will be said that we have basically transformed the entire country'.[6]

This ambition was realised, though not in the manner he intended. The cost of the policies of industrial and agricultural reform during the Great Leap Forward was punishing, and is still being accounted by historians. In order to attempt to meet his startling targets, the government mobilised men, women and children across the country to help with the production of iron and steel. Backyard metal furnaces were constructed in their hundreds of thousands, fed by any wood that could be found, including coffins,[7] whilst existing factories like Shougang ramped up their own production, supported by collective labour. Thousands of new modern steelworks were also planned. As a young married woman from Sichuan recalls: 'In 1958 we were sent to the iron factory. In our area, everyone was requested to take part in the mass production of iron […] Every day we hammered at stones. We were told that it was the way to make iron. […] Blocks of carbon, steel sheets, and tree branches were all fed into the furnaces'.[8] The British diplomat, Percy Cradock, travelling by train from the south of China during the period of the Great Leap Forward, recalled passing endless factories emblazoned with slogans: 'Quicker, Faster, Better' and 'We're going to overtake Britain in no time in the production of steel'.[9]

This relentless focus on metal production had a calamitous environmental effect, with forests ripped up for firewood, and the land around left eroded or barren. Ironically, much of the metal produced, particularly in the backyard furnaces, was of desperately poor quality: 'the entire labour force was sent into the mountains to make iron and steel. […] We tried to make iron and steel day and night, and in the end all we got was useless slag. We had to abandon the project',[10] one worker recalled.

It was not only manufacturing numbers for iron and steel, however, that were radically over-optimistic in Mao's plan for the Great Leap Forward; the same rationale led him to believe that harvests of staple crops could be increased equally dramatically. The cult of personality which surrounded the Chairman ensured that none close to him would admit the unfeasible nature of the targets set, and this refusal to speak truth to power cascaded down from the national level to the provincial leaders, and then down through the county cadres to the rural towns and villages, with leaders at all tiers of the hierarchy overstating the production figures for crops. This meant that the proportion of grain taken by the state wildly exceeded what was sustainable to ensure that locals kept enough in reserve to feed themselves and their families. The steel-making initiative had also taken rural workers from their land, reducing the labour force available to plant and harvest crops. This all led to unimaginable famine. The starving resorted to stripping the bark from trees, or boiling the leather from their belts, in the search for something to sustain them. Some ate soil, concreting their digestive system. Other stories, darker, sadder, and reflective of the utter desperation of those terrible years, tell of people who ate the flesh of others, often family members. Estimates vary, but historians in the West generally concur that in excess of 30 million people lost their lives between 1958 and 1962 as a result of the famine which resulted from the Great Leap Forward.

When researching such controversies, I often found it illuminating to consult my copy of the official timeline of the People's Republic, optimistically subtitled *The First Sixty Years*. Published by China's Foreign Languages Press, part of the nation's soft-power apparatus, it provides an instructive summary of the official version of these pivotal moments. Its entry for the Great Leap Forward is critical, if euphemistic: 'some leaders at the central and local levels … became complacent and boastful in the face of temporary victories. […] The "Great Leap Forward" disrupted national economic order, caused vast waste in manpower and resources, and caused serious imbalances in the development of industry and agriculture'.

Shougang's status as a flagship facility ensured, however, that it expanded significantly during this period, developing its steel-making capability by building new furnaces and drafting in rural and urban workers to help keep them running twenty-four hours a day. One contemporary account tells of factory leaders calling a meeting and declaring to their 5,000-strong audience the need for a new steel furnace. Without further prompting, the workers reportedly streamed from the auditorium to a nearby cornfield where, in fourteen days, they built a new workshop. Predictably, the writer admits, the quality of the metal produced left much to be desired.[11]

Chapter 1

Permanent jobs at Shougang were highly prized: there was cachet to working in the nation's vanguard industry at its most high-profile site, and the promise of the security of the so-called 'iron rice bowl', as posts in well-supported state enterprises were known, added to the appeal; working men from the plant were viewed as particularly eligible husbands by the local women. Communist Party leaders such as Liu Shaoqi and Zhu De visited regularly to rouse the workers and spur on the production figures.

However, beginning in the 1970s, the plant began to attract a reputation as a bad neighbour to Beijing. One local who had grown up at Shougang, talking to me of the government's new plans to make this a place for healthy living and eco-tourism, noted the irony: 'Before, when Shougang was still there', she said, 'it meant one thing: pollution'. The dust and smog generated by the workings was so bad that those living in the shadow of Shougang had to avoid eating outside or hanging out their washing, which would turn from white to black overnight. Each day they would have to clean their homes, and wipe up the black dust that had settled. As production capacity increased and the city suburbs spread out towards the plant over subsequent decades, this became even more problematic. According to figures released after the closure of the main production line at Shougang, the site was, at its worst, annually producing thirty-four tons of pollution for each square kilometre of the Shijingshan district,[12] and was cited as the greatest single source of pollution in Beijing. Eventually, after Beijing secured the hosting of the 2008 Summer Olympics in the year 2001, the decision was made that Shougang needed to go.

The initial intention was to ensure that the new plant was ready in advance of the Games, but the company ultimately missed the target and, instead, agreed to scale down production by almost three quarters during the Games, spending an additional 140bn yuan (£10.3bn) on 'reducing pollution and improving energy efficiency'.[13] Many industrial sites were shuttered for the duration of the Olympics, as is common during major national and international events in Beijing, but the need to close Shougang down for this period was exacerbated by its location close to a key Olympic venue – the velodrome and mountain bike track, which had been built just a few kilometres down Chang'an Jie. Looking west from here, the Shougang site formed an expansive industrial backdrop – a view which would not be enhanced, the city leaders felt, by chimneys spewing smoke into the sky.

Production finally ceased entirely on 13 January 2011. At the pithily named 'Shougang Beijing Shijingshan Iron & Steel Main Process Discontinuation Ceremony', Politburo member Zhang Dejiang brought the curtain down on nearly a century's production at Shougang, with the company chairman promising in his speech a new future for the site, focused on the promotion of 'a civilised Beijing; a technological Beijing; and a green Beijing'.

In line with this ambition, vague but expansive plans for the redevelopment of Shougang were touted in the media after the closure, with the proposed division of the site into different areas, including a cultural and creative area, home to a proposed 'Animation City', a high-technology zone and an ecological tourist area along the Yongding River, which flows along the western periphery of the site. Civilised; technological; green – it met all the buzzword criteria: now they just had to get on and build it.

Today, more than five years on from the closure, there seemed little sign of progress in these plans beyond the building of the new, forbidden road, and the demolition of some of the former workings along it. A few administrative buildings remained, their windows now obscured by virulent ivy, whilst away to the north much of the old industrial architecture seemed to be still standing. Reuters had reported in 2014 that the redevelopment of the site was proving to be complex and costly; the Beijing municipal government had established a joint fund with Shougang to shoulder the 200 billion yuan (£22.3 billion) cost, but 'squabbling over who should pick up the bill'[14] was delaying progress. Part of the site had apparently been retained as a tourist destination, intended to give visitors an insight into what life had been like as a Shougang worker. According to its website, tourists could explore a disused blast furnace, eat a meal in a Shougang canteen, ride on one of the factory trains and even drink authentic Shougang-brand cola.

From my corner, I wandered north along a side street to see if I could catch a proper glimpse behind the blue fence panels which ran around the perimeter of the site. On the opposite side of the road ran squat one-storey buildings that had once been factory sheds and dormitories, but which had now been repurposed into makeshift dwellings, many doubling as small shops or workshops. Dirt alleyways ran between these buildings, potholed and littered with the detritus of the lives of those who made this periphery of the city their home. In the ruts, fetid green water stood in pools from the last of the summer storms. On one open stretch of ground, a couple had established bee hives and were selling honey from the back of one of the tiny vans known in Chinese as *mianbao che*, or 'bread loaf vans', for their distinctive shape. Parked in the shade, the couple glanced dozily at me from a mattress in the back of the van as I passed.

I walked up the street until the pavement ran out, unable to spot a break in the fence anywhere. I doubled back southwards and went into one of the small shops to buy a bottle of water. Irrespective of where one travels in China, from sprawling megacity to tiny village, you will rarely be far from a *xiaomaibu*, the small convenience stores and kiosks which cater to one's most essential needs, selling a miscellany of goods including soft drinks, cigarettes and snacks – vacuum-sealed tofu, chicken feet, peanuts, sunflower seeds – as well as beer and small bottles of the potent white spirit *baijiu*. This xiaomaibu was tended by a girl of around twenty, who was determinedly shovelling noodles into her mouth whilst watching a soap opera on her laptop. She barely noticed my entrance. I rooted around in the slide-top freezer, found a bottle of water and paid the girl, who looked up just long enough to establish the cost of my drink. The transaction completed, I asked her what she knew about what was planned for the Shougang site. 'It's closed now. I don't know what they're doing', she told me matter of factly. 'Most of the men have gone to Hebei.' She appeared notably incurious, considering that whatever did end up being built would be about twelve metres from the shop's front window, and seemed relieved when I stopped asking questions and left her to her television show.

This sense of apparent indifference was shared by two older men whom I met as I walked back down towards Long Peace Street; their thinking seemed to be that, though they had heard that there was a plan for the site, no one had told them what it was, and it wouldn't make much difference if they did: the government would build what they wanted to build. I mentioned the ambitious proposals I had read of – the animation city, the hi-tech district, the eco-park – but they simply smiled and said 'Perhaps'.

2

New suburbia – The City in History – the hutong – Shijingshan Amusement Park

Returning again to the corner where my taxi had deposited me earlier, I waved to the police officer under his faded red parasol, and set off eastwards along Long Peace Street. This was the beginning of my journey proper, and the straightforwardness of my route created a curious illusion, somehow making the distance ahead seem shorter, though I knew I would be doing well to reach the halfway point of Tiananmen Square before late afternoon. There was no pavement, just a wide gravel path which took me past the headquarter offices of Shougang, and then the first signs of real redevelopment, in the form of the buildings of the 'Financial Street Chang'an Center', which promised to be a 'New Business Landmark in West Beijing'. The tall towers were of curved corners and blue glass; a butterflied suspension bridge in steel and wire added a flourish to the plaza in front. Along the bottom of one of the promotional signs for the as-yet empty towers ran English text in the cut-and-paste style one becomes accustomed to in China: 'approach of interior architect material and finish detail design', it ran incoherently, adding, 'important it will not be a versace'. To one side of the new development, in an old crumbling concrete pergola smothered with bougainvillea, a group of retired men played cards and dozed in the shade. Around them, the noise of crickets oscillated in the heated gusts of wind blowing in from the west.

Along the opposite side of the street, a strip of shops and old dormitories had been razed, and from behind the rubble were emerging skeleton blocks of apartments in China's distinctive utilitarian style: twenty-five storeys of protruding rectangular windows, hollow and dark, cast in the same grey-wet concrete. The suburbs of Chinese cities are densely packed with apartment compounds in this style, and whilst it is the esoteric, internationally designed glass and steel towers of the Central Business District in Beijing and Pudong in Shanghai which grace the covers of Western travel guides, it is these hive-like oblongs, built as walled compounds in peripheral bands around the city centre, which truly define the urban Chinese skyline.

Developments such as this lend China's urban spaces a startlingly homogenous look. Distinguished only by the occasional flourish – Doric columns here, an asymmetrical roofline there – this is a fundamentally utilitarian mode of architecture, making little concession to context.

This eruption of cookie-cutter architecture is particularly conspicuous outside the big cities. A week or so earlier I had been in Kangding, capital of the Garzê Tibetan Autonomous Prefecture in Sichuan, in China's far south-west. When I had visited a few years previously, this had been a relatively modern, but still distinctively Tibetan town, sequestered in a valley amongst high mountains; now, however, anonymous new apartment compounds were under construction all along the valley floor. Looking south from a hilltop above the town, the only reminder of one's location, aside from the ring of mountain peaks which stretched around the horizon, was the gold-tipped roof of a Tibetan Buddhist monastery at the foot of the mountains, shining brightly in the summer sunshine in defiance of the grey Lego-block architecture rising up all around it.

This model of high-rise compounds has the virtue of space efficiency – a necessity in China, where it is predicted that by 2030 one billion people will be living in its cities – and it is easy to lapse into sentimentality for more communal or traditional models of living whilst conveniently sublimating the inconveniences of such an existence. Yet this brave new world of concrete and steel, with its echoes of Le Corbusier's notion of the city as a machine and its tendency to isolate the individual, does seem not only depressingly unimaginative in style, but also sits at odds with Chinese culture, which has long been predicated on a tight-knit sense of community. Derived partly from traditional Confucian values, which place the needs of the social group over the desires of the individual, but also encouraged in the Communist era by the emphasis on collectivisation and the division of people into *danwei* or 'work groups' – evident in the communal living and working conditions of Shougang – it is a deep-rooted part of Chinese culture.

The archetypal American suburb is generally considered to be Levittown in New York State. Built in the late 1940s by the firm Levitt & Sons, the development employed techniques of mass-production honed during the years of the Second World War to quickly and cheaply erect identikit houses on a mass scale. The building process was simplified to twenty-seven steps, with the houses assembled on concrete slabs from a prefabricated kit. Each house came fitted with the latest appliances, including a washing machine and an eight-inch television. Outside was a driveway for the new car necessary to get to and from the grocery store – later models came with a carport – and a yard for the kids to play in, overlooked by the kitchen to allow mothers to keep an eye on their children.

Levitt & Sons were selling a way of life as much as a place to live; an escape from inner-city tenements and the privations of urban living during the war years. Chiming with contemporary aspirations, the development was a great commercial success, and would eventually grow to more than 17,000 houses; the company would go on to build another Levittown in Pennsylvania.

In his 1961 book *The City in History*, the historian Lewis Mumford would condemn the homogenous appearance of the American suburb which resulted from the rush of post-war building:

> A multitude of uniform, unidentifiable houses, lined up inflexibly, at uniform distances, on uniform roads, in a treeless communal waste, inhabited by people of the same class, the same income, the same age group, witnessing the same television performances, eating the same tasteless pre-fabricated foods, from the same freezers, conforming in every outward and inward respect to a common mould.[1]

In living these identical lives, such suburbanites had become isolated from each other, in Mumford's view, encapsulated within their car or house, travelling long distances to and from work in the inner-city – all in solitary communion. He believed that as cities expand outwards and, in particular, as the places where people live become more remote from central areas of the city where they work, a feeling of social isolation begins to afflict them.

Mumford was reacting to the spread of cities like Los Angeles in the 1950s, which had become 'walled off into sectors by many-laned expressways, with ramps and viaducts that create special bottlenecks of their own', with an 'environment befouled by smog'.[2] The new urban America had abandoned an earlier, more successful model of life outside the city, Mumford argued, when there were distinct and coherent neighbourhoods which were glued together by a sense of community.

However, it would be the house owners of the new suburbs who would help to drive the remarkable post-war economic development of the United States. William Levitt – one of the sons of Levitt & Sons – commented proudly in 1948 that 'No man who owns his own house and lot can be a Communist. He has too much to do'.[3] Too much to do – and also too much to buy. The houses, bought on credit, had to be decorated, and then filled with furniture – plus there was the cost of that car required to travel to and from work in the city.

What is being attempted in the building of these new Chinese suburbs is not just the creation of space to house the burgeoning urban workforce, then: it also seems to indicate the state's general desire to bring about cultural change, and to cultivate in these suburbs a more individualistic middle class, who will shift China into a new economic era, filling their individual new apartments with flat screen televisions, American-style fridges and IKEA sofas.

The new conurbations on the edges of the Chinese towns and cities may differ architecturally from their Western originals – stacked vertically rather than spread horizontally – but in their uniformity and their separation from the cities that they ring, they seem to mimic many of the problems identified by Mumford in *The City in History*.

The sense of isolation experienced by many of these new suburbanites living in the high-rises on the city edge is heightened by a lack of thought and care around how to provide for the requirements of life beyond a place to sleep. China's new suburbs tend to be absent of both those places which bring people together – public spaces, such as parks, markets, restaurants etc – but also more essential institutions such as schools and hospitals. They are often oddly sterile places, with little bustle or life. In a 2015 report on East Asian urbanisation the World Bank criticised this aspect of China's urban planning in particular, commenting that the density of these facilities 'should be increased, to create a city where most daily amenities are available within a five minute walk. [Cities in China] should mix commercial space, offices, and residential areas to reduce the distance residents have to travel to their jobs or recreational space'.[4]

Day one: Shougang Iron and Steel to Tiananmen

The distances to be travelled between home and work are particularly problematic. Commuting remains a painful experience in Beijing, despite ever increasing investment in the subway and road networks. In one survey, the Beijing commute was named the second most painful in the world, after only Mexico City, and tied in the standings with Shenzhen, the hyper-charged tech metropolis on the Pearl River Delta which has become metonymic of China's post-1980 economic boom. Since that survey was commissioned, the population of Beijing has grown by around another two million – with most of these incomers settling in distant residential areas like Shijingshan. According to a more recent study, the average length of a daily commute in Beijing is now ninety-seven minutes. Again, Beijing comes out very slightly ahead of (or rather behind) other Chinese megacities, with Shanghai, Guangzhou and Shenzhen all averaging around ninety minutes.[5] The time which is necessary for a real life – one beyond simply eating, sleeping and working – thus leaks away in the air-conditioned carriages of the car or subway, with individuals living the 'encapsulated life' which so worried Mumford.

The gravitational pull of China's urban centres is so powerful that it appears to be statistically unaffected at present by intangible concerns around quality of life; yet there are increasing rumblings of discontent in China's megacities.

In 2013, the Chinese magazine, *New Weekly*, compiled a list of China's 'alienated cities', fifteen years on from a similar edition which had extolled their charms. In the list, Beijing had moved from being 'The Most Magnificent City' to become 'The Most Miserable City':

> Over the last 15 years ... Urban public resources have become scarce, urban living has become suffocating.
> Over the last 15 years ... Metropolitan areas have become black holes that suck in everything.[6]

Capturing the frustration of those who have watched this change unfold, a novelist and blogger named Zhang Wumao wrote an essay in 2017 entitled 'Beijing Has 20 Million People Pretending to Have a Life Here'. Though jocular in tone, the essay contained some strident criticisms of life in the city. 'Beijing is a tumour, and no one can control how fast it is growing', Zhang wrote, adding that the city is 'too big; so big that it is simply not like a city at all'.[7] Lovers living on either side of the city were really in a long distance relationship, he playfully argued.

Zhang's essay struck a nerve, and racked up millions of views before being taken down by censors. He would later, seemingly under duress, apologise and be subject to a barrage of refutations and criticism from the state press and disgruntled Beijingers. Zhang is an incomer to Beijing from Shaanxi province, and some questioned his qualifications in offering an assessment of a city that was not originally his own. But something in his criticism of the city, and the increasing atomisation of life here, resonated.

Why, then, does China follow this road to urban reinvention? Apart from that desire to speedily cultivate an aspirational middle class, and the simple need to house incomers to cities, it is also the case that the Chinese state has a venal interest in these large scale suburban developments. All land in China is ultimately owned by the state, and local governments know that there is good money to be made in selling land for redevelopment, both in the city and just outside, to developers. The scheme is, seemingly, a win-win for the local Party cadres: they make money from the land sale, and can sit by and watch as developers modernise and expand their city.

The most lucrative land is, of course, that nearest city centres, which is in demand for new offices and malls, as Tom Miller has observed in his book *China's Urban Billion*: 'The flight from the urban core is exacerbated by government attempts to convert high-density city centres into commercial districts, which often requires kicking the original residents out into the suburbs'.[8]

In Beijing, those original residents of the central city traditionally lived in single-storey houses built around jealously guarded courtyards. Known as *siheyuan*, these dwellings are oriented around the cardinal points, and set along similarly symmetrical alleyways or hutong. From the viewpoint of those passing along the narrow hutong, the siheyuan enclose themselves, with small windows set high in the grey brick walls and a solid wooden door barring entrance to unwanted visitors. Siheyuan offer sanctuary from the outside whilst still retaining a fraternal inner space, in a manner not dissimilar to an Oxford quad. Steep, densely tiled roofs mark boundaries between the compounds, which nest tightly against each other: 'Like boxes within boxes, and puzzles within puzzles',[9] wrote David Kidd. In imperial Beijing the only buildings exceeding two storeys in height were a handful of ceremonial and religious buildings and, given that the city is also built on a plain with few natural hills or inclines, this ensured that no private space was overlooked.

In recent times, life in these courtyard houses has become increasingly communal, however. Compounds which would have once housed one family were divided up to be shared by many, their courtyards filled in to provide more accommodation, and left to decline into in a state of dilapidation by landlords. Few have bathrooms, and so families are obliged to rely on public toilets in the hutong. They went from being siheyuan to dazayuan – or 'big, messy courtyards'. Those who own the houses could, of course, invest in bringing the dwellings up to date – but given that the state owns the land on which the buildings sit and individuals only hold rights to usage, there is little incentive for owners to spend money on their property, particularly as they live in constant fear that their plot will be claimed when the government decide to sell the land for redevelopment. Those who actually live in these dazayuan are often poor out-of-towners, reluctant to stand up to their landlords.

There is thus a myriad of factors which count against Beijing's courtyard houses; to the cynical eye of the developer, they represent a dishearteningly inefficient use of space; to the local government they offer an opportunity for profit; to their owner, they seem a risky investment for the long term, and to those who live in them, attached as they may be to their way of life, they often fall notably short in providing modern comforts and amenities.

As a consequence, the city has witnessed the steady destruction of the hutong. In 1949, Beijing had around 7,000 hutong; by the 1980s this had dwindled to around 4,000.[10] Now, preservationists find it hard to keep track, but numbers are in the hundreds. For years, residents of the hutong have feared rising in the morning to find the character 拆 (*chai* – to demolish) painted on their front wall. There is no consultation, no real possibility of protest: such is the precariousness of life in modern China.

The state pays compensation to the evicted owners, and those who can afford the rapidly increasing prices tend to end up out here: in the new suburban apartments of areas like Shijingshan to the west or Changping to the north, many miles from their old homes and from the centre of the city. Often they find themselves part of an incongruous community: a mix of young professionals, farmers and rural workers who have been moved off their land in neighbouring counties, as well as a smattering of local families and retirees. These newest members of the new suburban China are held together in vertical isolation – with little in common besides the identical floor plan of their apartment.

More recently, those isolated patches of hutong that have survived the sweeping destruction, mostly in the square miles around the Drum and Bell Towers in the north of the city, have been subject to a coordinated campaign of prettification. Over the course of a summer, gangs of labourers swept through these old alleys with wheelbarrows and noisy cement mixers, bricking up windows and entrances that had been opened in the exterior walls with the aim of restoring the hutong to a more 'original' look. Over cheap red bricks secured with patchy mortar, the workers laid grey rectangular brick tiles in order to match the look of the old masonry. Roofs which were in need of proper repair were often simply tarted up around the edges to make them presentable from street level.

The small hole-in-the-wall restaurants and shops which had come to define the look and life of the hutong were the main victims of this campaign; some proprietors have had to resort to selling their goods through the identical small, red-framed, double-glazed windows installed in the wall opening on to the street. Others have left entirely. It is not all bad: some more substantial tidying up and repair work has been done in parts, and quite a few Beijingers I talked to – admittedly often those from elsewhere in the city – felt that the campaign made the hutong look cleaner and more civilised.

As I stood on a hutong in the north of the old city watching the renovations one summer afternoon, a middle-aged man with lined eyes came and stood next to me. His name was Mr Wang, and he lived with his wife and young daughter a little further down this hutong. I asked what he thought about all the building work.

'They're too lazy to do it properly', he said. 'Xi Jinping says he wants it to look better, so they'll come in and fix it up quickly.'

He had lived in his siheyuan for his whole life. He told me that his was still 'original', though exactly what that meant these days was hard to guess. But these big new apartment buildings were no good, he said: he wanted his eight-year-old daughter to finish growing up in the hutong, in his old house and amongst the people she knew. As we watched a grizzled, open shirted worker heave another load of roof tiles from a trailer, I wondered silently at the likelihood that he would get his wish.

I carried on past the unfinished apartment compounds, with each block's readiness for habitation increasing as I passed along the street. Cranes moved silently above them in smooth synchronicity. At around the eighth-floor, green safety nets had been rigged against the concrete skeletons.

Approaching Gucheng subway, the second most westerly station on Line 1, the hitherto empty streets were suddenly filled with life. Squat middle-aged ladies carried string bags filled with groceries; grandmothers chatted in the shade of a poplar tree and watched as their wards chased each other around the playground. On a quiet corner, a fruit vendor leaned dozily against the side of his flatbed van, t-shirt rolled up over his navel in an attempt to keep cool. As I strolled in the sunshine, the city was reduced once more to a manageable scale. Many of the apartments in this area were older: either big 1970s blocks or earlier 'walk-ups', buildings of five storeys or so sharing shabby communal stairwells – relics of a housing system which provided accommodation for individuals based on their *danwei*, the work group to which they were assigned. Between and below them were scattered small scruffy shops and restaurants.

I crossed a footbridge to walk on the north side of the street, and stopped in its middle, with the traffic rumbling below me. To the west, the road fell away imperceptibly below the horizon and, as it dipped, the landskein of the Western Hills rose hazily in the background. Framed by the gaps of the buildings, the bright hills silhouetted a pagoda which sat in the middle distance, somewhere out beyond Shougang. Out here, the signposts declare this thoroughfare to be Shijingshan Street; further east, it will become Fuxing Street, and then Fuxingmen Outer Street, and then Fuxingmen Inner Street, before finally being given the name of Chang'an Jie. It repeats the same pattern of name changing on its eastern stretch, but it is all one road, never deviating from its straightness, and even in this distant suburb it is three lanes wide on both sides.

I carried on along the northern edge of the street, passing by more blocks of old apartments. Banks of grass, well-tended and green, formed a barricade between the road and the buildings, and the frenetic sense of the central city, with its bustle and noise, was absent. In the gaps between cars the only noise was the crickets and the scuffing of my feet on the dusty pavement. I walked for fifteen minutes or so, past the neo-Gothic 'Sunrise Hotel', then a new electronics mall, whose automatic doors I approached deliberately to enjoy a few moments of cool from the interior's air-conditioning.

Just beyond the mall, a fairy-tale vision arose in front of me. Against the backdrop of the Fifth Ring Road flyover stood the gothic turrets of a Disney castle in miniature; alongside them were an immobile Ferris Wheel and a brightly colourful roller coaster. This was Shijingshan Amusement Park. Any visitors lured to this distant part of Beijing, however, were likely to be disappointed: built in the 1980s, and half-heartedly kept going by the local government, the park now looks distinctly tired. In all the times that I had passed the park, I had never seen a queue for the entrance, or many other signs of visitors. The only activity around the park came from the kite flyers who took advantage of the optimistically large plaza in front of the entrance to launch their kites, which, once airborne, hovered effortlessly above the traffic jams backing up around the intersection of Chang'an Jie and the Fifth Ring Road.

In 2007, the Amusement Park suffered the ignominy of becoming the focus of one of the media's periodic 'Only in China' stories, when the park's similarities to those of Walt Disney attracted the attention of the Western press. The original video, filmed for a Japanese TV report, 'showed children cavorting with characters resembling Minnie Mouse, Donald Duck, Pluto, Snow White and the Seven Dwarves and Japan's Hello Kitty and Doraemon'. By the time the rest of the international media arrived, however, many of the characters had mysteriously disappeared (as had a sign telling visitors: 'Disney is too far, please come to Beijing Shijingshan Amusement Park'), and those running the park were emphasising the cultural specificity of those who did remain on show: 'Take our Cinderella as an example', the deputy general manager told CNN. 'The face of Disney's Cinderella face is European, but ours is a Chinese. She looks like a young Chinese country girl.'[11]

China has since got its own, authentic Disney experience, as in 2016 the company opened their first mainland park in Shanghai. At a cost of $5.5 billion, and boasting the largest and tallest Disney castle ever built, Shanghai Disneyland is another large-scale example of the determination of Western brands to attract the increasingly disposable income of the Chinese middle class. Inauthentic relics such as Shijingshan Amusement Park simply don't make the grade any more; as the slogan of another American corporate behemoth put it, the new suburban middle class want the 'Real Thing', whether it is Coca-Cola, an iPhone – or the runaway thrill of a rollercoaster.

3

Change – ring roads and the new Beijing – Great Olympics

One spring morning, on descending from my apartment – in a block just down the road from the Amusement Park – I found, where once had been an entrance to a small shop at the foot of the stairs which led to my building, a cavernous opening into the ground that yawned like a portal into another world. Perhaps twelve-foot-wide and seemingly limitless in depth and darkness, the hole would take form over the subsequent weeks as the entrance to a vast, subterranean electronics mall. I asked the middle-aged man who ran the small kiosk in the car park to my building what was happening. 'Welcome to the new Beijing', he said with a shrug, echoing the somewhat unimaginative original slogan for the 2008 Olympic Games: *New Beijing, Great Olympics*. When the mall opened a couple of months later, I descended into the maw of the beast on a long escalator to emerge into an endless maze of connected subterranean plazas: carved from a space which had lain dormant and unknown beneath me all the time I had lived nine floors above.

About five months into my tenancy of this same apartment – five months of winter and spring in which I had indisputably settled in and begun to think of the place as my own – the landlords announced they were selling up and that I needed to pack up my things and move out as a matter of some urgency. From the front window of this apartment I had watched as the skeleton of three new blocks across the park to the south acquired tissue and muscle; their sleek glass and marble-effect tile exterior rather brought the walk-ups and 1980s and 1990s compounds which surrounded them into relief. I decided that, having been forced out, I quite fancied trying life in one of Beijing's slick new high-rises.

The estate agent attempted to show alternatives, including one nearby which seemed homely, convenient and cheap enough to convince me out of my desire, until I pulled back the living room curtain to reveal a view of a vast demolition site over which caterpillar-tracked diggers swarmed noisily. '*Mei wenti*', said the agent – 'No problem: in six months it will be a new building.' I got my way, however, and found a just-finished two bedroom place in one of the new buildings across the park. At night, only one other apartment's lights shone out in the Beijing haze; for the rest of my time there, the sound of drilling and hammering became my dawn chorus.

A week or so after I had moved in, however, I realised that I was missing a box of belongings. Thinking that I might have inadvertently left it at the old apartment, I decided to stroll over on the off-chance that someone might be in. I took the lift down from the seventh floor, walked past the steel and glass guard hut (the guard in regulation position: feet up on desk; peaked uniform cap pulled low over his closed eyes), out of the accordion gate, and up the street. It was a walk of only two hundred metres or so, but the disparity was acute. The courtyard of my new building was bereft of life, save for the few sad goldfish swimming in the murky water of the plaza fountain. Around the entrance to my old building, by contrast, there was the fuss and whirl of everyday life: locals popping in to the market, the tea shop, the cobblers, or diverting the grandchildren with a go on the mechanical rides – a vaguely terrifying goat and wolf from a popular cartoon, *Pleasant Goat and Big Big Wolf*, which moved in time to a hypnotic musical jingle. Without a magnetic entrance key for the main door, I waited on the outside steps until an old man, Pekingese in tow, came down and opened the door on his way out of the building. I slipped in and then walked the nine flights of dimly lit stairs.

The door opened the instant I knocked; a t-shirted man, covered in dust, looked at me questioningly. Behind him I could see that not a vestige of the walls, ceiling or floors of the place remained. In seven days it had been stripped back to a shell; any trace of previous habitation, let alone my brief tenancy, had been obliterated. Piles of rubble lay on the floor. Dust hung in the still air giving the place an ethereal feel. Slightly out-of-breath, I explained my errand; he and his work mate, bashing away near the back window, had not found anything they said, though I thought it unlikely that they would tell me if they had. I headed back downstairs and walked the two-hundred yards to my apartment compound. The guard still dozed, and from the open windows of my block the steady knock of hammers and whine of drills carried on the spring air.

Leaving the dreaming spires of the Shijingshan Amusement Park behind me, I passed under the rumbling flyover of the Fifth Ring Road, navigating my way through balanced racks of bicycles. Above a building of official purpose a little down the road, the red and gold of the Chinese flag moved like a flame in the hot air. From somewhere off in the distance, down a side street, came a car alarm; it sat just at the edge of audibility, vacillating in tone and volume on the same breeze which pulled the flag to attention and blew around litter at the dark subway station entrance. Along the narrow pavement an old man on a mechanical tricycle towing a trailer of plate glass passed me, pursued by the metronomic beat of his two-stroke engine. Behind everything: the sound of the traffic.

The city's main ring roads nest inside one another, drawing concentric parallel lines around the Forbidden City and Tiananmen Square, singling them out on a map like a bullseye. The so-called seventh ring road – the G95 highway – runs so far distant from Beijing's current periphery, however, that its relation to the city does not seem immediately obvious on the map. It gives the sense that it draws the circumference of a space to be filled – a guide line for urban planners to aspire to meet. It is another piece of the project to unify this part of north-east China, and only thirty-eight kilometres of the ring road's near one-thousand-kilometre length actually run within the Beijing city limits. The ring road forms one physical marker in a plan for the city and its province which will stall and restart, flex and twist – but the tide of urbanisation will inevitably rise to wash over the flat fields of Hebei, until it will soon be hard to conceive where each town and city begins and ends.

The Beijing authorities have announced a plan to restrict the population of the city itself to below 23 million, and to keep it at that level for the foreseeable future. Part of their plan is to use the surrounding area to soak up the overspill, moving out some industry and bureaucracy to Tongzhou, to the east, and the Xiong'an New Area, an entirely new city to be built to the south-west of Beijing in Hebei province.

After the announcement, to great fanfare in the Chinese media, of the Xiong'an development – the name combines the characters for 'brave' and 'peace' – there was a gold rush of developers and individuals trying to buy up land and property in the part of the province where the new city was to emerge. Much of this part of Hebei is functionally unlovely: small two-storey shops, restaurants and houses, often swathed with thick palls of coal-tar scented pollution, set out along grids of streets which fade into gravel tracks once they reach the countryside. At the heart of the area to be developed lies a network of marshes and wetlands; litter-strewn and polluted a few years ago, they have since been cleaned up into a tourist attraction famed for their waterlilies. That the area has been prone to dreadful flooding in the past nobody mentions.

Local residents in the area earmarked for development had endeavoured to maximise the compensation paid to them by the government, hurriedly adding makeshift extra rooms and floors to their houses – the government quickly banned them from doing so, as well as outlawing land deals – and ensuring that as many of their family members as possible were registered to their home address. They were being forced to move out, but the people I met when I visited what was to become Xiong'an seemed philosophical at the prospect, and tried to take the positives where they could. In any case, as one villager told me, 'What's the point in arguing? It's going to happen anyway'.

Linked by the sleek white projectiles of China's high-speed rail network, which has begun to resemble a subway system for the country, these satellites will provide alternative sites for the commerce and bureaucracy Beijing no longer wants. But what they likely won't offer is a new home to those people being forced out of the city as it struggles to keep its population in check. These are overwhelmingly the poorer members of the city's *waidiren* – the 'outside people' who are not officially resident in the city and who are increasingly not welcome there.

China's *hukou* system, a household registration scheme which effectively restricts those not born in a city from accessing its services, means that the aspiring poor who are drawn to Beijing from other towns and provinces find themselves living a second-class life when they arrive. They are hobbled not only by the hukou system, but also by prejudice: marked out by their accents, their clothes, even the tone of their skin, they are often subject to sneering looks and sharp-edged comments from native urbanites. These out-of-towners make up a substantial, though indefinite, proportion of the city's population, doing jobs that Beijingers generally have an aversion to. They are the city's delivery drivers, pedlars, street sellers, construction workers, factory labourers, cleaners, shop keepers.

After a 2017 fire killed nineteen people in a shabby two-storey apartment building housing migrant families in the city's south, the caterpillar tracks of demolition crews crawled to the edgelands of Beijing and, citing health and safety concerns, began to raze similar structures: the shops, markets, restaurants and homes of the migrant population. Combined with the redevelopment and gentrification of the hutong, which has meant the closure of the small businesses which they run, the message has become clearer and clearer for the poor migrant workers of the city: in the past, you were useful, but this new Beijing – civilised, technological, green – doesn't particularly want you here anymore.

Where they go, and how Beijing will change without them, remains an open question.

Along the southern stretch of this section of Long Peace Street, I passed an outcrop of building from the last wave of city regeneration, the nucleus of which was the blocky pinstriped towers of a shopping mall. The mall was, along with a monolithic hotel of similarly sharp edges to its east, the newest building in an array of construction which had filled in the empty lots of this western suburb of Beijing, blossoming from a seed planted in the years running up to the Olympics.

China had lavished money on the 2008 Games. It was a chance for the country to be a good-news story for once, and to force an impression, solidified by bold imagery and sporting success, onto the consciousness of the world. The Games were a series of grandly symbolic orchestrations of the kind in which China excels, its long history having cultivated a talent for pageant. Planners placed the principal venue – the so-called Bird's Nest Stadium – at the pinnacle of the north-south axis which cuts through the Forbidden City and Tiananmen Square: a telling choice which asserted the historical significance of the Games.

Their legacy – that intangible value so oft-referenced by those who oversee them – is harder to quantify. It is evident far more clearly in the infrastructure it provided for the city, and the national pride it provoked, than in any inspiration it seems to have cultivated for physical exertion. The city was bequeathed a new airport, new roads, new subway lines. As for sport, the venues are still present, but their usage varies wildly. Further along the northern edge of Long Peace Street, a broad squat block of ruffled gold sits back from the road: now known as the 'Cadillac Arena' it was built for the Olympic basketball competition and has hosted an eclectic range of musical artists including The Eagles, the Backstreet Boys (three times) and Iron Maiden.

Just above the section of the road where I now stood was the venue for the Olympic cycling events. The velodrome is a downed flying saucer, a sleek metallic ellipsoid hidden just north of Long Peace Street among the cypresses and dusty hills of the park where the Olympic mountain bikers had sweated and strained. It has taken on a somewhat unloved air since the Games, with weeds growing up in its dusty car park, but from the slatted wooden platform which sits above the track, one gains a grand panorama of the city; a view limited only by the sky's particular opacity that day.

The pathways around here I'd come to know well, a short stroll away from my old neighbourhood. In wintertime, the park felt like some abandoned munitions test site: black reaching limbs of trees; hard, parched and frozen ground, hard as concrete; the landscape all peaks and craters. The Beijing winter, dry and arctic in its cold-ness, permeates the ground, making it seem incredible that anything could ever grow again, but come spring, the grass gradually returns to greenness, the blossom emerges on the trees and once again it is difficult to imagine the land looking any other way. By the time the

Chapter 3

dense, tropical heat of summer arrived, my English sensibility, used to more modest shifts of climate, was in a state of trauma.

From up on the platform the sheer horizontal growth of the city is easier to assess. In his blog post, Zhang Wumao compared the spread of the city to a metastasising tumour, growing unmanageably, destructively. The phrase more often used to describe the development of the city is *tan da bing*, or spreading a big pancake; an apposite image given the frying-pan flatness of the plain on which Beijing is built. Looking out across it, the city's reach extends beyond sight. To the west, it hits the buffer of hill and mountain, but in every other direction beige apartment compounds and offices of grey and blue run off into the murk at the horizon edge. Across it all, Long Peace Street draws a long black line bordered by thickset architecture: a strike through the city's symmetrical sprawl.

4

Babaoshan ghosts – the cemetery – the life of Peng Dehuai – return to Hunan

I did not have time to linger long above the city.

I was on my way to Babaoshan Revolutionary Cemetery, China's national burial ground and the resting place of the founding fathers of China's Communist Revolution. On an earlier attempted visit, I had been refused entry at the gate by an overzealous teenage guard. Pressed for an explanation, he had simply observed '*Ni shi waiguoren*' – 'You're a foreigner' – and walked back to his hut, apparently seeing no need for further explanation. Though I knew there was no formal injunction denying me entry to the site, I decided for my return attempt to err on the side of caution and enlist my Chinese friend Christy, who, experience had taught me, could generally talk her way into most places, and out of most situations.

Chapter 4

Christy was initially not keen, however; she had heard stories about Babaoshan. 'My friend knows a girl who was possessed by spirits there', she had told me matter-of-factly when I first proposed our visit.

The girl in question had worked in a beauty salon in the local mall, Christy said. Early one evening, she and a young male co-worker had been sent by their manager to hand out promotional flyers on the streets around the mall. The pair were gone for hours. Closing time came and went, and their phones rang out. When they finally returned at around 11.30pm, both looked shaken and refused to tell their colleagues where they had been.

One curious co-worker followed them into the staff workroom, however, and overheard a whispered conversation between the two, in which the girl instructed her companion that he was not under any circumstances to tell anyone about their visit to Babaoshan cemetery. Even though the mall was, by now, long closed, both refused to leave the salon to go home – telling their co-workers that they were waiting for someone.

'So the manager of the salon called the girl's aunt, who wasn't surprised by how she was behaving at all', Christy told me. 'She said her niece had been possessed a few times before – she was skinny and weak, and an easy target for a ghost.' The aunt came to collect the girl, and everyone eventually left for home. The next day, both the boy and girl were unable to recall anything that had happened the previous evening.

'Isn't that scary?' Christy asked after she concluded her tale. Christy is herself rather skinny. I asked her, if she was to be possessed by a Communist leader, whom would she least like it to be? 'Lin Biao', she replied, without hesitation. Lin Biao had once been Mao's heir apparent; a PLA general who, after losing his patron's favour, had died in a mysterious plane crash that many assume was a politically motivated assassination. She said the name with a look of real fear.

The story seemed to me to leave a lot of unanswered questions, but I agreed that I would do my best to protect Christy from malevolent spirits – and buy her a coffee afterwards.

When I arrived at Babaoshan subway station, Christy was sheltering from the heat inside the squat concrete building, fanning herself with a flyer. As we strolled the short distance to the cemetery we reviewed our prepared cover story: she was visiting the grave of an uncle, a martyr of the revolution, and I was a sympathetic boyfriend.

The entrance to the cemetery sits back from Long Peace Street, marked by a chunky stone arch inscribed with gold-leafed characters. Two stone lions, open mouthed, guard the archway; just behind them a pair of cypress trees strike skywards.

My young acquaintance from that previous visit was not on duty, and we passed through the gates without attracting any notice. As we walked down the drive through the still heat, Christy whispered to me: 'This must be the quietest place in Beijing.'

The grounds of Babaoshan extend across a large hillside – the name translates as Eight Treasure Hill – north from the edge of Long Peace Street. Only a small section of the whole site is given over to the Revolutionary Cemetery; there is also a public crematorium and a large burial ground just to its west. Altogether, there are now around 60,000 memorials at Babaoshan.

The site was, for centuries, a Daoist temple: the 'Honored Nation-Protecting Temple' or *Baozhong huguosi*. It was provided by the Emperor as a place for retired eunuchs to live, with a special building given over to the housing of their severed genitalia. It was repurposed by the CCP in 1951, following a proposition by Zhou Enlai that China needed its own national cemetery: the eunuchs who remained were apparently handed their genitalia and sent on their way. Government guidelines drawn up at the time instructed that the site was to be dedicated to those 'revolutionary soldiers or personnel who had made distinguished contribution to the revolution and had been killed in some form of revolutionary activity or passed away later as a result of illness'.[1]

The cemetery is organised into hierarchical zones, with the remains of the highest-ranking figures interred at the top of the hill, or within private columbariums. These include: Bo Yibo, one of the 'Eight Immortals' of Chinese communism, and father of the disgraced former Politburo member, Bo Xilai; Zhu De, founding father of the People's Liberation Army; and Chen Yun, another elder statesman of the Party, well known for his significant role in the economic life of the country.

The most significant figures of the communist movement are, however, not to be found at Babaoshan: Mao's body continues to reside in the mausoleum built along the city's north-south axis in the centre of Tiananmen Square, whilst Deng Xiaoping and Zhou Enlai, the other two most prominent figures of the CCP leadership in the twentieth century, both had their ashes scattered elsewhere. Deng, ever outward-looking, preferred to have his cast into the sea, whilst Zhou's were dispersed by aeroplane across China's hills and valleys.[2] Both were sent for cremation at Babaoshan, however, and on the occasion of their final journeys the normal bustle of Long Peace Street was quieted by the hush of tens of thousands of mourners.

Amongst those who did find rest at Babaoshan, however, it was Peng Dehuai, Defence Minister of China in the early years of the People's Republic and once one of the foremost military men of the Party, whose story had drawn me here. The three-act tragedy of Peng's life seemed to me to exemplify the tumult of the Mao era, and the remarkable human cost attached to trying to do the right thing at a time when the simple virtues of morality and empathy counted for little.

Like Mao Zedong, Peng Dehuai was born in rural Hunan province at the tail end of the nineteenth century. Faced with the limited choices of a young man from a poor area, and with little by way of education, he had become a soldier at sixteen and, like many who would come to play an important role in the communist movement, ended up fighting for the National Revolutionary Army – the military wing of the Nationalist Party which would become the CCP's opposition in the Chinese Civil War.

Peng had always felt a connection with the plight of the rural poor, however, and became increasingly attracted to the fledgling Communists: eventually, he defected, bringing his troops with him when he joined the Red Army in 1928. One of his first acts was to lead his men in rescuing Mao Zedong, breaking through an encirclement of Guomindang troops to free the future leader and his soldiers. He would spend much of the early 1930s launching scrappy, often unsuccessful, raids against the Nationalist army.

The American journalist, Edgar Snow, met Peng the year after the Long March, the legendary trek from south-eastern to northern China undertaken by the Communist forces in the mid-1930s. The Long March has the qualities of some ancient epic: encircled by overwhelming numbers of Nationalist troops, the Red Army formulated a secret plan of escape, and broke out from their base in Jiangxi in China's south-east, arriving just over a year later in October 1935 in Shaanxi province in the north. The troops, one corps of which was commanded by Peng, had travelled nearly 6,000 miles. They had crossed rivers by raft and boat and bridge, and traversed treacherous mountain passes. They had suffered calamitous losses, and been forced from their strategic base, so this was not some grand military success, but it kept the CCP and their revolutionary ambitions alive.

Meeting Peng in 1936, Edgar Snow was clearly impressed by this young general who had played such an important role in the Long March, and dedicated a substantial section of *Red Star Over China*, the famous account of his stay with the Communist forces in Shaanxi, to him: 'There was something open, forthright, and undeviating in his manner and speech – rare qualities among Chinese – which I liked', Snow wrote. 'Quick in his movements and speech, full of laughter and a great wit, he was physically very active, an excellent rider, a man of endurance.'[3]

Peng was round-faced with close cropped hair, and even in photos from his youth he looks prematurely aged; his life was defined throughout by hardship of one kind or another. His upbringing had occurred in straightened circumstances. His parents owned a small-holding and a bean curd shop in a Hunan river valley village. Times had become hard, however, in 1905, when a drought hit the country-side. His mother passed away, his younger brother died of starvation at six months and he and his siblings were forced to beg and cast about for any job they could find in order to survive. All of his life, he would live frugally, modestly.

Born in 1898, he came to adulthood as the forces holding the country together were fracturing; his first post as a soldier had been in a local warlord's army. He was a military man through and through, hardened by conflict and revered by his men for his bravery and resilience. On the Long March, he had apparently often given up his horse to tired subordinates.

In the late 1940s, Mao himself composed a poem celebrating Peng's courage, as evidenced by the general's victory in a key battle of the Civil War:

> The mountains are high, the road is long and full of potholes,
> Many soldiers are moving to and fro.
> Who is the courageous one, striking from his horse in all directions?
> None other than our great General P'eng![4]

After the founding of New China in 1949, Peng played an important role in the administration, supporting Mao in his decision to intervene in the Korean War, which began less than a year after the Communists had taken charge of the country. He would ultimately lead the military during this conflict. He was made Defence Minister of the People's Republic in 1954 and was thus in overall command of China's armed forces.

Yet, Mao and Peng had long had a difficult relationship. Others within the higher reaches of the Chinese Communist Party talked of Mao and Peng as 'two bad tempered mules from Hunan',[5] and there had been disputes between the two in the difficult early years of the CCP's armed struggle; Peng was not a character who was afraid to speak truth to power. In 1933, Peng described Mao to one of the CCP leaders as 'a nasty character ... If you do not submit to him, he will without fail find ways to make you submit'.[6]

The anecdotal belief held by many Chinese is that the irrevocable damage to the relationship between the two was done by the death of Mao's son. Mao Anying was assigned to Peng's personal detail during the Korean War, and was killed by an American airstrike in 1950; the rumours said he had been frying rice during daylight hours, which gave away his location to American pilots. Mao professed not to hold Peng responsible, but the Chairman took the loss hard, brooding in an armchair all day and night and chain-smoking cigarettes.[7]

Yet the event which initiated Peng's tragic final act still seemed to come out of nowhere, blindsiding the Defence Minister and the leadership of the CCP as a whole. In the summer of 1959, at a meeting of the Chinese leadership near Lushan, a range of misty mountain peaks in Jiangxi province, Peng raised concerns about the policies of the Great Leap Forward – then a year old. He wrote a letter to the Chairman expressing his worries about the pace at which economic and social changes had been made and the over-exaggeration of agricultural and industrial results – those hyperbolic claims which led in part to the catastrophic famine which would afflict the countryside. Peng attempted to soften his criticism with self-deprecation, writing that 'whether or not this letter is of reference value or not is for you to decide. If what I say is wrong, please correct me'.[8] He also explained that he felt many of the problems had already been rectified. Peng was echoing language he had himself heard the Chairman use, and did not seem to view his contribution as especially controversial, particularly as Mao had opened the conference by encouraging the free expression of ideas.

Chapter 4

Peng sympathised with the plight of those who were struggling to survive under the strictures of the Great Leap Forward; he had seen for himself the difficulties faced by farmers and peasants – the very people, of course, whom the Chinese Communist Party had been founded to support and defend. In 1958, Peng had undertaken a number of inspection trips around the country, and was seemingly deeply affected by the hardships he encountered. At one point on his travels, he penned a poem reflecting the seeming hopelessness of the situation facing many in rural provinces:

> Grain scattered on the ground, potato leaves withered;
> Strong young people have left to make steel.
> Only children and old women reap the crops,
> How can they pass the coming year?
> Allow me to raise my voice for the people![9]

In raising his voice at Lushan, however, Peng made a colossal political miscalculation. Mao's response to Peng's criticism was swift and damning. He had Peng's letter printed and distributed to the other delegates and gave a vitriolic speech characterising Peng as an opportunist and questioning why he had not chosen to speak up sooner. He also gave a terrifying hint of what was to come:

> I never attack others if I am not attacked. If others attack me, I always strike back. Others attack me first, I attack them later. [...] Now, I have learned to listen, listen with a stiffened scalp, for one or two weeks, before I launch my counterattack.[10]

Peng was utterly taken aback by the ferocity of Mao's response. It is easy to forget that, for all the leaders of the CCP at this time, relationships went well beyond that dictated by their jobs governing the country. For all their disagreements, he and Mao had been fellow-travellers in the revolution for more than three decades; they were neighbours at Zhongnanhai, the compound housing the Chinese leadership. Peng would struggle to sleep for days afterwards, the awareness of the enormity of what had happened haunting him.[11]

Day one: Shougang Iron and Steel to Tiananmen

In the immediate aftermath of the conference, he was stripped of his position as Defence Minister, exiled from Zhongnanhai, and sent to live in the western suburbs of Beijing, with only his secretary and bodyguard for company. As with the other hardships of his life, however, he took this exclusion stoically, busying himself with gardening, and, as events began to prove his assessment of the Great Leap Forward correct over the following years, he began to try to nudge his way back into public life.

Finally, in 1965, after six years on the sidelines, he was invited to meet with Mao – for what would turn out to be the final time – and was appointed to a role overseeing industrial construction in China's south-west. It was a minor post compared to his previous position in the higher echelons of the Party hierarchy – but it suggested that he was no longer a pariah. He moved to Chengdu, the capital city of Sichuan province, in November of that year.

'Rehabilitated' is the English word generally used by historians to describe those restored to Mao's favour. The word derives from the Latin *habilis*, and reflects its verbal root, which means 'to hold'. Literally, to be habilitated is to be easily held; to be rehabilitated is to be made so again. The word seems particularly apt for those whose destinies Mao did seem to hold, puppet-like, at his fingertips.

Peng's rehabilitation did not last long. In 1966, the chaos of the Cultural Revolution was unleashed: Mao's desperate attempt to consolidate his power, and to smash – both literally and figuratively – the remnants of the traditional and the bourgeois in Chinese culture. In December of that year, Peng was seized. He was taken to Beijing, where in January of 1967 he was paraded in chains and a dunce hat. Over the subsequent months, he was subjected to violent interrogations aimed at provoking a confession to various crimes; his torturers operated in two-hour shifts to avoid developing any degree of empathy for their victim. In August of 1967, he was paraded at another 'struggle session' in front of tens of thousands of soldiers at Beijing's Workers' Stadium and forced to kneel for hours as the litany of his crimes was recited to a baying crowd. The accusations made against him were typically non-specific; he was a 'great warlord'; a 'great ambitionist'; and a 'great conspirator', who had sided with foreign states against the Party. The veracity of such accusations was irrelevant; your choice in such a scenario was either to make a public self-criticism, to commit suicide – a not uncommon option – or to maintain your innocence and suffer the consequences.

Peng chose the latter and remained in prison for most of the subsequent seven years of his life. His health had been drastically weakened by his ill-treatment, and he went on to develop colon cancer, which would spread throughout his body. In 1973, he was relocated to Beijing's 301 Military Hospital; the windows of his room were covered in newspaper and his requests for a radio to break the silence were refused.[12] In 1974, he wrote to Mao, but received no reply; the fact that he was seemingly denied any substantive medical treatment despite his illness speaks to Mao's lingering resentment. In her memoir, *Wild Swans*, Jung Chang recounts that Peng's last request was for the paper to be removed from his windows so that he could once again see daylight.[13] It was denied.

Peng died on 29 November 1974. He was seventy-six years old. His body was cremated in secret, along with the sixty-two books he had read in his last few years, and his ashes sent to Chengdu – the site of his last official posting, but a city with which Peng otherwise had little connection. His ashes were stored at a suburban funeral home, accompanied with a label: 'No. 327 – Wang Chuan, 32 years, from Chengdu'. 'Even in death', his biographer Jürgen Domes observed, '[he] remained a non-person for the ruling élite'.[14] News of his death was kept so quiet that many in the Party were unaware of his fate and even his widow, caught up herself in the machinations of the Cultural Revolution, did not learn what had happened to her husband until 1978.

By this time, Mao himself had died, and the ring-leaders of the Cultural Revolution – the so-called 'Gang of Four', which included

Mao's fourth wife, Jiang Qing – had been imprisoned awaiting trial. The reckoning with the terrible cost of Mao's final revolution was beginning.

In December of that year, under the leadership of Deng Xiaoping, who had himself been purged from the Party during the years of the Cultural Revolution, the CCP considered and corrected the 'erroneous conclusions'[15] reached on a number of their former colleagues – Peng amongst them.

A few days later, the Party held a funeral for Peng Dehuai, with Deng Xiaoping delivering the oration, confirming that the Party had undertaken 'a total and just evaluation: his honour is herewith restored'.[16] Peng's ashes, having been retrieved from Chengdu, were transported to Babaoshan Revolutionary Cemetery, where he was laid to rest amongst the comrades from whom he had been forcibly estranged for so long.

Cypress trees shaded the dusty path through the tombstones; only the oscillating noise of crickets – their 'urgent whir' as a poem by the Tang dynasty poet Wang Wei describes it – disturbed the peace. The air was utterly still. From the top of the hill, neat rows of gravestones cascaded down the incline. 'It isn't scary at all', Christy said.

It wasn't. It was orderly and human. At the bottom of the hill, neat ranks of white tombstones marked the graves of the foot soldiers of the revolution. Here at the top were enormous bespoke marble and bronze edifices, made personal to the memorialised by carved portraits or epigraphs; they must have cost enormous sums. 'Which do you think is better?', Christy asked me as we looked at one particularly elaborate memorial, 'Communism or capitalism?' I said I thought that communism was a good idea that had never worked very well in practice. 'I don't think everybody wants to be the same', she commented.

Try as we might, however, we could not find a memorial, big or small, to Peng. Finally, we asked one of the gardeners. Peng used to be here, yes, he said – but I don't think he is anymore. I was some-what incredulous – surely the state would not have moved him again? Besides, I had read numerous accounts which claimed Peng as one of Babaoshan's most high profile residents.

Yet, digging through Chinese-language news after my visit, I found that, after twenty years at Babaoshan, he had indeed quietly departed the Revolutionary Cemetery. In recent years, partly to help with the increasing demand for space, a number of the high-profile resi-dents interred at Babaoshan have been returned to their hometowns, including Hua Guofeng, Mao's anointed – and politically short-lived – successor, and the military leader and former Vice Premier He Long. In 1999, apparently according to his final wishes, Peng's ashes were quietly sent on one final journey – back to his home province of Hunan, where he had been born a century before.

There was almost certainly a more cynical reason for this reloca-tion however – one more commercial than political or personal. In recent years, a burgeoning industry has emerged in China known as 'Red Tourism', in which selected sites from CCP history have become destinations for pilgrimage. Local politicians searching for a way to increase revenue in far-flung parts of China have begun build-ing memorial halls and museums dedicated to the memory of the key people and places of the revolution. Hunan has a great advantage in this endeavour, with Mao Zedong, Peng Dehuai and Liu Shaoqi – once the third most important figure in the CCP hierarchy, but who was also persecuted to death during the Cultural Revolution – all hailing from the province. Peng's tomb now features as part of a series of attractions oriented around his former residence, just outside the city of Xiangtan in Hunan. Entrance costs 25 yuan, or about £3.

Christy and I stood silently in the heat for a moment, and I thought about the stories which swirled like ghosts around Babaoshan. In particular, I thought of the remarkable human cost which this place attested to; the sacrifice and betrayal, the refusal to let the perceived fripperies of life – love, loyalty, friendship, personal happiness, parenthood – get in the way of the political will to reforge a nation. The motivations of those whom this place memorialised remained opaque to me, but their stories here at least seemed once again to have been made their own.

Finally, Christy broke the silence. 'Let's go and get a Starbucks', she said.

We found a coffee shop nearby, and I kept my side of the bargain, taking secret pleasure from the opportunity to escape for half an hour into the mall's crisp air. When we had finished our drinks, I walked Christy back to the subway station and then set off alone again down Long Peace Street.

Cottonwood poplars dappled the pavement with shade, their bark a brittle off-white etched with dark diamond patterns. Each spring, these trees generate clouds of white fluff: it carries on the April breezes, building in small drifts against pavements and walls, and coating the water of Beijing's lakes like rime. In the breeze, the friction of their large, leathery leaves sounds like a rain shower starting, and many times along the walk I found myself unconsciously glancing at the sky in anticipation of a downpour.

On the approach to Jade Spring Road, patients from the hospital on the northern side of the street had come out to take the air; one sat beatifically in her wheelchair on the pavement corner, whilst an older man, stubbled and in striped blue pyjamas, squatted on a low wall and smoked an illicit cigarette.

From a footbridge, a red and gold banner hung, proclaiming how with one heart and one strength, a civilised city was being developed. Across the intersection, I passed a row of single-fronted shops below low-rise apartments – walk-ups of blue-grey. Across the road were bigger buildings – new offices and a scattering of old housing blocks, their ice-cream colours failing to distract from an increasing decrepitude. Below one, a frontage of plate glass and high arched windows was being stripped of its signage by men on scaffolding; its long facade – formerly a restaurant perhaps – showed a dark, empty interior. Scholar trees were set out at intervals of twelve feet or so, next to the hooped white fence which divided pavement and road, their trunks supported by trusses. The regularity of this arrangement was disturbed only by junctions or bus stops, which had queuing lines and corresponding bus numbers painted on the floor. Looking back, a large blue road sign indicated what Long Peace Street would lead you to out west: *5th Ring Road – 5km; Mentougou – 14km; Laiyuan – 240km.* I wondered why anyone driving out here would need to know how far distant Laiyuan sat – a small, comparatively insignificant town to the south-west of Beijing. I turned back around to confront my own journey. Ahead, the ever-unspooling distance of the road pulled me forward.

三座门

5

A diversion – straightness –
the road as metaphor

On a whim, I wandered off into one of the old apartment compounds sitting to the north of the road. The buildings here were painted in ox-blood red with white detailing. A small lean-to with a corrugated iron roof was fronted with a panel of red-on-white characters offering lock repair and replacement. Cars parked at an angle and strewn in front of the buildings blocked the entrance steps to the apartment buildings, and brightly patterned flowered quilts were hung out to dry on lines amongst them.

Though I don't ordinarily smoke, I had a packet of cigarettes in my pocket with me, part of a plan to alleviate the monotony of the route, but also because cigarettes were a currency between men in certain scenarios here – particularly after they had knocked back a few glasses of baijiu in the course of an evening meal – and I tended to keep a pack with me just in case. I had lived here when the government first tried to ban cigarettes in restaurants and bars. I recalled a poster campaign accompanying the ban, telling smokers that 'The gift of cigarettes is the gift of cancer'. It had had little discernible effect. I bought 'Pride' cigarettes, for no other reason than that the logo, a cartoon baby panda, made them easily identifiable under a glass counter top. I sat down on a small four-seated plastic picnic table painted bright blue and yellow and lit one up. Behind me on a red brick wall ran painted white characters: 'Traffic safety – Friends for life'.

I took a few puffs and let the rest of it burn down; two days walking along China's busiest street would doubtless put enough strain on my lungs. For the few minutes before I stubbed the cigarette out, I was entirely alone. Though I could still hear the traffic on Long Peace Street and the whine of air-conditioners, all else was quiet. I felt a curious sense of separateness, of the oddity at finding myself alone here, in an unremarkable apartment compound in the suburbs of this huge city which I was passing through: a place I would likely never see again, but where countless people who were not me would live in a perfectly ordinary happiness for years or decades more.

Then, a grandmother came around the corner with two small girls in identical Disney t-shirts who looked at me sidelong as they passed – and the spell was broken.

I had craved this diversion: though only a few miles into my walk, the straightness of Long Peace Street had already begun to feel unhelpful. In the simplicity it had earlier suggested – all I needed to do was keep going, putting one foot in front of the other – there was also a sort of relentlessness, with a lack of the respite offered by turns and decisions, or the surprise of a new streetscape greeting the rounding of a corner. The limit of one's horizon on Chang'an Jie is generally defined by pollution haze rather than any physical obstacle. It seemed as if by looking hard enough I might be able to catch a glimpse of my destination miles away on the other side of the city, like Marco Polo in thirteenth-century Beijing, with its streets so 'straight and wide that you can see right along them from end to end and from one gate to the other'.

Noted by Marco Polo, the affection for symmetry and straightness in city planning long predates the Communists. The bureaucratic manual known as the *Rites of Zhou* had set out some basic rules of city planning in the second century BCE, stipulating that a city must be square, and contain nine north-south and nine east-west streets: the north-south streets were given prominence in this description, with their width fixed at nine carriage tracks. These guidelines influenced the design of many of China's ancient cities, including the different incarnations of Beijing.

The CCP, however, have adapted and exaggerated the legacy of this tradition in their city planning to the point of near absurdity. New towns and cities are routinely oriented around wide main avenues running down to oversized squares, with little concession to former thoroughfares or byways; often eight or ten lanes wide, these roads create a central urban space which eschews consideration of the human in favour of scale and symbolism.

Long Peace Street was not always so long or so straight. Indeed, at the beginning of the twentieth century, it was in fact two short streets running only a few blocks to either side of the centre of the old city, and separated by Tiananmen Square. The square was at that time not really a square at all, but rather formed a T shape, with red ochre walls all around. The eastern section of Chang'an Jie ran about one hundred metres to the south of its western equivalent, with four gates interposed between either side. In 1913, under the fledgling Republican regime, the doors were removed from the paired gates, and for the first time, Beijingers could walk between the two streets. In the 1920s, in an even more striking concession to the modern world, crosstown trams were installed along the avenue.[1]

The design of this central section of Chang'an Jie was, however, displeasing to the Communist leadership when they took power in 1949. The substantial gateways which remained between either wing of the avenue, though doorless, still obscured the view of parading soldiers, and flagpoles had to be lowered when passing through them.[2] In consequence, over the course of the 1950s, city planners undertook to join up the fragmented horizontals which ran across the centre of the city, constructing a thoroughfare along which the forces of the People's Liberation Army could parade without obstruction. Refinements to the street were particularly significant in the run up to the tenth anniversary celebrations for the People's Republic in 1959; the tram lines were removed – the gates had been demolished in their entirety in the early 1950s, to much protest – and the central section of the street widened to eighty metres, paved with granite blocks. Wider, and longer – by this point reaching out to the suburb of Shijingshan in the west, though remaining abbreviated in the east – Chang'an Jie was lined on 1 October 1959 by 700,000 people, who watched a parade of just over 11,000 soldiers.[3] Chang'an Jie had been remade into a symbol: a 'wide, open, and straight road, a visible metaphor for China's bright socialist future'.[4]

The Belgian correspondent, Jacques Marcuse, was unimpressed when he saw the revised street in the early 1960s: 'The avenue itself was curiously un-urban', he wrote. 'It suggested the middle stretch of an important highway linking two major hypothetical towns. Actually, it still leads nowhere and, at both ends, becomes a primitive country road with a bad surface.'[5] The obvious and intentional cost of all this revision was in the fabric of the old city; courtyard houses were destroyed along its outer lengths, and the imperial architecture in front of the Forbidden City razed, sweeping away the 'feudal pattern' it apparently represented.

The reshaping of Chang'an Jie into its current form is perhaps allied to the Party's general affection for metaphors of travel. Well-liked by politicians generally, China's Communist leaders seem particularly drawn to them, perhaps partly because of the foundational role which that most arduous journey – the Long March – played in the foundation of the Party. Examples abound: the period leading up to Communist rule has been stretched, straightened and labelled as the 'Road to Rejuvenation'; those who strayed from the Party line in Maoist China were said to be 'deviationists' or later 'capitalist roaders'; whilst in 1965, on the cusp of the Cultural Revolution, Mao would comment that the urgent task was to 'grasp the struggle between the two roads of socialism and capitalism'.[6] Peng Dehuai was said, after the Lushan Conference, to be guilty of right-deviation; that is, of straying from the straight road of Maoist thought to the right, towards a view that seemed to favour less collectivisation and state control of the economy.

Peng was one of many tarred by similar accusations in the late 1950s and during the Cultural Revolution. It was a time when symbolism was everything – when the sublimated meaning of actions or events was far less important than how they could be interpreted and portrayed by those in power. It did not matter that the accusations against Peng were fabricated, or indeed that everyone knew that they were fabricated. He was reduced to a warning of what happens if you drifted from the straight socialist road.

Minded to keep my own deviations to a minimum, as the day continued to ebb away, I found my way back to the compound gate and set myself once more towards the east.

6

Military markings – Tomb of the Princess – new regime, new capital? – the Military Museum

I reached the busy intersection of the Fourth Ring Road. Pedestrian crossings count down the seconds remaining for people to secure safe passage across the street, requiring some rapid arithmetic on Beijing's broader avenues. Even then, however, cars turning right onto the road are able to continue, often leading to an inelegant, hesitant dance between vehicle and pedestrian. Most Chinese streets of decent size also have a dedicated lane for cyclists, which must be navigated before the main road itself; few rules seem to apply. Most dangerous of all, however, are the electric bikes, whose indeterminate status as a vehicle allows them seemingly to choose which, if any, of the ordinances of the road they are required to obey. Their potential to cause harm is exacerbated by their silence and, as I crossed, I was nearly blindsided by a white scooter carrying a young man and woman. Sharp-cheeked, with the bouffant hairstyle beloved by real-estate agents and hairdressers here, the man seemed to barely notice the clumsy foreigner; the woman, sitting side-saddle, gazed impassively at me from beneath a rulered fringe as they disappeared onto the ring road.

I crossed over again, more cautiously this time, to walk along the other side of Chang'an Jie, where a large military compound spreads southwards. From behind a low blocky arch which marks the entrance to the compound, an alabaster figure of Mao, hand raised in benediction, watches the crosstown traffic. Chinese military sites are marked with an emblem bearing, in red and gold, the symbols 八 (ba) and 一 (yi), eight and one, representing the first day of the eighth month, i.e. 1 August, the date in 1927 on which the Nanchang Uprising took place and the Red Army was born. Generally, these are the only markings borne by military buildings, leaving one to speculate as to their actual function – most are also censored on maps of the city, appearing as a blank collection of buildings.[1] These sites are equally inscrutable in person; the immobile young sentries in olive uniform who watch from raised platforms at the entrance gates dissuade any passers-by who linger too long – in English, simply telling one 'No!' – though their darting eyes betray a nervousness which makes one wonder how they would deal with a threat more substantive than a passing tourist with a camera.

There is a preponderance of such sites in western Beijing. In Ming times, a number of ministries and headquarters related to security and the military had been located on the western side of Tiananmen Square, and the distinction had been perpetuated by subsequent administrations. My next way-marker on Long Peace Street was to be a building celebrating China's martial might: the broad-shouldered, Soviet-ornamented Military Museum a little further down Chang'an Jie. First, however, I had to navigate the swirl of overpasses which make up the Gongzhufen intersection, its storybook name – meaning 'Tomb of the Princess' – belying a distinct lack of romance.

The prosaic explanation for the name of this confused cloverleaf, which connects Chang'an Jie with yet another of the city's ring roads, is that two daughters of a Qing dynasty Emperor were buried here. As so often in China, however, an alternative legend has grown up around the name and the place.

The story goes that the Qianlong Emperor, who ruled China for much of the eighteenth century, one day travelled from the Forbidden City to explore the countryside beyond the walls of his great capital. Becoming hungry on his travels, he and his attendants stopped at a village and asked a local man for food. The villager sent his teenage daughter to prepare a meal for the visitors and, shortly afterwards, she delivered them a bowl of steaming noodles and some roasted sweet potatoes. Though dressed in tattered clothes, the girl's beauty and good nature was evident to the Emperor. Having eaten, he spoke to her father and offered to become her godfather, giving the girl the gift of a handkerchief to mark his commitment.

Some years later, the countryside around the capital was beset by famine. On the brink of starvation, the daughter recalled her godfather, and set out to the palace with her father to find him. Arriving at the Imperial City, she encountered a minister of the Emperor who recognised the girl. The pair were duly invited into the Forbidden City, and given food and accommodation. Shortly afterwards, however, the father succumbed to the ravages of famine, and the girl sickened herself with crying. She found little succour or friendship within the palace: the ladies of the court viewed this beautiful peasant girl with a mixture of suspicion and disdain. Eventually, she too died and, unsuited as she was to residency in the royal tombs amongst the mountains to the east of Beijing, her body was taken a short distance to the west of the city, outside the walls, to be buried. Her tomb stood separate and alone in the open farmland, as isolated as she had herself been in the palace.

Day one: Shougang Iron and Steel to Tiananmen

The fairy-tale world of this story seemed long distant as I edged around the hectic north-west corner of the junction, speakers blaring promotional slogans from outside the small shops which arced around the corner, arrayed below the mismatched towers of the Beijing 'Urban-Rural Trade Centre'.

I stopped to buy a coke, and sheltered from the heat under the street-seller's parasol for a few minutes. The xiaomaibu was a flimsy rectangle with a canvas roof, bordered on each side of its central window by racks of magazines and in front by a large, colourful chest freezer. The man behind the counter had close-cropped hair and a cigarette balanced on his lower lip. He spoke with that burr of the Beijing accent, which elongates words with a final 'arr', turning sentences into a blurred drone of soft consonants.

'Where are you from?' the wiry man in the booth asked after returning me my change.

'England', I said.

'Ah ... Really?'

'Really.'

'You don't look English.'

'I am English', I said.

'It's something about your face', he said. 'Are you sure you're English? You look American.'

I dug my passport out of my bag and showed him the front cover, tracing my fingers over the embossed text as I said it in Chinese: 'United Kingdom of Great Britain'.

'Ah. The English are okay. I mean, we remember that you burnt down the old Summer Palace, but that was a long time ago. And all countries have some good, some bad in them.'

'China too?' I asked.

'China too.'

The rumble and thud of traffic on the flyovers, the exhortations of the loudspeakers, the metallic tang of exhaust fumes and, above all, the heat meant Gongzhufen was not a place to linger long. I offered him a cigarette, which he took and tucked behind his ear as he finished the one still dangling from his lip, said my goodbyes – 'Goodbye Englishman' shouted the shop keeper as I walked off – and headed for the other side of the intersection.

This cloverleaf junction has another hidden story, however: one of an alternative vision for modern Beijing. In the aftermath of the Communist takeover in 1949, debate had raged fiercely as to how best to organise and develop the city, restored as the capital after more than twenty years as Beiping – Northern Peace – while the Nationalists ruled from their capitals in the south.

The challenges were obvious. Beijing had changed little in its fundamentals over the last few centuries. The high city walls had kept out the modern world and Beijing had become a beautiful relic of a bygone age. David Kidd, one of the few Westerners to remain in Beijing through the tumultuous first years of Communist rule, felt he was living 'near the timeless heart of Cambaluc itself' in the late forties[2] and, for all the orientalist romance Kidd's invocation of Beijing's ancient title conjures, the historical integrity of the city was remarkable – and problematic. China's seemingly interminable state of conflict, and Beijing's loss of status as the country's capital, had meant that, after a brief period of modernisation in the post-Qing era, little substantial improvement had occurred. As the historian Stephen Haw points out: 'When the Communists took control of Beijing, it was in a parlous state [...] Less than a third of the city's population of about 2 million had running water. Most still relied on wells. Most also had no electricity in their homes, which were lit instead with oil-lamps'.[3]

Alongside the need to improve the city for residents, there was also the pressing matter of transforming Beijing into a capital suitable for running the country. One key question to be answered was where those buildings essential to a modern administration – the various ministries and central offices of a national government – should be placed; over the centuries of imperial rule, decisions had tended to be made inside or in close proximity to the Forbidden City.

When the Japanese arrived in 1937, they did begin the attempt to formulate a solution to Beijing's need to modernise, proposing the building of an entirely new urban area just to the west of Gongzhufen, and about six and a half miles from the centre of the old city. This would be a special enclave, reserved purely for the Japanese, and would allow the old walled city to be preserved as a cultural destination.

After the Communists took control in 1949, a similar proposition was mooted, in which the essential functions of the government would be sited to the west of the city, with Gongzhufen as the furthest edge of a new administrative zone, where nearly forty ministries and commissions would be based. At this time, the area around Gongzhufen was sparsely populated farmland, and the proposers of this scheme, the architects Liang Sicheng and Chen Zhanxiang, felt that starting with a blank slate had a number of advantages: it would allow the old city to be preserved as a cultural site; it would reduce the need for government workers to commute across the city, as the new area would consolidate the major bureaucratic functions with accommodation; and it would offer the opportunity to build 'a new capital city with an artistic demeanor' which was also 'congenial to live in'.[4]

The trouble was that at this point in the early 1950s, CCP leaders were determined followers of the advice of the Soviet Union. Leading a guerrilla movement to seize control of a country was quite different to running one day-to-day, and there was much hand-holding done by the troupe of Soviet advisors who arrived from Moscow shortly after victory in the Civil War was secured: 'The Communist Party of the Soviet Union is our best teacher and we must learn from it', Mao had said in 1949. Drawing from the perceived lessons of redeveloping their own capital, the Soviet group advocated keeping the administrative buildings of the government within the old town, and

Chapter 6

dismissed suggestions of a new urban area to the west of the walled city as uneconomical.

Ultimately, and after a debate which failed to result in a final, coherent plan for the capital, the political centre of China remained at the physical centre of Beijing, with the new government installing itself around the Forbidden City and Tiananmen Square and along the wings of Long Peace Street running east and west. Mao would elect to sequester himself in a former imperial park just to the west of the Forbidden City, seemingly unconcerned by the metaphorical weight of inhabiting pavilions ghosted by the Emperors of the Ming and Qing dynasties. Gongzhufen would become just another busy and anonymous intersection along Chang'an Jie.

Flitting wobbily in front of me on the pavement, a magpie fights with a discarded food wrapper, prodding and turning it with its dark beak. Plumping finally to leave its investigations, and with a great noise from flapping its oil-slick feathers, it launches itself first on to the hooped white metal fence which runs between the pavement and the road, and then up on to the gantry of CCTV cameras which bridges it, its head a gun-turret turning between me and the road; me and the road.

A breeze picks up; this stretch of Long Peace Street is more open, the claustrophobia of Gongzhufen behind me, and I set my stride purposefully in the knowledge that Tiananmen Square is still four miles or so ahead.

Most tourist maps of Beijing fix their westerly edge at around this point, treating the city I had spent the last few hours walking through as something of an irrelevance. This is the beginning of a city that is not just a space for everyday living; the smooth concrete projectile of Beijing's TV tower just to the north, stretching a striped antennae high above the city, declares that this part of Beijing concerns itself with outward show as well.

This is an impression confirmed a little further down the road, when the star-topped spire of Beijing's Military Museum appears above the roof tops, its Soviet bluster testimony again to China's uncertainty as to its own identity in the early years of Communist rule. The museum – the Military Museum of the Chinese People's Revolution, to give it its full title – was built in the late 1950s, and was one of the so-called 'Ten Great Buildings' which were constructed to commemorate the decade since the CCP had taken control of the country. Many of these were built along Chang'an Jie, intended to shore up the east-west thoroughfare's status as China's most important road: 'If the Anniversary Projects were primarily exhibition halls to display the achievements of the previous ten years of socialist construction', the architectural historian Shuishan Yu has observed, 'Chang'an Avenue was the main exhibition space for these halls, a showcase of the showcases'.[5] The most high-profile of these projects were the Great Hall of the People and what is now the National Museum, which stare across Tiananmen Square at each other, sharing the distracting almost-alikeness of twins.

The main building of the Military Museum was closed for renovation, as it had been since late 2011; it would reopen again in 2017 with great fanfare, in time for the 90th anniversary of the founding of the Red Army. Outside, a few dusty tanks and planes sat under a temporary metal shed, including the proudly displayed wreckage of a 1962 US drone. Out-of-towners milled around the entrance, clutching their identity cards – China's propagandising museums tend to be free with the only stipulation being that you prove your identity on entry. A young boy in a vest dashed around holding a plastic machine gun, face screwed up as he sighted targets. The electronic rat-a-tat of his gun cut through the low hum of the crowd. Spotting me as he swept the barrel slowly from left to right, he lowered the gun, perhaps aware that shooting a foreigner, even in play, might give the wrong impression. I was reminded of a recent long journey on a sleeper train from China's south, during which I had

Chapter 6

shared a cabin with a friendly mother and her two young daughters of perhaps four and ten. They were returning from a visit to the family home – and all were attired in identical People's Liberation Army branded t-shirts and shorts.

Diaoyutai State Guesthouse – December 1980 – 'To rebel is justified' – Chairman Mao's dog

Behind the Military Museum sits a broad stretch of parkland, famous for its April cherry blossom and for its lake, which draws water from springs rising in the Western Hills and after which the park is today named: Deep Jade Lake. On the banks of the lake, willows nod and droop, and plastic paddle boats knock hollowly against one another.

To the east of the lake, part of this imperial garden – known as Diaoyutai, or 'fishing platform', for its origins as a favoured angling retreat of a Jin dynasty Emperor – has been walled off for official use and repurposed as the nation's State Guesthouse. It is here that presidents, prime ministers and other dignitaries are housed when visiting the Chinese capital. It too was designated as one of the Ten Great Buildings constructed in the late 1950s, though its design of scattered pavilions set amidst a landscape of narrow inlets and weeping willows consciously echoed China's imperial past rather than its socialist present.

Amongst the 1,300 heads of state who have visited Diaoyutai since its opening in 1959 are Queen Elizabeth II, Mikhail Gorbachev, Boris Yeltsin and Margaret Thatcher, as well as multiple American presidents.[1] Famously, Henry Kissinger, then US Secretary of State, met secretly with Premier Zhou Enlai at Diaoyutai in 1971, paving the way for a reopening of diplomatic and economic relations between the US and China.

Kissinger had arrived in Beijing after shaking off the press following him on an ostensibly routine tour of Asia. Feigning illness, and to everyone else's knowledge holed up in a Pakistani hill town, Kissinger jetted in to Beijing for forty-eight hours of talks. When they concluded, with an agreement that President Nixon would undertake an official visit to China the following year, Zhou Enlai told Kissinger that their announcement would 'shake the world'.[2]

For many Chinese, however – particularly those of a certain generation – the name of Diaoyutai is inextricably linked not to the foreign dignitaries who have stayed there, but rather to the calamitous drama of the later Mao years – the Great Proletarian Cultural Revolution, which rumbled on for a decade between 1966 and 1976.

The story of the Cultural Revolution is less easily told than that of modern China's other defining events. Partly, this is because of the striking disconnection between the declared political and cultural aims of the revolution and the personal motivations, insecurities and grievances which began and sustained it. It also lasted for an awfully long time, moving through different phases in which different elements of Chinese society were held under the magnifying glass. As the historian Jonathan Spence has commented, the Cultural Revolution is that rare historical event that seems to make less sense with the passage of time.

Trouble in the CCP had been brewing for some years by the time the Cultural Revolution began in 1966. The unmitigated disaster of the Great Leap Forward had led to Mao's being pushed aside within the Party by the early 1960s, with many of his economic and political initiatives shelved in favour of more pragmatic options. Mao had become troubled, too, by events in the Soviet Union where, after Stalin's death in 1953, the country's new leader Nikita Khrushchev had set about dismantling his predecessor's reputation, exposing his brutality and abuse of power. If this could happen in the Soviet Union, why not in China?

The Cultural Revolution was Mao's response to this perceived threat to his authority and his legacy. The Chairman argued that in order to counter the possibility of any deviation from the journey towards true socialism – a course to be piloted by the Great Helmsman alone – a programme reforming the thinking of the masses needed to be embarked upon. The values of the past must be overthrown – forcibly if necessary.

Diaoyutai became notorious as the headquarters of the political faction who oversaw many of the key directives of the Cultural Revolution, handing down diktats which aimed to limit and change the behaviour of the Chinese populace in a range of different ways. This group became known around the world as the 'Gang of Four' and was led by a woman who would become one of the pantomime villains of modern Chinese history, Mao's fourth wife Jiang Qing: the 'White Boned Demon'.

In recent years, Diaoyutai has begun to open to wealthy paying guests; 'with an attitude of "chasing perfection" and quality service', its website blurb runs, 'we are welcoming friends from home and abroad'.

I doubted, however, that this welcome would extend to me as a curious Westerner unable to afford the prohibitive expense of the place. Walking up the northerly avenue which ran along the edge of the grounds of the guesthouse, I could see tiled roofs peeking over the low wall, and guessed that this was probably as near as I was likely to get. I thought it worth a try, however, despite a somewhat dishevelled and overheated appearance.

The smartly dressed attendant at the entrance looked at me questioningly as I approached his plinth; behind him, two young guards, in dress uniform, stood motionless at the gate.

'A friend of mine is staying here; I'm supposed to meet him at reception', I said.

'You can call him, and he can come and meet you here at the gate', he replied.

'Well, he asked me to meet him inside', I said, 'so maybe I can just go through'.

He paused, considered me again slowly, and then repeated himself: 'You can call him. He can come and meet you here at the gate'.

I gamely took out my phone and went through the motions of calling. I held it to my ear and let a suitable amount of time pass. 'He's not answering', I told him with faux-bemusement, 'I'll have to come back later'.

'Okay. When you get through to him, tell him to come and meet you here at the gate', he said, a faint smile on his lips.

That was that, I thought. I walked back down the street a little way and decided I had had enough for a while. I sat down on the pavement, propped myself against a low fence in the shade of Diaoyutai's famous avenue of Gingko trees and watched the light filter through the leaves to play on the high perimeter wall.

December 1980: four years after Mao's death and the end of the Cultural Revolution; dry and cold in Beijing, with the temperature barely creeping above zero. The White Boned Demon herself, Jiang Qing, dressed all in black, her short hair brushed back, sits behind a plain wooden dock in the centre of a packed courtroom listening to the emotional testimony of Liao Mosha, a former official imprisoned for eight years during the Cultural Revolution. Suddenly Jiang erupts: 'This is really outrageous, asking the renegades and bad elements to come and speak in court'. Gan Ying, a female judge, tells Jiang to be quiet; that she is adding to her crimes by interrupting in this way. 'What the hell do you mean by crimes?' she retorts. 'You bitch.'[3]

Her hostility has been unremitting since the trial began; of the ten defendants, she stands alone in her vitriolic refutation of everything the court stands for – and her interjections and objections make for compelling viewing. China's new leadership have elected to put the Cultural Revolution on trial in a very public way, and across the country, at 7.30pm each evening, families gather to watch the summary of that day's events in court. What unfolds on their television screens over nearly five weeks is a carefully orchestrated investigation of some of China's darkest recent history, in the professed attempt to exact justice: a public reckoning of the unspoken terror of the Cultural Revolution. Peng Dehuai's widow would comment that, having seen the defendants led in handcuffs to the dock, she finally felt she would be able to console her husband's spirit in heaven.[4] Though the most extreme elements of her testimony are censored, Jiang Qing is indisputably the main attraction in the most high-profile trial in China's history.

The trial takes place, fittingly, at No. 1 Justice Road, which runs south from Chang'an Jie just to the east of Tiananmen Square. The Chinese state wish the trial to act as a means of drawing a line underneath the chaos and fear of the Cultural Revolution; ticketed audience members are invited to watch the proceedings. They include representatives from all over China, and from numerous branches of the government. For an administration as secretive as the CCP, this relative transparency testifies to the government's desire to control the narrative; to lay the blame for the Cultural Revolution at the feet of those in the dock – and, particularly, Jiang Qing.

In its early days, Jiang's main concern was with the cultural aspects of the Cultural Revolution. It was she who, in 1965, helped to orchestrate the writing and publication of the article which in many ways fired the starting gun on the whole debacle; a critique of a play titled

Chapter 7

Hai Rui Dismissed from Office, which has been referred to as the most influential theatrical review in history. The play tells the story of a Ming Emperor who takes umbrage at the honest criticism of an official in his court, dismissing him from his post despite the minister's good intentions. Irrespective of its historical source material, it was hard not to read *Hai Rui Dismissed from Office* as anything other than an allegory for the dismissal of Peng Dehuai at Lushan in 1959 – the diligent underling courageous enough to tell the truth. The review of the play which Jiang Qing organised – and which was revised by Mao himself – explicitly drew out its perceived politics, asserting that not only did the play criticise Mao and glorify Peng, but that Wu Han, the playwright and deputy mayor of Beijing, was himself a supporter of the private economy. The article became a dividing line for the upper reaches of the Party hierarchy; Wu Han would later die in prison.

In the aftermath of the article's publication, Mao established the Cultural Revolution Group, with Jiang Qing as one of its key members. The group swiftly moved into Diaoyutai 'with a crew of telephonists, typists, recorders and other assistants'.[5] Jiang co-opted one villa for her living quarters, another for her office. From behind the walls of the State Guesthouse, they would orchestrate the Cultural Revolution, Mao periodically visiting to support, or chastise – or sometimes just to escape the chaos.

'To rebel is justified', Mao said in 1966; it was the only way, he asserted, to overthrow the 'demons and monsters' he perceived lurking still in Chinese society. It was to the youth that he turned, encouraging students across the country to engage in debate and expose these malign elements. Under the encouragement of Mao and the Cultural Revolution Group, young people across the country formed themselves into groups of Red Guards, who would act as the stormtroopers of the revolution, dressing themselves in cobbled-together military uniform. The instructions handed down to the Red Guards were vague enough to provide impunity in carrying out the stated aim of combatting the 'four olds' – old ideas, old customs, old culture and old habits – and harrying the demons and monsters hidden away. Madame Mao argued that 'when bad people get beaten by good people, they deserve it';[6] one of several statements by her and others which seemed to sanction violence.

In Beijing, and across China, the summer of 1966 saw the young turn upon the old, students upon teachers, children upon parents. The centrifugal forces that kept social order began to lose their power, and those hot days marked the end of innocence for many in China. David Kidd recounts that at night in the city 'the screams of the beaten and dying made sleep impossible. … By the end of that month the dead were piled so high that they could not be burned fast enough in the huge new crematorium to the west that, then as today, is the last destination of all those who live and die in Peking'.[7] This outpouring of violence – an uprising against authority in all its forms – became known as Bloody August. Artists and intellectuals were hounded beyond the limits of endurance; many committed suicide. Homes were ransacked. Professors and school principals were tortured and beaten to death. People were arbitrarily labelled – landlord; counter-revolutionary; careerist; black gang element; local despot – and humiliated in mass rallies, forced to wear dunce hats and placards spelling out their sins.

An interview with one of the Red Guards captures something of their giddy abandon in this new topsy-turvy world:

> I took part in pretty much all the big events: being reviewed by Grandad Mao in Tiananmen, destroying the four olds, the great link-ups, armed struggle: anything that involved beating people up and smashing things and taking stuff. Man, it was fantastic! Me and my buddies got baseball bats and worked our way up the street from south to north. We must have busted every damn shop sign along Xidan. Just try doing that today![8]

The enthusiasm was real; a collective madness which seems inexplicable in cool-headed retrospect. Few people are willing to talk of it, even today.

Chapter 7

The intensity of this early phase was ultimately unsupportable, even for Mao; in the following year he would denounce the violence, and, in the last years of the 1960s he would pack many of the Red Guards off to the countryside to learn from the peasantry. Like a comet, however, this burst of heat and light drew a tail behind it, and the Cultural Revolution continued in a new form – this time more political, and focused on the rooting out of undesirable elements from the Party, including those at the highest levels. Jiang Qing and the Gang of Four would be intimately involved in the political witch-hunt that unfolded, with Madame Mao taking the opportunity to enact revenge against the many she felt had wronged her over the years. She also kept a close grip on acceptable forms of artistic pursuit, imposing strict regulations on the theatre, literature, opera, music and film, though she herself took great delight in the films of Greta Garbo, which she would screen in the privacy of her villa at Diaoyutai. Her favourite book was said to be Dumas' *The Count of Monte Cristo* – that paean to long-held grievances and the visceral delight of revenge. In Dumas' novel, the Count mentally condemns his enemies 'to every torment that his inflamed imagination could devise, while still considering that the most frightful were too mild and, above all, too brief for them: torture was followed by death, and death brought, if not repose, at least an insensibility that resembled it'.

Jiang was arrested in 1976. Mao had died at the beginning of September, a few days after suffering another major heart attack, and an inevitable power struggle followed his death. The Gang of Four were called to a meeting on 6 October; hidden behind screens in the meeting room were security guards, who handcuffed each member as they arrived. Jiang, however, never turned up. Late that night, a military detachment arrived at her villa and broke in. Jiang was arrested in her nightgown.

She was kept at Qincheng, the famed Beijing prison in the city's northern reaches which still today houses China's high-ranking and high-profile miscreants. She took her imprisonment resolutely, eating and sleeping without obvious anxiety as to her fate, practicing *tai ji quan*. 'I tried to keep myself healthy and strong', she would say later, 'so that one day I could stride properly to the execution ground.'[9]

She almost got her wish; the sentence passed down at the end of her trial in 1980 was that of death – but suspended for two years to assess her behaviour; China's new leaders were perhaps cautious of making a martyr of her. As she was sentenced, she cried to the court 'It's no crime to make revolution!'

Jiang Qing stuck unrepentantly to her principles until the end; she took delight throughout in pointing out to the court the essential hollowness of the proceedings. And there was, of course, one figure noticeably missing from the roster of defendants accused. It was Mao Zedong, she argued repeatedly, who had orchestrated the violence and chaos of the period: 'I was Chairman Mao's dog', she famously told the court. 'Whomever he told me to bite, I bit.' As one television viewer of the court proceedings in China observed at the time 'Everyone knows it was really Mao who gave the orders in the Cultural Revolution, and it is he who should be on trial'.[10]

The official history in my People's Republic of China timeline also lays a little of the blame at Mao's door, but there is no ambiguity about whom the CCP wish to be remembered as the true villains of this particular episode:

> The 'cultural revolution' was a political movement mistakenly launched and led by Mao Zedong who misestimated China's class situation and political circumstances. Unfortunately, it was exploited by two counter revolutionary cliques respectively headed by Lin Biao and Jiang Qing, and caused serious damaged to the Chinese Communist Party, the nation and all peoples. In 1976, after Zhou Enlai and Mao Zedong passed away, the Politburo of the CPC led by Hua Guofeng smashed the Jiang Qing counter-revolutionary clique, bringing an end to the calamity.

I walked slowly southwards through the grove of Gingko trees. As I wandered, I wondered. I thought about Jiang, safe behind these

Chapter 7

walls, and the chaos that unfolded on the streets of Beijing during those first months of the Cultural Revolution. I thought about guilt and memory and how it haunts a place. I thought about the chasm the years of Mao's rule had opened between China's future and its past, and whether, after a diversion such as the Cultural Revolution, way merely leads on to way, and one can never go back. I thought about the almost unfathomable chaos; the complete absence of logic; and what it must have been like not to know, from day to day and week to week, whether the invisible lines separating good and bad would shift once more. I thought about the final outcome of all of the conflict, and the new start that China made, for better or worse, once Mao was dead and Jiang put behind bars.

And I thought about the final act of Jiang's drama in which, like Lady Macbeth, she quietly, offstage, took her own life. After her death, her ashes were interred not at Babaoshan, or back in her home province of Shandong as she requested, but, like the peasant girl in the story, she was placed out of sight and mind in a sprawling cemetery in Beijing's north-west, under a modest grey headstone inscribed with one of her many pseudonyms.

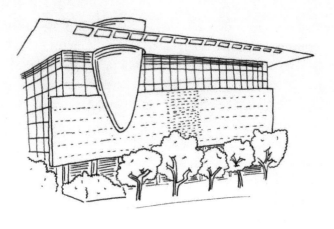

8

Big roofs – Capital Museum – *pailou* – some history

I crossed the road from the slew of Gingko trees, electing to wind my way to Chang'an Jie through back streets which I had previously only glimpsed through a taxi window; here I could ink in another section of my mental map of the city.

Running south, back down towards Long Peace Street, I found a phalanx of stately buildings, bruised grey and with an air of official-dom. Atop them perched sweeping rooflines of glazed tile, with up-ticked corners – the traditional hipped roofs of old China; the roofs a schoolchild would draw atop houses if asked to sketch a Chinese scene. These particular buildings, I discovered later, were relics of the early 1950s, when the ubiquitous Soviet advisors were advocating a national architectural style which mixed modern and traditional elements. The Chinese 'big roof' or *dawuding* was the most obvious symbol to signal a link with the past. The incongruity of such roofs on top of twentieth-century structures did not go unremarked; earlier in the century the style had been referred to as 'wearing a Western suit and a Chinese skullcap'.

A number of significant buildings adopted the 'big roof' style in the early 1950s, before an abrupt and characteristic change of heart from the Party leadership in the middle of that decade, when such rooflines were suddenly deemed to be wasteful – they were, of course, also visual motifs redolent of the feudal past. These buildings running south just a little across the city from Diaoyutai were remnants of that brief architectural phase when it seemed as though the new and the old might continue to rub along passably – in architecture at least. They were also the only memorial to those abandoned plans of a new political centre for the city – that which would have run out to Gongzhufen. The small, dark windows hid ministries and bureaus of obscure function. Despite their slight awkwardness, the buildings have a certain sturdy charm – and seem indisputably preferable to the massed ranks of anonymous, perpendicular boxes which line the wings of Long Peace Street and today house most government bodies.[1]

I arrived back onto Long Peace Street at Muxidi intersection. Back west, banks of old, pale-peach apartment blocks ran along either side of the road. At a hotel on the corner, a group of businessmen huddled by the entrance to the marble foyer, swiping frantically at their smartphones as they talked. Away to the south, I could see a reaching industrial chimney; it marked the site, I knew, of an unseen and more venerable partner: the Tianning pagoda. The pagoda's ridged octagonal silhouette has marked the city skyline for nine-hundred years; its industrial counterpart was erected during the Cultural Revolution as part of the workings of a Thermal Power Plant and, so I had heard, was soon to be demolished.

Day one: Shougang Iron and Steel to Tiananmen

On the opposite corner from where I stood sat Beijing's Capital Museum, a sleek metal and glass rectangle resembling an upscale airport terminal, built to house vestiges of the city's past and to tell of Beijing's storied history. I crossed the bridge and entered a vast hall which dwarfs its main feature: a great colourful archway or pailou – one of the punctuation marks of old China's towns and cities. They are carved wooden archways with three openings, and were often erected to venerate worthy citizens, particularly chaste widows who remained unmarried after the death of their husband. One traveller in nineteenth-century Sichuan, for example, recorded the story of a pailou which had been put up to memorialise a woman who, so over-come with grief at having lost her magistrate husband, swallowed a concoction of gold and lead before dressing herself in her state robes and retiring to patiently await the arrival of death. Once a defin-ing feature of Chinese streetscapes, providing geographical markers which live on in many place names, most pailou have long been brought to ground, viewed by the CCP as remnants of the old China and, more practically, an impediment to traffic flow. One is almost as likely to encounter a pailou in New York or London, marking the entrance to those cities' Chinatowns, as in Beijing.

There is pleasure in their sheer decorativeness: vivid geometri-cal motifs are picked out in blue, turquoise and gold, with images of dragons and phoenixes in relief on the archway's horizontals. Fundamentally lacking in utilitarian function, they simply brightened the streetscape, marking passage through the city. The Jingde arch-way in the Capital Museum is one of a pair, pulled down in 1954. The architect Liang Sicheng thought it one of the most attractive in the city, and the museum's own description offers a bittersweet evocation of the manner in which they graced their original home – the Street of Respect for Virtues: 'if one stands at the eastern archway and looks westwards, they would find the Fuchengmen gate tower as the background and see the Western Hills if the weather was fine, and the scene was extraordinarily beautiful at the sunset'.

Chapter 8

On another floor, visitors from out of town can experience Old Beijing on an exhibition floor built to resemble the city's traditional hutong. Children scamper through the fake alleyways, whilst their parents, smartphones out, snap away at the faux-traditional details of cast-concrete doorways; they could see the crumbling reality just a couple of miles down the road. As one caption has it: 'The most impressive thing about Beijing City are Hutongs – the lanes'.

The museum's main exhibition, however, tells the story of Beijing's unlikely journey to becoming, and remaining, China's capital city.

Beijing has always been an outlier, perched on the northern edge of the territory which has historically constituted China. It is to the nomads from the north, and not to the native Han Chinese, that Beijing owes its status as the country's capital. Kublai Khan, grandson of Genghis Khan, established it as the political centre of his Yuan dynasty in the thirteenth century. The Mongols had swept in on horseback from the northern grasslands; after a long siege, Genghis Khan had the city, then named Zhongdu, razed to the ground and everyone in sight killed. A rival visited some months afterwards to see if the rumours that the city had been captured were true; he found there a scene of utter horror: 'the bones of the slaughtered formed mountains ... the soil was greasy with human fat'. A number of his men died of illnesses picked up from the rotting corpses.[2]

The devastated city would eventually be rebuilt by his grandson, a little to the north-east, as Khanbaliq, the city known to Marco Polo, and would become the capital of the largest unbroken land empire in history: it was also known as *Dadu* or 'Great Capital'. It was convenient for the Mongols, whose traditional lands lay north of the city.[3] China, however, ended up with a capital city which was somewhat awkwardly sited.

The heartland of China has always been well to the south of Beijing, concentrated on the fertile plains of the Yellow and, latterly, the Yangtze Rivers, which wind from west to east in a parallel dance, away and then together, across the country's middle, from the Tibetan plateau to China's eastern seaboard. It was in the vicinity of the Yellow River that, for the previous two millennia, China had located its capitals, whilst the river cities of the Yangtze became the established economic and cultural centres of the country – a distinction which they retain today, with the area of *Jiangnan*, meaning 'South of the Yangtze', still the most dynamic, wealthy and sophisticated area of China.

Beijing is ill-suited as a capital for other reasons. It sits on an arid plain which suffers dry, cold winters; this makes growing staple crops and even ensuring a basic water supply difficult. There was a reason that the nomads called the land north of Beijing their own, as China's traditional forms of agriculture were not well suited to that terrain; the Great Wall, just forty or so miles outside of the city, marked off the boundary between competing forms of subsistence, as well as those of culture, language and politics. The Mongols restored and rejuvenated the Grand Canal, a long ribbon of water stretching to the fertile south, to keep the city fed. Likewise, elaborate systems of water management were required to ensure that the city did not run dry.

The Mongol nomads had laid waste to the city and built a new one in its place. Just under a hundred years after the Yuan dynasty's establishment, the city was subject to another upheaval. The conquest of the city by soldiers of what would become the Ming dynasty brought fire and destruction once more; even worse, the first rulers of the Ming would cast the city into relative irrelevance by relocating the capital to Nanjing, in the Yangtze river delta. However, in 1402, the fourth son of the first Ming Emperor wrested control of the throne from the anointed successor.[4] Naming himself the Yongle Emperor, he restored Beijing as the nation's capital, rebuilding the city in his own image. It is he who named the city Beijing; and who built much of the architecture for which the city is famed, including the vast palace of the Forbidden City.

The subsequent Qing dynasty – the last custodians of the Dragon

Throne – were also impostors from the north, though they took the city without the blood and fire which had accompanied the last two changes of regime. When they came to power in the mid-seventeenth century, they chose to retain Beijing as the national capital, leaving much of the Ming city design and architecture unchanged.[5] To show their authority, however, they evicted the Han Chinese residents of Beijing from the old walled city, forcing them to a new district to the south. There were suggestions in the late nineteenth century by those wishing to reform the declining Qing rule that the capital be moved to Xi'an due to Beijing's vulnerability to foreign attack.[6] But at Beijing the capital remained, up to and beyond the final, anticlimactic demise of the dynasty in 1912.

Through the turbulent years which followed, with warlords vying for control of the nation, Beijing's status as capital was often more theoretical than actual. After the Nationalists under Chiang Kai-shek eventually gained control of the country in 1928, Nanjing became the official capital of the Republic: Beiping, or 'Northern Peace' as it was renamed, was back to being a provincial town.

The war years from 1937, with the Japanese waging a ruthless campaign, would see China's capital becoming itinerant, drifting up the Yangtze river: first, briefly, to Wuhan, and thence to Chongqing, where the vertiginous cliffs of the city offered some slight protection from the nightly onslaughts of the Japanese bombers. These were capitals in name only, however; the reality was that they were entrenched positions of weakness, reflecting the emerging reality that Chiang Kai-Shek and his Nationalist government had lost their grip on the nation.

In Beijing, the Japanese had taken control of the city, establishing it as the seat of the 'Provisional Government of the Republic of China'. The Japanese rule of the city ran from 1937 to 1945 and was a time of hardship; indeed times had been tough throughout the 1930s. The sinologist Derk Bodde would report on the poverty he found on returning to the city after the Japanese occupation. The buildings, he wrote, 'look drab, gray, and unpainted. Traffic on the streets seems slow and thin compared with former days, and business appears to be in a somnolent state. Goods in the shops are in general meager in quantity and variety, high in price, and poor in quality'.[7] To him, it felt that he was witnessing the end of an ancient civilisation.

Bodde was writing in 1948; that same winter, the People's Liberation Army laid siege to the city, by now back in the hands of the Nationalists after the end of the Second World War. Eventually, the general in charge of the city gave way, and negotiated a deal in which Beiping was handed over to the Communist forces peacefully; it would be restored later that year (1949) as the nation's capital, and renamed 'Beijing' once more.

It was a tumultuous story – of shifts in power, unlikely restorations and frequent calamity for the city and its people. It testified to a remarkable tenacity, and of the gravitational pull of the place. The Capital Museum's synopsis made it sound as if it had all happened over the course of a long afternoon: 'Beijing experienced various stages of development from primitive settlement, feudal town, prominent center of northern China, dynastic capital, and finally to the capital of the People's Republic of China. Today, Beijing aims to develop herself into an international metropolis with a harmonic integration between traditional and modern cultures'.

I left the museum alongside a cluster of school children who looked bored beyond relief and walked up onto the steel bridge which straddles Chang'an Jie. Looking west from the bridge, the middle lane rose smoothly to an overpass meeting a main road coming from the north. I counted across: ten lanes altogether from left to right. In the slow lane of the east-bound carriageway, a man in his late sixties was piloting an electric wheelchair in a determined fashion, doing his best to evade the rumbling diesel buses which would occasionally sweep in to a bus stop.

9

Muxidi Bridge – petitions and protests – May Fourth – Democracy Movement – 1976 – 1978 – 1989 – the aftermath

As the day had progressed – it was now into the early afternoon – the relative brightness had been gradually occluded by a settling miasma of pollution, which robbed fine edges of their definition. The constancy of at least some haze in China's cities, even on clear days, meant that after a time you didn't tend to notice it very much; I found that it was upon my return to Europe that the opacity through which I had been viewing China was discernible. Emerging from the terminal back in England was like that moment when the optician slots in the final lens and the world suddenly gains a new found, and rather magical, level of definition and clarity.

Disappearing in the haze back to the west of where I was standing,

Day one: Shougang Iron and Steel to Tiananmen

Chang'an Jie crossed a modest canal running south out of the waters of Diaoyutai. This was Muxidi Bridge.

I could not tell the story of Long Peace Street without mentioning those days on which it has resounded with shouts of protest, and the steady footfall of those drawn here by the desire for change. The subject is unavoidable. The dense square miles at the centre of the city – political and judicial authority writ large in architecture – have long exerted a gravitational pull on those with grievances against the state. The protests Long Peace Street has witnessed over the course of the twentieth century speak of the swirling forces of frustration which have repeatedly threatened the status quo, and which make a mockery of the street's given name.

In the Ming and Qing era, those seeking to complain about corruption or injustice would, if unable to secure redress with their local magistrate, travel to Beijing's centre to petition the court bureaucracy directly; some persistent souls even managed to carry their petitions to the Emperor himself. A version of this system exists still, though those who pursue petitions in today's China rarely secure justice, becoming locked instead into a Kafkaesque proceeding which often seems to demand and encourage a sort of monomania. As in imperial times, petitioners will often arrive in Beijing from hundreds or thousands of miles away, having been frustrated by local, official channels. The most dogged amongst them will take their case to Xinhuamen, the Gate of New China, which marks the main entrance to the Chinese leadership compound, or the Great Hall of the People, in order to appeal directly to their leaders. There, they are inevitably rounded up by police and sent back to their provinces, often to face restrictions on their liberty once at home.

Sometimes the protestors who are drawn here arrive not as individuals, but bound by some common ideal. The mass protests which have periodically occurred in the capital are divisible into two broad types: those whipped up by the country's leaders in order to make a particular political point – such as the gatherings of the Cultural

Revolution, cultivated and managed by Mao and his underlings, or the anti-Japanese protests of 2012 – and protests which occur organically and over which the state has no control. The history of this latter form of popular protest in the modern era can be said to begin, chronologically and intellectually, with the May Fourth Movement.

Named after a student protest which began on that day in 1919, the May Fourth Movement crystallised a set of emerging beliefs that had developed in the aftermath of the Qing dynasty's demise. Specifically, the protests were against the outcome of the conference in Versailles, which had set the terms of peace after the First World War. The Chinese were aggrieved that a former German territory on their north-east coast would be handed over to the Japanese rather than returned to China, which had thought itself a valued ally. Around 3,000 students from Beijing's universities marched to the Gate of Heavenly Peace to protest the deal. Blocked from marching on towards the Japanese Legation, they instead surrounded, broke into and set fire to the home of a government official apparently sympathetic to the Japanese. Anti-Japanese sentiment would rise sharply in the aftermath: a boycott of Japanese goods was encouraged, and rickshaw men refused to haul Japanese passengers.

More generally, however, the May Fourth Movement became synonymous with an intellectual trend against the value system of old China, emerging out of a concern over the country's place in the modern world and the direction in which it was moving. The broader ideas which were expressed by the movement advocated a shift away from the long-established traditions and hierarchies, towards a freer, Westernised system of political leadership and the embrace of science and technology. The twenty-year-old Qu Qiubai – later to become one of the leaders of the fledgling Communist Party in China – wrote of the strength of emotion amongst those who identified with the movement: 'Feelings alone, however, ran so strong that restlessness could no more be contained. That was, so far as I can see, the real significance of the student movement. There was a demand for change, and that demand erupted in an outburst'.[1]

The date 4 May 1919 casts a long shadow. Many and various are those who have subsequently claimed kinship to its ideals: the Chinese Communist Party presents it as a significant staging post on the nation's so-called 'Road to Rejuvenation', but those who took to the streets in protest against CCP rule in the 1970s and 1980s also traced their descent from the May Fourth Movement. By then, the Communists had become the status quo to be queried: the young upstarts had become the staid old men, and the need for rejuvenation – but perhaps not wholesale change – needed to be asserted once more.

The so-called 'Democracy Movement' which took up the mantle of the May Fourth protestors began in earnest in the late 1970s, with public expressions of frustration at the pace of development in China and the restrictions on liberty and individuality. It would end dramatically in June 1989, with pitched battles fought between the state and its people along both wings of Long Peace Street.

'Democracy Movement' is a translation of the Chinese *minzhu yundong*. Minzhu can be translated as 'rule of the people', sharing a similar etymology to the Greek derived 'democracy': *demos* meaning people, and *kratos* meaning rule or strength. Yet there is a gap between the political notion minzhu suggests, and the idea of democracy as commonly referred to in the modern Western world: it does not, for example, necessarily imply a majority decision-making process, but carries historical connotations of centralised rule based on the collective will of the masses, who act as a scrutinising force – a rule *for* the people and not *of* the people. In the post-Mao era, its specific meaning was far from clear, muddied by its employment in Communist political rhetoric.[2]

The use of the label 'Democracy Movement' also suggests that those involved in it were united behind an ultimate goal and the means by which it was to be achieved. In reality, those who took part in the restiveness of this era were diverse in their views and backgrounds. Some were simply frustrated by economic uncertainty and governmental corruption, whilst some did indeed want a more representative form of government. Some wanted greater freedom of expression; others simply the freedom to eat the food of their choice in the university cafeteria.

To understand the complex story of this period of restiveness we must begin in 1976. It was a momentous year for China; the rumblings of change made geological by the sudden tectonic shift which triggered the deadly Tangshan Earthquake, its epicentre not far from Beijing, in July of that year. The lives lost to the earthquake ran into the hundreds of thousands, but it was the deaths of two ageing men which would have the most significant long term repercussions in China that year. The Great Helmsman, Mao Zedong, would die in September aged eighty-two, whilst the year had begun with the death from cancer of Premier Zhou Enlai.

Zhou had managed to weather the storms of the Great Leap Forward and the Cultural Revolution – practically the only high-level leader to do so – endearing himself to the Chinese people in the process as a pragmatist who restrained Mao's more impulsive tendencies. On a clear, cold January day shortly after his death, Long Peace Street was lined metres deep by mourners dressed in drab uniforms of blue and grey and revolutionary green, there to watch Zhou's final journey. A curtained blue and white bus would carry his coffin west to Babaoshan for cremation along the emptied lanes of Chang'an Jie. Despite having spent decades fighting and working alongside one another, Mao Zedong would not attend his memorial, nor would he issue any public message of condolence, jealous perhaps at the deep reservoirs of affection Zhou's death had tapped.

The crowds would return later that year, the catharsis of the funeral seemingly not enough. On the eve of the solar term of Qingming, or 'Clear Brightness', in early April, a period traditionally marked by visiting and tending the graves of loved ones, people began to arrive at Tiananmen Square, laying wreaths and pasting up poems commemorating Zhou – and stridently criticising Jiang Qing and the Gang of Four:

> You've got together a little gang
> To stir up trouble all the time,
> Hoodwinking the people, capering about.
> But your days are numbered.[3]

Thousands turned out to the square to read these poems and share in a collective outpouring of emotion after the long, restrictive decade of the Cultural Revolution. Uncomfortable with the increasingly forthright tone of the memorials, the government had all the wreaths and poems removed, resulting in an enormous political demonstration of more than 100,000 people which led, ultimately, to the police and soldiers sweeping in to clear the square with force.

Calls for greater freedom and political reform continued to grow in the following years. Two years after the protests in Zhou Enlai's honour, Chang'an Jie once again became the focal point for calls for change, with Xidan, a junction just to the west of Tiananmen Square, turned into a forum for public protest. On a 200-metre-long brick wall at Xidan, large handwritten sheets – known as 'big character posters' or *dazibao* – began to be pasted up, calling for a range of reforms related to both political and cultural openness. Democracy Wall, as it came to be known, provided a focal point for the promotion and discussion of new political ideas. It was a far more sustained protest, motivated by intellectual debate rather than raw emotion. Unofficial, homemade newspapers were distributed each week, dense with radical poetry:

> A white stone brick wall at Xidan
> calmly stands by Changan Street
> [...]
> The cry of a new arrival
> echoes all around, forcefully.
> 'We want democracy!'

Chapter 9

'We want science!'
'We want a legal system!'
'We want the Four Modernisations!'[4]

In late 1979, the authorities would close down Xidan's Democracy Wall, and relocate it to a park further west of the city; anyone wishing to post a dazibao would now have to register their details with the authorities. By this time, one of the leaders of the movement, an electrician named Wei Jingsheng, had been sentenced to fifteen years in prison, having called openly for the fifth modernisation – of democracy. His prosecutor declared that although the Chinese constitution did protect certain democratic rights:

> It does not mean absolute freedom for one to do as one likes [...] Freedom of speech of the individual citizen must be based on the four basic principles of insisting on the socialist road, the dictatorship of the proletariat, the leadership of the party, and Marxism-Leninism-Mao Zedong thought. The citizen has only the freedom to support these principles and not the freedom to oppose them.[5]

The rulers of Communist China have demonstrated over the years a tendency to, tacitly and often retrospectively, redraw the red line marking out what is politically acceptable. The protests of 1976 after Premier Zhou's death were initially condemned as counter-revolutionary and dangerous. Later that assessment would be overturned: they were in fact satisfactorily revolutionary, the Party decided. The protesting voices of 1978 at Democracy Wall were initially welcomed by then leader Deng Xiaoping, who observed that China's rulers did not have the right to criticise people for promoting democracy[6] – before being abruptly silenced as they became more vociferous. Sometimes this ambiguity is unintentional, reflecting a power struggle at the heart of government, or within the mind and conscience of one leader. Sometimes it is calculated – intended to lure people into the open. Yet the cumulative effect has been to encourage confusion and ambiguity as to where the thin red line might actually be drawn.

Day one: Shougang Iron and Steel to Tiananmen

This uncertainty was palpably evident in the events of the dramatic concluding act of the Democracy Movement: the protests of May and June 1989. As with the Qingming revolt of 1976, it was the death of a popular political leader which vented the simmering discontent; in this case, the passing of Hu Yaobang. Hu – a modernising figure who advocated eating with a knife and fork, rather than chopsticks (for reasons of hygiene) and who was one of the first of the senior Party members to eschew the Mao suit in favour of a Western-style outfit – had been forced to resign his position as General Secretary of the Party a few years earlier because, according to hardliners, he had failed to quell another eruption of pro-democracy student protest at the tail end of 1986 with sufficient decisiveness. His death from a heart attack in April 1989 acted as a release valve for another outpouring of dissatisfaction amongst young people about the restrictions imposed by their government; they strode out from the universities and descended upon Tiananmen Square once again. In the coming weeks, the vast, inhuman granite and marble of the square would be turned into a place of the people, its careful symmetry disordered by the makeshift festival which emerged: colourful banners tied up; tents erected. Wall posters appeared again across the city. These protestors knew their history too, and would mark the seventieth anniversary of the May Fourth Movement with one of the largest marches the country had seen for decades.

The protests developed their own momentum; a sense emerged that their scale was too large to be ignored. In the middle of May, thousands of protestors began a hunger strike. In major cities across the country – Nanjing, Chengdu, Guangzhou and numerous others – similar uprisings were taking place. It felt like change was almost palpable in the spring air.

As with earlier protests, the government's response was initially hesitant. The higher echelons of the Party were split, with some leading politicians sympathetic to the calls for greater openness, whilst others advocated a robust response which would send a clear message. On 20 May, a month into the protests, the governmental hardliners announced that Beijing would be placed under martial law. The assumption seems to have been that the mere presence of the army on the street would be sufficient to bring popular involvement in the protests to an end.

It was not just students who supported the movement; whilst those encamped on the square were mostly young people from Beijing's universities, the protests had developed broad support amongst the people more generally: a fact that had become patently evident during the government's first attempt to bring the PLA into the city as night fell on 19 May. 'Every military column the Army dispatched – and they came from all points of the compass – was blocked', writes the historian Timothy Brook, 'first by hundreds, then thousands, then tens of thousands of ordinary people'.[7] Chang'an Jie was one of the main routes along which the army travelled; at major intersections like Gongzhufen and Muxidi, and even out at the Capital Iron and Steel Works in Shijingshan, they encountered makeshift barricades manned by ordinary Beijingers, which brought their vehicles to a halt.

The last time that the People's Liberation Army had entered Beijing, they had been hailed as heroes. On the last day of January 1949, as their final victory over the Nationalists neared, they were greeted in the streets of Beijing by crowds, some waving flags and some simply curious. The soldiers were led by a truck carrying a speaker blaring slogans – 'Congratulations to the people of Peiping on their liberation' – and 'had a red-cheeked, healthy look and seemed in high spirits. As they marched up the street, the crowds lining the sidewalks ... burst into applause'.[8]

People were relieved at the conclusion of the siege to which the city had just been subjected and the prospect that privations of recent times – they had had no electricity supply for many of the recent weeks – were over; Beijing, after all, had suffered a tough couple of decades, having first been marginalised by the Nationalists, then occupied by the Japanese.

Day one: Shougang Iron and Steel to Tiananmen

Over the course of the war years the PLA had developed a reputation as a respectful army, not to be feared by ordinary people, and with a strict set of values which governed their behaviour. Codified in the early days of the army, these included instructions to: 'Replace all doors when you leave a house'; 'Return and roll up the straw matting on which you sleep'; and 'Be courteous and polite to the people and help them when you can'. Now they seemed to be the enemy, sent in to frighten the people of Beijing back into their homes.

The protestors stood strong, however, and in the face of the barricades and hostility, and after a stand-off lasting a few days, the army retreated. A seeming victory had been secured. Some said that now was the right time to consider bringing the campaign to an end.

Then came the erection of the Goddess of Democracy. The thirty-three-foot statue was sited to gaze sternly at the portrait of Mao hanging on the Gate of Heavenly Peace across Long Peace Street, and right on the intersection of both central axes of the city. It was controversial in design as well as location; some said it was too American, in its indisputable resemblance to that national icon of freedom from oppression, the Statue of Liberty. The Goddess was intended partly as a way of signing off; a final flourish and a summative articulation of ideals. It had almost the opposite effect however – just as the movement seemed to be losing momentum, the appearance of this assertive, female figure facing down Mao provided a symbol which inspired and galvanised, drawing new protestors to the square.

She also drew a forceful rhetorical response from the government. An editorial in the *People's Daily* on 1 June laid down the law:

> All citizens have a duty to cherish and protect Tiananmen Square. This is equal to cherishing and protecting our motherland and to cherishing and protecting our own rights. The Square is sacred. No one has the power to add any permanent memorial or to remove anything from the Square. Such things must not be allowed to happen in China.

Chapter 9

The denouement was approaching; the power-holders in the CCP had indeed decided that such things must not be allowed to happen in China. The Goddess would last only three more days.

Over the course of those days, soldiers began being secretly moved into the centre of the city, donning civilian gear and travelling in small groups to evade detection. They set up camp at sites along Chang'an Jie, including the Military Museum and the Great Hall of the People. Outside the city, troops also massed, awaiting instruction. On the late afternoon of 3 June, the orders came: the city was to be taken by force, and Tiananmen Square to be cleared by dawn.

A wall of flame halted the soldiers at Muxidi. As before, the army had moved in along the central axis of Long Peace Street, from both east and west. Stopped by the barricade at Muxidi, this time they had the means and authorisation to overcome the obstruction. Buses and trucks had been lined across the road to halt the soldiers' advance; as the army approached, these were set alight by the protestors.

It was around 11pm, and behind the barricades, a crowd of a few thousand had assembled. Those present had expected rubber bullets and, when the firing started at Muxidi, many refused to believe the reality of the situation. The injured and dead soon testified to the seriousness of what was unfolding, however. The soldiers were armed with AK-47s: the People's Liberation Army were shooting its own people.

The journalist John Pomfret was at Muxidi Bridge on the night of 3 June:

> 'Live fire! Live fire!' a student shouts moments after he's hit in the leg by a bullet. Soldiers fire into the crowd.
> They are shooting low, hitting many in the legs and stomach. Blood, pooling on the pavement, splatters the bridge at Muxidi.
> The night, balmy with a calm breeze, echoes with the explosion of blank shells. The blank rounds send the crowds fleeing up a nearby side street. They quickly return, rocks in hand to face the oncoming troops.[9]

Day one: Shougang Iron and Steel to Tiananmen

From Muxidi, the army moved slowly toward Tiananmen Square along Chang'an Jie, halted at almost every intersection by barricades. 'The Avenue of Eternal Peace was packed with angry people and everyone was weeping [...] They followed the troops, and shouted, "Bandits! Bandits!"'[10] recalled one witness. Stray gunfire peppered the apartment blocks that line Chang'an Jie, many of which housed government officials and their families. The roadway was covered in dirt and debris: charred and broken bits of metal; concrete fragments from the makeshift barricades; and, increasingly, patches of blood.

The army arrived at Tiananmen Square itself shortly after midnight. On the square, there was uncertainty amongst the masses who had gathered there as they awaited the approach of the soldiers: should they stay or go? In the end, an organised retreat was negotiated, and the students filtered out of the south-east corner. As dawn broke in the early morning of 4 June the square was empty of people, with just the detritus of the protest remaining: tattered tents, clothes, sleeping bags, banners. The Goddess of Democracy – built intentionally so it could not be removed without being destroyed – was gone. In the early summer light, the tanks and armoured personnel carriers rolled onto the square, crushing whatever the students had left behind.

Now, on and around 4 June each year, police in uniform and plain clothes are dispatched to Tiananmen Square and other sensitive sites around the city. At Muxidi subway station, certain of the exits are reliably closed for renovation. References, both overt and obscure, are censored on social media. These tacit acknowledgements are the only commemorations made by the Chinese state. It is the great unmentionable: any revision or review of these events seems unimaginable under the current administration.

The most enduring image of the student protest, at least in the Western world, is not that of the violence on the streets, the clearing of Tiananmen Square, or the destruction of the Goddess. It was, in

Chapter 9

fact, recorded on 5 June, on the stretch of Chang'an Jie running east from the square. In the footage, a line of tanks rolls towards a man, dressed in a white shirt and holding two shopping bags, who deliberately obstructs their progress. He shouts and gesticulates at the tank, before climbing on top of it. Afterwards, he disappeared into the crowd; no one knows with any certainty what eventually happened to him. On the Chinese news, however, the treatment of this lone protestor was held up as evidence of the moderation with which the army had dealt with the protests: 'Anyone with common sense can see that if our tanks were determined to move on, this lone scoundrel could never have stopped them. This scene recorded on videotape flies in the face of Western propaganda. It proves that our soldiers exercised the highest degree of restraint'.

I left Muxidi smothered in a settling gloom. Walking east once again, the buildings became more obviously of official function; blue-glassed and white-walled, they line up along Chang'an Jie like ocean liners waiting to dock: an interminable procession pulled slowly toward the centre of the city. The heat was close and cloying, and the noise of the road was a persistent and enervating rumble. There were few people on the streets here; this stretch of Long Peace Street is absent of the bustle of everyday life, with fewer and fewer apartments, restaurants or public spaces, and more and more office buildings, government bureaus and hotels. On my walk from Muxidi to the next main intersection at Fuxingmen, I passed only a few office workers and a couple of street sweepers, dressed in loose pale blue and prodding half-heartedly at dust and litter with their straw brooms.

The final triumph of the machinery of state power over the fragile and uncertain hope of the Democracy Movement left an indelible mark on Chinese society. The China we see today, encouraging of individual wealth and economically liberal in ways unimaginable to Mao, is a consequence of the calculated gamble Deng Xiaoping doubled down on after 1989: that people would care less about abstract political rights if they saw an uptick in their personal circumstances. Its legacy is also obvious to any visitor to China in the care and control the state exercises in managing freedom of thought and expression. It is the source of the paranoia, which seems ever-increasing, of the state evident in their policing of public spaces: no one would get anywhere near Tiananmen Square with a tent and a protest banner today.

Those boisterous days of early summer, when China seemingly teetered on the brink of a change which, later that year, would sweep across the Soviet Union and Eastern Europe, have become embedded memories in the Western consciousness. Partly, this is due to the coincidence, unfortunate for Deng Xiaoping and the CCP, that the world's press was on hand to witness and film the unfolding drama of the 1989 protests; in town to cover a Sino-Soviet summit, they arrived in the midst of what seemed to be a revolution. Images were beamed back to living rooms across the world; images which would indelibly alter the West's view of the Chinese state.

Yet, for those Chinese tourists who arrive in their thousands each day at Tiananmen Square, their visit is not freighted with such concerns: it is a highlight of an organised tour of the capital; an opportunity to snap some pictures in China's most famous space to show the family at home. The dissimilarity between the Chinese and Western understanding of the events of 1989 is remarkable: utterly taboo in China, it is one of the few things that Westerners reliably know about the political history of the country. The Democracy Movement of 1989 provides a paradox for anyone trying to garner a serious sense of modern China: its significance undeniable but easy to overstate; its legacy both vividly present and oddly, dispiritingly remote.

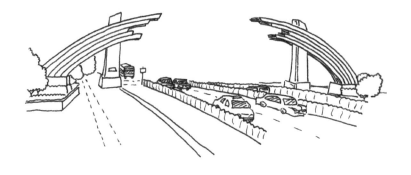

10

Rainbows – walls, walls and yet again walls – breaches – New Year's Day in Xi'an – demolition – Core Socialist Values

A little walk east, no more than fifteen minutes from Muxidi, and a broken rainbow reaches across the breadth of Long Peace Street, the gap missing from its arc framing a first view of Beijing's centre. On the city's eastern side is a matching arch: both were erected to commemorate the transfer of Hong Kong from Britain to the People's Republic of China in 1997.[1] A few years before the handover, a clock had been erected in Tiananmen Square, ticking down the seconds until the archipelago was returned to the embrace of the motherland.

Illuminated at night in Las Vegas neon, the jagged, colourful symmetry of the rainbows seem to signify a reaching for wholeness; for completion, but their arms are left grasping in mid-air – a metaphor uncompleted.

On both east and west of the city, however, they are a tacit reminder of the threshold being crossed; of the transition from *wai* (outside) to *nei* (inside). The line drawn by the rainbow's arc was once a boundary which marked off a sense of identity; of community; of security – for here ran Beijing's city wall.

Along with the symmetry of which they formed a crucial part, walls were long the defining feature of China's towns and cities; indeed the Chinese character for wall – *cheng* 城 – is also that for city. As the art historian Osvald Sirén observed in his 1924 book, *The Walls and Gates of Peking*, 'Walls, walls, and yet again walls form, so to say, the skeleton or framework of every Chinese city. They surround it, they divide it into lots and compounds, they mark more than any other structures the common basic features of these Chinese communities'.[2] Walls provided a comforting sense of enclosure, as they did in medieval Europe; when the gates closed at sundown, the city was a self-contained unit fortified against the outside world. They also defined the limits of the city and, by implication, of the countryside around it, with the gatehouses the point at which these two worlds met.

The oldest of Beijing's walls, as they existed when Sirén saw them, dated predominantly from the Yongle Emperor's fervour of construction in the early fifteenth century. They were explicitly constructed – like the Great Wall – to keep out those nomads from the north who, history had taught, formed a constant existential threat to the city and the country: 'Do not fear the cock from the South, but the wolf from the North', an old Beijing saying went. Running outside the walls was another defensive layer in the city moat – though in places this was often more of a stagnant ditch. The size and scale of the walls was remarked upon reliably by visitors to Beijing – almost every account mentions them, from the earliest missionaries and diplomats to those last witnesses in the 1950s – emphasised as it was by the flat and featureless countryside around them. Ellen La Motte's comment from her residence in the city in 1916–17 is typical; she wrote of the 'tremendously impressive' approach to Beijing: 'Lying in an arid plain, the great, gray walls, with their magnificent towers, rise dignified and majestic'.[3] The towers sat on the wall's corners and atop the gates: storied pagodas with pointed arches and square hollow openings, far grander than the simple arched apertures below which allowed ingress and egress to the city. Through these openings passed all manner of goods, fuel, food and animals, soldiers and tradesmen, city folk and villagers. Houses, inns and shops mushroomed around them, spreading out into the countryside. The gates also watched on the final journey of Beijingers, as funeral processions from the city passed on their way to family burial sites outside the walls.

'Walls, walls, and yet again walls'; anyone attempting a Ming dynasty stroll across Beijing would find their route regularly impeded by city walls, palace walls, temple walls, fences and gates. At the centre of Beijing lay the Forbidden City, sequestered behind its own high wall and moat. Beyond that lay the walls of the Imperial City, enclosing other buildings and gardens of the court. The next layer of Beijing's fortifications was that of the high crenelated walls of the Inner City, which defined the limits of the whole city until the mid-sixteenth century. The Inner City would later become known as the Tartar City, after the Manchus of the Qing dynasty pushed the native Han Chinese into the winding alleys of what became the Outer or Chinese City to the south; this was edged by its own lower, oblong wall. The Inner City was protected space, not to be sullied by commercial enterprise, and it was left to the Outer City to fulfil the daily needs of Beijing's population – both prosaic and profane. The gates leading between the two cities were closed at nightfall, but briefly reopened at midnight to allow errant officials who had been adventuring in the alleyways of the Outer City to scarper homeward.

Barriers and thresholds thus defined Beijing life; much of the city was off-limits and entirely unknown to the ordinary city dweller, with the various imperial altars, palaces and pleasure grounds all protected spaces. Even outside the areas reserved for the spiritual and political, the city was somewhat hidden; entrances to the hutong were often fenced off, whilst the siheyuan which lined them were themselves a closed world. The only point of elevation in the city from which one might look down into the courtyards and gardens of the city – named Scenery Hill, and located just to the north of the Forbidden City – was restricted to the Emperor and his court; thus, what was behind many of the city's walls remained a mystery for most, the glories to be imagined and not seen.

The main city walls remained intact until the early twentieth century, when the encroaching modern world made its first incisions into Beijing's outer shell. The arrival of the railway required breaches in the city wall, not least because in 1900 the foreign community in Beijing had endured a siege by hostile Chinese rebels of their home in the Legation Quarter, the space carved out for foreign diplomats to reside and work in just east of Tiananmen Square. After this, they demanded safeguards enabling them to exit the city quickly if necessary, and brought the railway station as close as they possibly could. After the siege, foreigners in the Legation Quarter kept a bag packed ready and a ladder to hand, just in case they needed to make a speedy escape.[4]

Once breached, walls lose their rationale. They have purpose and power only if they remain intact. After the first gaps had been made in the wall, further changes became hard to argue against. Through the early decades of the twentieth century, a slow process of deliberate destruction occurred; indeed, Fuxingmen, the site of the rainbow arches that I had reached, was not one of Beijing's original gates, but had been punched through during the years of Japanese occupation to allow access to the new areas planned to both the east and the west of the city – it was given its current name in 1945, after victory over the Japanese, becoming the 'Gate of National Revival'. By the time Mao Zedong and the CCP came to survey their new city in 1949, the walls were grand relics, imposingly redundant in practical terms.

The Communists had ideological issues with the city walls; they had, after all, protected the mechanics of imperial rule for centuries, and, at the centre of its nested squares, encased the Emperor. They were thus potent symbols of feudal power and authority; an authority which the Communists wished to give back to the people.

There were pragmatic reasons contributing to the decisions to bring down Beijing's walls, as well; the argument was that they would impede traffic flow and limit the development of Beijing as a modern city. The rational voice of China's preeminent architect Liang Sicheng – he who had planned the new district out near Gongzhufen – pleaded for adaptation, rather than destruction; tunnels could be dug to allow cars to pass more freely, and the walls could be turned into a public space, with the gate- and corner-towers as teahouses or exhibition halls. It seems now some sort of utopian dream: to imagine I could stroll from the busy roadway here up onto the battlements, to linger amongst landscaped gardens of magnolia and lilac and pause in the cool shade of a gate tower for a pot of chrysanthemum tea.

A few years ago, I had spent a brisk 1 January on the city wall at Xi'an, walking the northern edge of the old city amongst families wrapped up against the winter chill, and dodging the enthusiastic youngsters on rented bikes who made directly for the foreigner: 'Hellohowareyooooou', they would exhale as they flashed past. From here, I looked down on courtyards and gardens silvered with frost. The hovering notes of a *gucheng*, the Chinese zither, moved around in the still January air, broadcast from hidden speakers along the wall. Across the city, heavy frozen droplets of grey mist hung.

Looking down on the squat buildings of the inner city, one could almost conjure a vision of the Ming dynasty Xi'an that the current wall marked off.[5] At the least, one's elevation above the noise and bustle of the streets to this orderly point of perspective offered a novel respite from the Chinese city as usually experienced. The wall in Xi'an has been restored to a state of uncanny newness – there are no missing bricks or crumbling parapets here – and it lures hordes of domestic and international tourists to the city each year, who pay just over 50 yuan (about £5.60) to walk or cycle the fourteen-kilometre circumference. Today – early on a New Year's Day I had toasted on a sleeper train from Beijing with a small bottle of champagne, much to the confusion of my Chinese cabin-mates – the crowds were largely absent.

I had rented a room in a faux-Ming era building pressed up against the wall. On the lanes which run inside its edge, these buildings rise sheer and tall, with reassuring solidity, dampening the noise of the city outside. Apart from the occasional gate towers, there is no other way in or out; I rather liked the sense of impregnability they conveyed. On the occasions I had visited the city, I bemoaned the traffic which congeals at the large archways carved through the wall, but I cursed the traffic in every Chinese city, and it was hard to feel that the walls made a substantive difference.

The final destruction of Beijing's walls occurred in stages. By the end of the 1950s most of the Outer City wall had been destroyed, whilst that around the Inner City survived until the mid-1960s, when it was decided that, in order to build Beijing's first subway line, it was better to bring down the ancient southern wall than to demolish homes or other buildings.

When the writer and Sinophile David Kidd returned to China in 1981, having left behind a Beijing as yet largely untouched by the Communists thirty-two years previously, there was nothing left of them: 'I expected to feel a pang, but when I looked down at the oddly empty highway and the blocks of ugly new buildings, where the walls had stood, stretching north and south along the perimeter of what had been the most fabled walled city in the world, I experienced for the first time the anger that would save me from despair during the days to come',[6] he wrote.

The empty highway he was looking at was the second ring road. From the bridge, I looked down on the same road – now dense with traffic, as it always was. Here, the only reminder of the grand battlements which had once ringed the city is in the official street name, which switches from *Fuxingmen Wai* – 'Outside the Gate of National Revival' – to *Fuxingmen Nei* – 'Inside the Gate of National Revival' – as one crosses the bridge. The border marked by the ring road, though not quite as imposing as the nearly fifteen-metre high city wall, still marks off an important line; the part of the city I was now entering had, for most of the last five centuries, constituted the entire city of Beijing; almost everything I had just walked past was less than seventy years old – substantially so in most cases. Traffic-squeezed lanes moved clockwise and anticlockwise, orbiting the city. Looking out from the bridge, the northbound lane ebbed and flowed, brake lights illuminating with the synchronicity of starlings in flight or the ocean's phosphorescence; at a distance, and on foot, the sight had a strange beauty. As I stood I tried, and failed, to imagine the old Beijing wall, now lying as the foundations of this multi-lane highway, bordered by characterless offices and apartment buildings which would have dwarfed it.

One other marker announced the boundary about to be crossed. On either side of the street, just before the bridge which spanned the second ring road, stood a broad sign of six interlocked red circles, each perhaps two metres across and bearing, one above the other, a pair of words in Chinese characters and English: *Prosperity – Democracy; Civility – Harmony; Freedom – Equality; Justice – Rule of Law; Patriotism – Dedication; Integrity – Friendship.* These are known as the Core Socialist Values, as decided upon by the Party under President Xi Jinping's guidance, and are relentlessly promoted across the country, appearing on posters and billboards – often decorated with a soft-focus vignette of Xi and a tag line such as 'When the People have belief, then the Nation has strength' – and recited repetitiously by Chinese school students. The sign, unmissable as it is, seems to function as both reminder and warning for those crossing the boundary into this, the seat of political authority in China.

Day one: Shougang Iron and Steel to Tiananmen

The twelve are split equally into national, social and individual values; *minzhu* or democracy is thus the second most significant of the nation's self-declared principles. An editorial from the government mouthpiece *Xinhua* attempted to clarify how, in a country controlled by a single party and with a closed system of political organisation, democracy can be foregrounded in this way:

> In China, democracy means 'the people are the masters of the country'. [...] What distinguishes socialist democracy with Chinese characteristics from the West's largely money politics and power-for-money deals is its solid foundation of public opinion, which highlights the people's interests and aspirations.[7]

This echoes the Chinese constitution, a somewhat utopian document which, among other laudable claims, contains as its second article the statement that 'All power in the People's Republic of China belongs to the people'. Partly, justification for the idea that China is a democracy comes from the fact that, at a local level, the state does hold direct – though not free – elections. This electoral process then cascades upwards, with those directly elected choosing the delegates for the next tier of the hierarchy, and so on, until one reaches the national level. Thus there are elections, and there are individuals involved in those elections; thus the Chinese state can claim it fosters democracy.

I passed on, reflecting on the individual values incumbent upon me here – *Patriotism, Dedication, Integrity* and *Friendship* – and crossed into the old city.

11

A hungry refrain – little grey streets – reform and opening-up – state-owned enterprises

The odd meditative quality of my route, with its lack of diversions and decisions, had kept me from properly considering the passage of time; I realised suddenly that I had not eaten since breakfast, and it was now getting on for 3pm.

Ordinarily, this would not be problematic; in any global index, China must take a medal place in terms of restaurant density. Generally, the problem was not finding somewhere to eat, but rather deciding between competing options: do I feel like hotpot or barbecue? Sichuanese or Hunanese? Noodles or dumplings?

The stretch of Long Peace Street on which I found myself was, however, unpromising territory for decent food. On both sides of the broad avenue were ranks of bluff office buildings, recessed from the road a little behind banks of neatly tended grass and flowers. There might be a Starbucks hidden in a basement somewhere, but I would find little else here without diverting my route.

I consoled myself instead with imagining. I planned to eat that evening at a Uyghur restaurant in my old neighbourhood, one of my favourite spots for food in the city, and which served food from China's most north-westerly region, Xinjiang – its name, meaning new border, reflecting the contested nature of its status.

The province is still populated in the majority by the Uyghur – Turkic in ethnicity and followers of Islam – but the story of Xinjiang today is one of the gradual erosion of Uyghur culture as increasing numbers of Han Chinese have relocated there as part of an effort by the central government to more securely incorporate the province; this numbers game has been backed up by draconian policies restricting the freedom of the Uyghur population in all sorts of ways.

Uyghur food is distinct from that of the provincial cuisine of Han China – itself deliciously diverse. Foregrounding flavours of cumin, it connects more to the Middle East than to the Middle Kingdom. In my head, I ran through the litany of dishes I planned to order later; as I walked, their names became almost a mantra, their separate syllables playing in my head like a refrain, falling in with the rhythm of my footsteps: ...*zhi*...*ma*...*yang*...*rou* (sesame lamb) ...*yang*...*rou*...*chuanr* (barbecued lamb skewers)...*la*....*mian* (pulled noodles)...*kao*...*nang* (naan bread)...*da*...*pan*...*ji* (literally 'Big Plate of Chicken' – a jointed chicken cooked in a rich sauce heavy with chilli and cumin, along with potatoes, peppers and long, broad wheat noodles). Though far from satiating, this repetition at least provided a distraction as I trudged through a part of the city that I found unappetising in a number of ways.

This stretch of the city is a place where fewer and fewer people actually do any living; it is bureaucracy, politics and commerce writ large in architecture. All along the central east and west wings of Chang'an Jie are imposing hunks of concrete, steel and glass, all right angles and polish: bank headquarters, government and company offices, shopping malls and slightly tired looking hotels with elaborate fountains and circular driveways. The hutong neighbourhoods which traditionally ran to the south and north of this part of the street are on a forced retreat, crowded in from all sides by muscular new constructions. This is not what China is, but rather what it is gradually becoming: broad avenues lined with anonymous buildings, and the streets quiet save for the background drone of traffic and air-conditioning. In her book, *The Long March*, Simone de Beauvoir looked out from her hotel window onto Chang'an Jie in 1955 and worried: 'When they have demolished the little grey streets, will all of Peking look like this boulevard?'[1] The answer increasingly seems to be: yes.

In their 1982 city plan, Beijing's leaders dictated that Chang'an Jie's function should be as follows: 'Leading organs of the party center and the nation, as well as some significant large-scale cultural institutions and other public buildings, should be arranged here to form a solemn, beautiful, and modernized central square and main thoroughfare'.[2]

In the 1990s, this plan was adapted to allow for the building of property of a commercial bent on the street, in keeping with a desire both to develop Beijing as an international metropolis and the general attitude of the state, which in the aftermath of Tiananmen had begun to refashion itself, further easing restrictions on the pursuit of commercial gain generally.

The truth was that, whilst a yearning for political reform had been one motivation for those who protested in 1989, economic issues had also played a significant role in cultivating the conditions for protest. On the back of tentative and often ill-considered changes to the economic structure of the country, inflation had escalated to double-digit rates in the mid-to-late 1980s. Frustration had also grown at the widespread corruption evident in the Party itself, exemplified in part by the advantage cadres would take in buying goods at advantageous prices and reselling at the inflated market rate.

Day one: Shougang Iron and Steel to Tiananmen

The first loosening of the economic reins had taken place in the late 1970s, with the beginning of the process known as 'reform and opening-up'. In the early winter of 1978, eighteen farmers in Xiaogang village in Anhui province came together to sign a secret document: an agreement that, rather than farming collectively, with land combined and jointly managed, as they were required to do by the government, they would instead divide it up into family plots and allow themselves to keep surplus crops.

'We all secretly competed', one of the original farmers said in 2012. 'Everyone wanted to produce more than the next person.'[3] They were eventually found out by the state, but rather than receiving the punishment they expected, the villagers were showered with the Party's glowing approval. The small family plots of Xiaogang were held up as a model for the rest of the country to follow, and sweeping change of the way China tended its land marked the first stage of the country's post-Mao economic reform. Today, the village has become a point of pilgrimage, housing a museum complete with a large sculpture of the original eighteen farmers discussing and scrutinising the secret contract.

It was the beginning of a swathe of changes to the economy, which came with attendant growing pains. Deng Xiaoping famously called the approach of the government 'crossing the river by feeling for the stones', which was a poetic way of conveying their uncertainty and inexperience. He was restricted somewhat by Party hard-liners, who stubbornly resisted the new ideas, but change was also slowed by the unintended side-effects of the reform, including the loss of jobs for young urbanites and the trying issue of inflation, both of which fed into the protests of 1989.

In the aftermath of those protests, Deng came to more fully understand that the aversion to loss which kicks in when people are prospering can be a powerful force in the preservation of the status quo. During the so-called 'Roaring Nineties', the Chinese leadership opened China up to a greater range of market reforms, which drove astonishing economic growth, establishing a strata of Chinese society who, by virtue of the money they were making, had a vested interest in letting the good times roll.

In 1992, Deng, like an ageing rock star on one last tour, went on a high-profile expedition around China's southern provinces, during which time the now eighty-seven-year-old paramount leader made the case for reform, visiting sites that had, beginning in 1979, been designated as so-called Special Economic Zones – the technology hub of Shenzhen, just across the water from Hong Kong, being the best known today. He declared on this trip: '*Rang yi bu fen ren xian fu qi lai*' – 'let some people get rich first', repeating to a Western audience a phrase he had first used in 1985. In the West's parsing of this statement, it became 'To get rich is glorious'. This pithy version had the force of truth common to many misquoted aphorisms; it really did seem, and has seemed consistently since, that the pursuit of money should be the highest of ambitions. Over the next four years, the economy grew at breakneck pace, and opportunities abounded to make money, particularly for those with the inside track on reforms. Controls on lending were relaxed, the urban housing market was opened to private buyers, and foreign investment was further encouraged, particularly in the Special Economic Zones. There was a *quid pro quo* here, though, for as making money became acceptable, the trade in the currency of ideas was further restricted.

All along this part of Chang'an Jie, there are symbols of the economic changes that have swept across China since those early years of the 1990s. The glossy international headquarters and financial centres which cluster here ooze a muscular self-confidence. Running north from Long Peace Street here is Jinrong Jie or Finance Street: 'China's new Wall Street'. Spilling over onto Chang'an Jie are countless bank headquarters: the People's Bank of China, the Industrial and Commercial Bank of China, the Bank of China, the China Development Bank, the China Minsheng Bank, all sharing a similarly brutalist approach to their architectural design.

The most pertinent metaphors for the country's economic recalibration, however, are found in the equally imposing head offices of China's state-owned enterprises. These huge organisations are the legacy of the iron grip the Communist Party took on all economic activity when they came to power, and hold the monopolies on major industries in China – telecommunications; oil and gas production; transportation. Since the mid-1990s, these companies have begun to reform in ways that seem to bring them more in line with the behaviour of Western corporations, and have spun off profitable subsidiaries to float on international stock exchanges. The state-owned enterprises include the China National Petroleum Corporation, the state oil company Sinopec and the electricity supplier State Grid: respectively the fourth, third and second ranked companies in the Fortune Global 500, behind only Walmart in terms of revenue.

These organisations are kept in check by the 'State-owned Assets Supervision and Administration Commission of the State Council'[4] or SASAC, which convenes itself in a building as bland as its name one block south of this stretch of Long Peace Street: a vast pinnacle of blue mirrored glass and white tile. The combined size of the hundred or so companies SASAC oversees is almost inconceivably large – in 2016, their revenue topped 23 trillion yuan or 3.5 trillion American dollars. SASAC exists as a buffer between the Party and the companies, and has been tasked with leading the firms into more modern ways of thinking and working, but it must do so within the bounds of what remains a centrally controlled system. In reality, the state-owned enterprises are like the pandas who live at China's vast breeding centre down in Sichuan province: they are offered the illusion of liberty, whilst in reality the government ensures that their boundaries are securely fenced. The reaching SASAC headquarters embodies the contradictions which have characterised China's economy since the early 1990s; there is increasing freedom to make money, but that freedom has not been accompanied by the fundamental changes in China's political and economic approach that some in the West declare as essential for long-term success. This remains not a liberal, market-driven economy, but one in which the state retains a firm hand on the tiller.[5]

On one of the landscaped verges outside another glossy head-quarters, an old man pushed a petrol lawnmower, and the tang of the fuel and the clean chlorophyll scent of grass cut through the heavy afternoon air to bring me back to the present. It was a smell sitting in counterpoint to that which I had encountered on my walk so far. One Western visitor to the city wrote in 1900 that 'a whole story-book could be written about the Peking smell';[6] she took, like many of her foreign peers at that time, a critical view of this facet of city life, finding the atmosphere full of disagreeable dampness and contamination. Perfumers might categorise the dominant character-istics of today's air along Long Peace Street as follows: top notes of car fumes; hints of stale air-conditioner exhaust; occasional sugges-tions of tobacco smoke, and the subtlest touch of tree sap. On other Beijing streets, more specific elements might be added to the mix: on the narrow pavements outside the Buddhist Lama Temple in the north-east of the old city, the air is heavy with the smell of burning incense from the small shops selling offerings for visitors. On Gui Jie, or Ghost Street, the floral notes of Sichuan pepper float on the hot air from the extractors of the countless restaurants which line the street.

I walked along to the junction at Xidan, where a pailou framed a view of modern buildings stretching north. This part of Beijing had been given its name by the archway – Xidan means 'first west pailou' – but it had been absent for some decades. In 2008 it was dusted off, painted up and placed at the front of a new 'Cultural Square', complete with an elaborate circular fountain. The square today was empty save for a few scampering children. Ranks of malls bannered with colourful advertising hoardings filled in the view framed by the pailou.

Day one: Shougang Iron and Steel to Tiananmen

The sound of hundreds of cars moving east and west merged into a low and persistent rumble, drowning out the resonant sound of my own empty stomach as I drifted on towards the imperial centre of the city.

12

An assassination – Middle and Southern Seas – imperial pretensions – Xinhuamen – paranoia – hidden places – Mao at Zhongnanhai

1913: a spring evening in Shanghai. In the city's railway station, a slender young man stands on a platform, awaiting a train to carry him back to Beijing. His name is Song Jiaoren and he is China's presumptive new Prime Minister – a young idealist, just thirty years old, whose party has recently emerged victorious from the country's first ever democratic elections.

On what subject he is musing when the first gunshot rings out, we can only speculate. Gravely wounded by two bullets, he is rushed to hospital, where he dictates a telegram to the President of the new Republic of China, Yuan Shikai. 'I die with deep regret', it reads. 'I humbly hope that your Excellency will champion honesty, propagate justice and promote democracy.'

Day one: Shougang Iron and Steel to Tiananmen

The association of Yuan with concepts of honesty or justice was somewhat undermined by the material facts of the day – for President Yuan was the man who had organised the assassination.

Song Jiaoren would die two days after his shooting; Yuan would remain president for the next three years.

A pragmatic military leader, who had successfully ridden the waves of China's stormy last decades, in 1912 Yuan Shikai had, after taking the reins as president,[1] installed himself in the old imperial garden of Zhongnanhai – the 'Middle and Southern Seas' which form part of a chain of lakes flowing into one another on the west side of old Beijing. Zhongnanhai had been a place of relaxation and refuge for many of China's imperial rulers, dating back through the centuries, who dotted pavilions amongst willows on the lakeside. It is dominated by the lakes, which were expanded at the beginning of the Ming dynasty, with the earth from their excavation piled up to create Scenery Hill rising behind the Forbidden City. From above, the lakes of Zhongnanhai resemble the upright and dot of a fat exclamation mark. The base of this dot rests against Long Peace Street.

Yuan would have preferred to occupy the Forbidden City next door, but was unable to evict its current inhabitant – the last Emperor of the Qing dynasty, the young Puyi who, despite having his imperial title wrested from him in 1912, continued to live in closeted opulence, six-year-old master of an empire that extended merely to the walls of his limited section of the palace. Puyi would remain there, with his diminished court, until 1924. Puyi's British tutor, Reginald Johnston, characterised the illogicality of the situation thus:

> In the heart of Peking were two adjacent palaces. In that which still retained the distinction of being the 'Forbidden City' dwelt a titular monarch; in the other resided the chief executive of the republic. In the latter was a presidential chair occupied by one who exercised the powers of an emperor without the name; in the former was a throne on which sat one who was an emperor in name alone. He who ruled the vast realm of China was called a president; he whose rule did not extend an inch beyond his palace walls was called an emperor. Surely

in no other land could circumstances so anomalous have lasted more than a week; yet they lasted in China for thirteen years.[2]

Safe behind the walls of Zhongnanhai, despite the trail of evidence leading his way, Yuan managed to avoid the consequences resulting from Song's murder in 1913, undertaken, it was speculated, as a result of Song's declared desire to limit presidential authority. Those who had been suspected of conspiring in the murder either died or disappeared in mysterious circumstances. It may not have made much difference had they been brought to justice; there were, in reality, no viable alternatives to Yuan as president; his Beiyang army was the military powerhouse of the north, and most pragmatists, though noting his worrying propensity to act with the sword rather than the pen, accepted that he was the best of a limited number of bad options.

Yuan faced a number of problems when he took charge in 1912, not least of which was a fracturing China, in which the military and political leaders of its provinces paid little heed to the demands of their new leader. Convinced by events that China was not ready for freedom from central control, he began to envision himself as China's leader in perpetuity, and in 1915 forced his way to being declared the country's new emperor. Yuan adopted many of the Confucian rituals of earlier dynasties, visiting the Altar of Heaven to perform the rites necessary to secure a good harvest. The symbolic power of this imperial pomp was undermined somewhat by the manner in which it was carried out, however, for Yuan was uncertain enough of his personal safety at the time to demand travelling to the Altar by armoured car.

Yuan and his advisors believed that China needed a figurehead, but power would not simply and unquestioningly return to the centre. An invisible thread had been severed with the Qing dynasty's ouster in 1912, and despite many agreeing that China had proved itself unready for democracy, Yuan had a hard time establishing himself as the Son of Heaven. Provinces in China's south-west began to rebel against him, declaring independence from this new empire, and the constitutional uneasiness was only brought to an end by Yuan's unexpected death in June 1916.

In the years after his death, China would fragment, in yet another affirmation of the famous first line of that foundational epic, the *Three Kingdoms*: 'The empire, long divided, must unite; long united, must divide. So it has ever been'. An era of warlordism would settle on the country, the centrifugal pull of Beijing seemingly terminally weakened. The grounds of Zhongnanhai, which had housed the office of the president, would subsequently be opened as a public park – but Yuan's brief reign there had established its lakeside villas as an alternate centre of power in China.

Yuan had also established the symbolic main entrance of Zhongnanhai, which opens on to Long Peace Street: Xinhuamen – the Gate of New China. The two-storey pavilion is coated in the same deep, matte red which graces the walls of all Beijing's imperial buildings and which was reserved for use by the Emperor, with a roof of glazed yellow tile and detail on the panels which run below the roofline picked out in blue and gold. It had been built by the Qianlong Emperor for a homesick lover, a Muslim from Xinjiang taken as part of the spoils of war, and named 'Precious Moon Tower'; from here the concubine would gaze south at a mosque and bazaar the Emperor had especially built to assuage her longing for home. Yuan would refashion this pavilion into the main entrance to his compound, and establish a tall watchtower just to its east, with a lookout stationed in a crow's nest at its top.[3]

Today, there is no sign indicating what lies behind the ornate frontage of the Gate of New China; two long banners either side of the gate, however, suggest the significance of the entranceway: *Long Live the Great Communist Party of China* reads one; and *Long Live the Invincible Mao Zedong Thought* the other. On a screen wall recessed behind the entrance way, and which hides a view of the circular south lake, characters in Mao's own calligraphy declare: *Serve the People*. Perhaps the most telling signifier of what hides behind the Gate of

Chapter 12

New China is the ever-present security personnel, whose dark sunglasses follow the footsteps of those who pass by.

In front of me, the city opened like the pages of a pop-up book; finally I could snatch glimpses of the Gate of Heavenly Peace and Tiananmen Square itself. I was increasingly conscious of the heat and dust, and the ever-present noise of the road. The pavements, now soaked in hours of August sun, radiated warmth from below. As I walked towards Xinhuamen, I was reminded of the still, quiet winter image of this part of the street from one of my favourite Beijing novels, Lao She's *Camel Xiangzi*:

> Near Xinhua Gate, the wide street thinly covered with snow seemed to stretch away to infinity, and everything around took on a more solemn air. Changan Arch, the gate tower of Xinhua Gate and the red walls of Nanhai were all wearing white caps which contrasted with their ruby pillars and red walls. Still and quiet. Under the glow of the street lamps, they displayed all the stateliness of this ancient capital. The time and place made it seem as if Beiping were uninhabited, composed solely of sumptuous halls and palaces with a few ancient pines silently receiving the falling snow.[4]

Lao She was the bard of post-imperial Beijing, and his novel *Camel Xiangzi* – better known in the West as 'Rickshaw Boy' – was the bleak account of a Beijing rickshaw puller trying to make a life in 1920s Beijing, and constantly beset by the headwinds of fate: 'No matter how hard you tried to get on', he realises as misfortune greets his every move, 'you must never get married, fall ill or take one false step'.[5] The novel was so unremitting that, when first translated into English, it was altered to conclude with a romantic reunion between the protagonist and his lover: in the original, she had committed suicide in the novel's final act.

As I crossed a junction to walk the stretch of Long Peace Street which runs outside the southern wall of Zhongnanhai along to Xinhuamen, I was greeted by a checkpoint manned by two young police officers dressed in blue. '*Huzhao*', they demanded gruffly: 'Passport'. Beyond the barrier, an old man wearing a cheap polo shirt and carrying a pink plastic shopping bag had been taken to one side; they were not letting him through, and I overheard his impassioned negotiations with the guard who, typically, was showing no signs of revising his opinion. This diminutive elderly man with his ill-fitting clothes seemed little threat; however, he was poor and quite obviously not a Beijing native, which seemed to be enough cause for the young officer to hold him up.

The paranoia around security on this stretch of Chang'an Jie has its roots in those multitudinous political protests which have converged here across the course of the twentieth century, but has been encouraged by events in recent years. In 2013, despite all the fences, barriers, police, soldiers and scrutiny, a car managed to mount the pavement just down from the Gate of Heavenly Peace; driving at speed, it knocked down and killed two bystanders. The car then burst into flames with the three passengers inside, just beneath the portrait of Mao Zedong which looks out over Tiananmen Square. The densely packed pavements were cleared of tourists; a screen was erected around the smouldering remains of the car to shield it from view. The Beijing police announced later that they considered it a premeditated terrorist attack and named those who died in the car as a Uyghur family from Xinjiang.

Evidence of the state's nervousness proliferates today. CCTV cameras grace every lamp post, and peer over the top of the long, red wall of Zhongnanhai. Police vans park in the shade of the trees which line the pavement outside the wall or on side streets; some carry decals announcing them as 'Tiananmen Emergency Management'. In the shade of the broad tree-lined pavements and in Tiananmen Square a mix of uniformed and plain-clothes officers hover around trying to look nonchalant. There is another security checkpoint further towards Tiananmen; this equipped with X-ray scanners and generating enormous queues.

Chapter 12

The increased monomania around security is not merely limited to Beijing. At a train station in China's east, I had recently waited for nearly an hour in 35 degree heat just to pass through the same routine checks before entering the main building. As we had shuffled across the large shadeless plaza, a grandmother in front of me quietly toppled onto her stuffed plaid luggage sacks; her family crowded round and sprinkled water on her face. She eventually came to and tenaciously continued to queue.

Hidden places are always alluring. They hold a pure form of imaginative power, uncorrupted by dull reality. Chinese rulers have long understood the import of maintaining such mystery by screening themselves from the world, in both life and death. Qin Shi Huang, the Emperor who is considered the first ruler to have led a unified China, continues in isolation, 2,200 years after his death. His tomb, built over decades by tens of thousands of men, is said to be a microcosm of the world over which he ruled: rivers flowing with mercury; the stars and planets mapped on its roof; palaces in miniature across its floor – and spring-loaded crossbows designed to skewer any would-be intruders. As the historian Sima Qian recorded, it was thought essential that the mystery around the Emperor's final resting place be maintained:

> After the interment had been completed, someone pointed out that the artisans and craftsmen who had built the tomb knew what was buried there, and if they should leak word of the treasures, it would be a serious affair. Therefore, after the articles had been placed in the tomb, the inner gate was closed off and the outer gate lowered, so that all the artisans and craftsmen were shut in the tomb and were unable to get out. Trees and bushes were planted to give the appearance of a mountain.[6]

Despite the discovery of the site in the 1970s, the tomb has still not been entered and the secrets of the First Emperor remain intact, at least for now. He continues to be guarded, of course, by the fearsome warriors of his terracotta army.

Today, the formerly hidden home of the Ming and Qing Emperors being open to anyone who can afford the entrance fee, Zhongnanhai now functions as China's true forbidden city. The state is regrettably unable to prevent Google's satellites from flying over the compound, but on both digital and paper maps, the separate areas and structures within the sprawling site are unmarked. Indeed, even looking behind the walls from the birds-eye-view of Google's cameras is confounding, for, due to China's adoption of an electronic mapping frame designed to protect national security, the map and satellite images fail to match up when overlapped, suggesting rather surprisingly that there is a main road running through the centre of the Zhongnanhai lakes.

Accounts from those few who have seen inside suggest that the interiors of Zhongnanhai manifest a distinct lack of mystery or glamour; and indeed, the CCP approach to decoration does often meld a sort of pseudo-traditional ostentatiousness with brightly lit functionality. For much of its time, the compound has functioned in as dully bureaucratic a manner as any of the faceless ministries and commission buildings along the rest of Long Peace Street.

But Chairman Mao's long inhabitance of Zhongnanhai imbues its pavilions with an alluring quality: the tales of his time there are of lavish and eccentric customs; of intrigue and politics at a time of enormous social upheaval; and of a life lived just as eccentrically and whimsically as any of those of the earlier inhabitants of the palace next door.

Mao moved in to Zhongnanhai in 1950; he had initially taken residence in Beijing's Fragrant Hills to the west after the liberation of the city in 1949. Behind high walls which screen one from the world, it is perhaps unsurprising that a reversion to baser instincts might occur: to indulgence and to whim; to the exercising of an authority which creates an unchallenged alternate reality. Mao seemed aware of the potential for such a change, and refused to ever set foot within the Forbidden City, feeling presumably that it had some manner of innate corrupting power. Accounts of his life at Zhongnanhai, however, testify to a slow disconnection from normality, which exacerbated his already somewhat unusual personal habits. Mao had always been a man with strong convictions regarding how to live. Partly, this was driven by a professed desire to preserve a connection to the life of the peasants on whose behalf he had led the revolution; he maintained a rough frugality, in some aspects of his life at least. Edgar Snow had commented when visiting him at Yan'an that his manner could be considered somewhat coarse and vulgar, and that he was 'careless in his personal habits and appearance but astonishingly meticulous about details of duty'.[7] He cared little for style in his clothing or living arrangements, desiring instead to live in a comfort which was simple in appearance, if not necessarily inexpensive.[8] He rarely bathed and never brushed his teeth, simply swilling his mouth with green tea each morning. Over time, his teeth took on a distinct greenish tinge.

In Zhongnanhai, Mao was free to indulge his whims without scrutiny. A long-term sufferer from insomnia, he created his own schedule, working late into the night. He would summon colleagues at any hour, expecting an instant appearance. A love for swimming led him to move into the compound housing Zhongnanhai's indoor pool in 1967; here, bobbing around in the warm water, he would hold court. When Russian leader Nikita Kruschev visited in 1958, Mao held one of their meetings in his pool; his visitor, however, could not swim, so a pair of inflatable arm-bands were produced for him to wear.

The privacy of Zhongnanhai also allowed Mao to indulge his sexual appetite. Despite Jiang Qing's presence in a nearby villa in those years before she moved to Diaoyutai, the two lived increasingly separate lives, and Mao was free to pursue his enthusiasm for young women. In imperial times, concubines would be delivered to the foot of the Emperor's bed, naked and draped in a silk shawl. In the Mao era, the selection of sexual partners took place at the weekly balls the Chairman organised. In his detailed autobiography, Mao's personal physician, Li Zhisui, gave an account of the special arrangements made for these dances: 'In 1961, one of Mao's specially made beds was moved to the room adjacent to the ballroom where Mao would retire to "rest" during the course of an evening of dance. I often watched him take a young woman by the hand, escort her to the room, and close the door behind them'.[9] His doctor also noted that the sexually transmitted infection Mao passed on to these women was held as a badge of honour, proving their intimacy with the Great Helmsman.

Mao lived at Zhongnanhai for the majority of his time as China's leader, with periodic restorative escapes, particularly to his lake villas at Hangzhou in the south (he had a swimming pool especially built there, as well). It was at Zhongnanhai that he died in 1976, prompting a comical panic to preserve his body; the doctors in charge initially injected him with twenty-two litres of formaldehyde, which bloated him beyond recognition. Eventually they massaged him back into shape – but a wax replica was also made, just in case irrevocable damage had been done.[10]

The end of his story at Zhongnanhai was just the beginning of another, of course; power struggles over his succession rumbled on over the coming years, with Deng Xiaoping eventually emerging as the country's *de facto* leader. Since Deng, the pavilions of Southern and Central Lakes have continued to house China's presidents; today, President Xi and his wife, the celebrated folk singer Peng Liyuan, call Zhongnanhai home.

I had met my day's aim, and reached the city's centre. On both the wide pavement ahead and Tiananmen Square itself were crowds of people, their excited cries carrying on the wind, and their sun parasols bopping almost in synchronicity. Beyond Tiananmen to the east, faint outlines of the skyscrapers of the Central Business District interrupted the flat, milky sky.

I doubled back, cut down a side street and flagged down a *hei che* – literally a *black car* – one of Beijing's dwindling crop of illegal taxis,

Chapter 12

their status signalled by the hanging of a red LED light from the rear-view mirror. Authentic Beijing taxis are restricted in where they can pick up and set down around Tiananmen, and would doubtless try and overcharge me in any case, refusing to use the meter. My driver was around thirty, with a pot-belly and tight-fitting zip-up synthetic jacket. I got into the front seat and we set about our negotiations; we got the price down to a reasonable figure, but I was by this point happy enough merely to be both sitting down and air-conditioner cooled. My thoughts turned once more to barbecued lamb kebabs and the promise of a cold bottle of Yanjing, the capital's ubiquitous beer.

We found our way on to Long Peace Street, heading west. It was late afternoon now and the traffic was slow; the driver weaved between the lanes without signalling, searching out gaps and the chance to make a few yards. The water truck had just passed along the street, spraying a fine mist of water onto the broad tarmac to keep down the dust. As the grey nothingness of the sky cleared a little, the sun was once more visible; a ring of pure bright light dropping towards the Western Hills, unseen in the distance. Suddenly, the city took on a fresh look: the taxis which sped alongside us looked a little cleaner; the trees a little greener; the red walls of the imperial city a little more vibrant.

As we drove out past Zhongnanhai, the driver noticed my interest and asked me if I knew who lived there. I said I did, and asked him what he thought about President Xi. 'He doesn't really care about us', the driver said and gestured dismissively towards the Gate of New China. 'Anyway, they're all the same.'

We branched off Long Peace Street. The taxi driver stabbed at the radio-buttons – a news programme; a Chinese pop-song – and then turned it off all together. We sat in the quiet of early evening as the city rushed past in blurred frames of colour.

Day two

Tiananmen to Sihui Dong subway station

1 Fishing at Shougang

2 Railway lines, Shougang

3 Looking east across the city

4 Gravestones at Babaoshan Revolutionary Cemetery

5 Military compound on western Long Peace Street

6 The entrance to the Military Museum after its reopening in 2017

7 Traffic lights near Muxidi

8 A Beijing pailou

9 Outside the wall

10 Long Peace Street and the Gate of New China (Xinhuamen), 2012

11 Outside Tiananmen

12 The Monument to the People's Heroes

13 The archery tower and gate tower of Zhengyangmen, with Mao's mausoleum behind

14 A shop in Mao's hometown of Shaoshan, Hunan province

15 Inside the Forbidden City

16 The Conger family process towards the Meridian Gate, 1901

17 Fortifications and gateway near the British Legation off Chang'an Jie, by the northern end of Canal Street, Peking (Beijing). Est. 1928–29

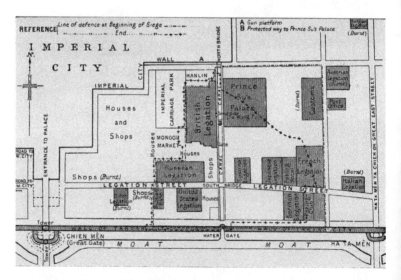

18 A map of the Legation Quarter, showing lines of defence during the Boxer siege

19 Peking dust at Yongdingmen

20 Rainbows at Jianguomen; the Observatory can be seen behind

21 The Observatory instruments today

22 The Imperial Examination Halls. 'As I look at these examination halls, sympathetic feelings mingled with sad admiration go to these scholars who come to them.' Sarah Conger, *Letters from China*, 1909

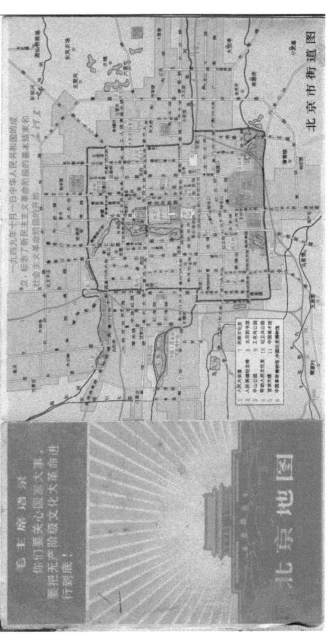

23 Cultural Revolution-era city map, showing some of Beijing's changed street names. Dongjiaominxiang – the Chinese name for what had been Legation Street – became Fandi lu (Anti-Imperialism Street)

24 Skyscrapers under construction, 2016

13

The middle of the Middle Kingdom
– hidden tales of Tiananmen – the
Great Helmsman

The river eddy swirls. The wind grows
in the pines.
On old roof tiles an ash-white rat scurries.
Which king built this palace, here beneath the cliffs,
nobody knows.
In moonlit rooms, ghostly green fires flame.
Grief has washed its paths to ruin.
The sound of ten thousand flutes catches on the wind
as russet leaves whirl.
His powdered courtesans are yellow dust.
Of his servants and gold chariots, nothing remains;
a stone horse is all now that tells of his memory.
As I sit on the ground, sorrow overcomes me;

Day two: Tiananmen to Sihui Dong subway station

a song comes to my lips, but my eyes fill with tears.
A pause on this unhurried journey.

Who knows what the long years will bring?

('Jade Flower Palace' by Du Fu, 757 AD, author's translation).

Stand on Tiananmen Square, just behind the flagpole which flies the national flag, looking north. In front of you, Long Peace Street conveys an endless stream of cars, taxis and buses, blurred as they speed across from west to east, east to west. Beyond that, the flat red walls of the Gate of Heavenly Peace rise to meet a falling sweep of yellow tiles at the balcony from which Mao Zedong announced the founding of the People's Republic in October 1949. Just below the balcony hangs an enormous painted portrait of the Chairman, a faint smile at the edge of his lips.

To either side of Mao's visage run a pair of slogans: *Long Live the People's Republic of China* and *Long Live the Great Unity of the World's Peoples.* Around you likely congregate some of the World's Peoples, snapping photos to share back home when they once again can access Facebook, Instagram, Twitter. Here I am, at the middle of the Middle Kingdom.

Invisible behind the Gate of Heavenly Peace, waves of gold-tiled roofs run north, an ocean of imperial grandeur: the Forbidden City stretching back along the central axis of the city. Behind it, the tree-covered mound of Scenery Hill blocks the view, a pagoda perched on its top. From there, one can look further north to see the Drum and Bell Towers and, on a clear day, the five flat-headed iron nails of the Olympic Tower, hammered into the imperial axis of Beijing in 2014, not far from the National Stadium.

The sense of physical space is overwhelming; Tiananmen Square is no longer the biggest public square in the world – that honour now belongs to Xinghai ('Sea of Stars') Square in the port city of Dalian, tucked away in China's north-east – but its relentless flatness still dwarfs the individual. Even on a busy day the square cannot transcend its inhuman scale: it never seems truly busy and fails to cultivate any sense of communal experience. It is not the piazza or public square of Europe, lined with cafes, a fountain in its midst, bustling with trade and thoroughfare: its design and history dictates that it crackles with a different kind of energy.

Turning around to look along the southern axis will present you with the Monument to the People's Heroes, an obelisk nearly forty metres high, made – so the factual plaque just beside it tells you – of more than 17,000 pieces of granite and white marble. It is dedicated, as its name implies, to those who gave their lives in the revolution. Contrarily preferring the vertical in a cityscape defined by the horizontal, it has the look of something designed by committee: indeed, its final form had been subject to intense debate. Facing north, it is inscribed with Mao's calligraphy: 'Eternal Glory to the People's Heroes'. Jacques Marcuse noted that his official 1962 guidebook to Peking asserted that the monument 'commands the respect of all who see it'[1] – though he was personally not so sure.

Behind the monument, and dividing the square into northern and southern halves, is the final resting place of Mao: the mausoleum constructed after his death in 1976. Like the National Museum and the Great Hall of the People to either side of the square, this is a building which makes subtle nods to Chinese architecture, but seems to be mostly aiming for an august neoclassicism, with ranks of tall columns running parallel on each of its sides. It faces the Gate of Heavenly Peace – twin symbols of the beginning and end of Mao's rule.

Beyond that, marking the southern boundary of the square, is the Gate of the Pure Sun, of which two towers still stand – together, they are better known as *Qianmen* or Front Gate. This was the main entrance into the Inner City; beyond it to the south spread the Chinese City, narrow alleyways serving the business and pleasure of life.

Autocracies like to tidy the mess of history and human behaviour into order and, since the founding of the People's Republic, the traditional layout of the space in front of the Gate of Heavenly Peace has been razed and rebuilt in order to ensure that it tells just one story.

In undertaking this refashioning, scale and symbolism were of paramount concern. The trees which lined the so called 'thousand-step corridor' which joined the Front Gate with the Gate of Heavenly Peace were uprooted, and granite slabs laid in their place to make a plaza of nearly 450,000 square metres. The section of Long Peace Street which runs north of the square was widened and reinforced to convey the National Day parade and, in response to the early paranoid thinking of the CCP, to allow aeroplanes to land should a swift getaway be necessary. When the Great Hall of the People was built in 1958 on the western side of the square, its construction utilised an almost inconceivable amount of raw materials: 127,700 cubic metres of reinforced concrete; 24,000 square metres of marble; and 27,000 square metres of granite, with these materials drawn from twenty-three different provinces and municipalities.[2] The same principle was applied to the construction of Mao's mausoleum, in which hundreds of thousands of 'volunteers' from across China helped during the six-month construction. The obsession continues today; when the National Museum opposite the Great Hall of the People was being refurbished, – it reopened in 2011 – one of those consulting on the redesign was called up first with a query as to the square footage of the Louvre, and then ten minutes later as to that of the British Museum – all to ensure that Beijing's was greater.[3]

The eight carved marble panels around the base of the Monument to the People's Heroes depict scenes of protest and rebellion, which outline the founding myth that the square and its surrounding buildings represent: one of a linear struggle against the old order and the impositions of foreign powers in which the CCP emerge as heroes and liberators. The fight against imperialism in the First Opium War; the fight against feudalism in the revolution against the Qing dynasty of 1911; the fight against the Nationalists in the Civil War: these and other similarly distinct historical moments are arranged in cartoon-book order around the base of the monument. It is the telling of history backwards, trying to join the dots to show the inevitability of China's current political situation.

A permanent exhibition at the National Museum expands on this pictorial representation, telling of 'the explorations made by the Chinese people from all walks of life who, after being reduced to a semi-colonial, semi-feudal society since the Opium War of 1840, rose in resistance against humiliation and misery, and tried in every way possible to rejuvenate the nation'. The CCP are, of course, the secret ingredient in finally overcoming all the humiliation and misery; it was under their leadership, we learn, that 'all ethnic groups joined forces to achieve national independence and liberation'. The Great Hall of the People opposite embodies this claimed unity of the nation, with rooms named after every Chinese province – including Xinjiang, Tibet and Taiwan. Mao, now reclining in his crystal coffin at the centre of the Square, looms large in this story of national rebirth, of course. When the museum first opened, visitors to the main exhibition were greeted by an enormous bust of the Great Helmsman.[4]

Yet, particularly in a place as dense with history as this, there is always another narrative waiting quietly to erupt and contradict the official version, pointing up the transience of the truth that the state has built from granite and marble. Looking at Mao's portrait on the Gate of Heavenly Peace – indubitably the most famous picture in China – one might recall that his was not the first portrait to hang thus; an image of Sun Yat-sen had been mounted there in 1929, and a picture of Nationalist leader Chiang Kai-shek painted on welded scrap metal had been positioned on the platform in the 1940s. Photos from the 1930s show a clock, declaring Republican time, on the balcony balustrade.

Looking at the images of protest and popular uprising around the base of the Monument to the People's Heroes one might remember the protests of 1989 or 1976, unmentioned by the carvings or the monument's adjacent plaque, but perhaps tacitly acknowledged by the perimeter fence which now surrounds it and the uniformed guard at its base. In 1976, it had been piled with wreathes to commemorate the death of Zhou Enlai. In 1989, the monument had become a platform from which leaders of the movement addressed the crowd, and banners had been tied around its base: 'The people will not forget 1989', read one.

Or one might turn to thinking of the famous story of the workmen who, in the early days of the fledgling republic, were sent to take down the sign on the Great Qing Gate which stood where Mao's mausoleum was later to be built, only to find that their predecessors, sent to do the same job at the end of the Ming era, had preserved the old sign – *Great Ming Gate* – just in case.

Who knows what the long years will bring?

The squat block of Mao's mausoleum itself, aiming for timelessness, but achieving merely a drab neoclassical symmetry, tacitly asks the same question. Mao has just passed his fourth decade on Tiananmen Square: how many more anniversaries he will see there is hard to predict.

The eventual fates of those other seeming immortals of the communist movement offer illuminating comparison. Lenin, of course, remains in stately repose in his underground tomb near the Kremlin in Moscow; Ho Chi Minh is entombed in a building even uglier than Mao's in Hanoi, and Kim Il-sung, the 'Eternal President' of the North Korean Republic is housed alongside his son and successor, Kim Jong-il in a vast palace which makes Mao's mausoleum look humble by comparison.

Stalin had likewise been preserved for posterity after his death in 1953, and installed in the same mausoleum as Lenin. However, one overcast night in October 1961, as the USSR was in the throes of de–Stalinisation, a convoy of military vehicles pulled up outside the tomb; soldiers entered and emerged some time later with the uniformed corpse of the General. They took his body to a cemetery notable only for the relative obscurity of its inhabitants and buried him in a modest grave. The news of his relocation was announced by identical back-page reports of the scantest detail in the Soviet newspapers.[5]

In recent times, there have been intermittent calls by intellectuals to cremate Mao – as was his original wish – and return his ashes to his hometown, in keeping with the return of other leaders to their places of birth around China. Mao's childhood village of Shaoshan, set amongst the hills of Hunan Province, would in many ways be suited as a permanent home; it is already established as a shrine to the Chairman, with every square foot of the once quiet village now given over to Mao history, worship or commerce. Every village restaurant sells the same over-priced version of his favourite dish, *hong shao rou*, cubes of fatty pork belly in a sweet red sauce; each shop carries effigies of him in bronze, plastic and porcelain alongside other over-priced *memaorabilia*; and in the centre of the town, another of China's broad plazas has been constructed, headed by a large bronze statue of Mao, in front of which visitors come to genuflect.

Mao himself returned only twice to his hometown during his adult life: once in June 1959, after an absence of thirty-two years, and again in 1966, in the early days of the Cultural Revolution, when he retired to nearby Di Shui Dong – 'Dripping Water Cave'. When the deification of the Chairman began in earnest, Shaoshan became a place of pilgrimage for the Red Guards.

Now, the visitors come in their millions. They visit his family home, a modest thatched house the colour of custard where Mao was born, and plod diligently around the museums dedicated to the Chairman. Shaoshan is a key stop on the 'Red Tourism' trail of significant Chinese Communist Party sites. As well as Shaoshan, Red Tourists can visit the caves of Yan'an where Mao and his fellow leaders lived in the years after the Long March; the small Shanghai alley house, now nestled amongst some of the city's most exclusive boutiques, where the Chinese Communist Party held its first congress in 1921; and the mountains of Jinggangshan in China's south-east, the Communist's first base and the 'cradle of the Chinese revolution'.

Whether the Chairman will ever be returned to the red soil of Hunan is an open question. His mausoleum in Tiananmen Square, architecturally so much of its time, has always seemed to me to have a look of impermanence and incongruity about it, an impostor on the dragon vein running north to south through the city. Yet it opens at 7am each morning to lines of visitors from across the country; pilgrims who are not entirely unaware of Mao's missteps, but are willing for whatever reason to overlook them. As my official CCP history has it, 'As one of the founders of the People's Republic of China, he performed immortal feats in the development of China's socialist cause. Although he wrongly launched the "cultural revolution" in his later years, his merits outweighed his mistakes'.

14

A walk to Tiananmen – into the Forbidden City – intruders

A few weeks earlier, I had walked with my English friend Ed – a China first-timer – down to the Gate of Heavenly Peace. Overnight the sky had been cleared by a persistent wind, and the morning air was fresh. Slow-paced, we found our way out of the narrow hutong where we were staying, and headed south along the central axis of the city, before diverting into Beihai Park, where the wind blew the willows iridescent in the sunlight and raised miniature white-caps on the lake. Beihai means North Lake, and it sits just above the government compound at Zhongnanhai.

A bridge runs across the narrow neck of water which join the two, high-fenced and policed by squat young men all in black. As we walked east across the bridge, cutting back towards Tiananmen, we briefly stopped and looked down at the schools of fleshy carp writhing and fighting in the water of Zhongnanhai. Instantaneously, a guard was upon us, hand held out as a gesture to stop.

'No', he said in English.

'We are just looking at the fish', I replied in Chinese.

'You cannot look at the fish', he said, trying to move his body in between us and the view of the lake.

'They are important fish?'

'Yes, they are.'

We arrived at the Gate of Heavenly Peace as the day was heating up. A mass of people waited to get through the security check, where IDs were scrutinised and bags cursorily scanned by young guards with a cultivated lack of interest. We finally reached a point from which we could gain some perspective; across both the plaza outside the Gate of Heavenly Peace and Tiananmen Square clusters of people were scattered across the broad emptiness of the cityscape.

Like Ed, most of those who congregate here are first-time visitors. Bussed in on tours, or having arrived under their own steam and struggled through the confusion of the Beijing subway, they come from all over China, as pilgrims to a shrine. The day is carefully structured. First comes the flag raising at the square's north end. Each morning the flag is raised anew on Tiananmen Square. From a safe distance, the visitors wait in the dawn light as a troop of soldiers emerge from the Gate of Heavenly Peace and cross the marble bridges over a small stream in front of it, and then Chang'an Jie itself. The flag is secured and then, with a flourish and flick of the wrist which sends it out into the breeze, it is raised to coincide exactly with the sun breaking the horizon. Following this marker of the day's beginning is a visit to Mao's mausoleum; then into the Forbidden City and to the Dragon Throne of the Emperor in the Hall of Supreme Harmony.

The out-of-town groups are distinguished by their matching outfits – generally they are made to don a colourful cap or matching t-shirt – and follow a leader equipped with an umbrella and loudspeaker, from which instructions and historical details spew at the same distorted volume. As we approached the Gate of Heavenly Peace, a teenager on one of these tours spotted us, and peeled off from the group. 'Hello, I am Bruce, welcome to China', he said in English. 'May I take a photo with you?' We agreed and Bruce positioned himself between the two of us. 'Smeel', he said, flashing a broad grin at both of us before pressing the shutter button on his smartphone.

'You are very handsome and strong', he said to Ed, who is 6 foot 7 inches tall, and broad-shouldered. From even the few hours we had spent together in Beijing, it was clear that he would be the focus of a good deal of attention during his time here. 'You are very handsome and strong and *tall*', he said again to Ed. He turned to me. 'You are handsome', he said grudgingly, and after a pause.

Bruce was from Xinjiang, though was himself Han Chinese; he was on a four-day school trip and wanted to take every opportunity to practice his English. His accent was excellent, on the whole, with the unfortunate exception of the word he uttered every ten seconds or so as he snapped another selfie with the two of us: 'Smeel!' he would tell us. 'Smile!' we would echo.

Eventually he spotted that his group, wearing yellow t-shirts with a cartoon monkey on the front, were in the process of crossing the bridges leading to the tunnels underneath the Gate of Heavenly Peace. He said his goodbyes, told Ed once more how handsome, tall and strong he was, took one last selfie and disappeared after them. We watched him become part of the crowd and disappear through the tunnels leading towards the Forbidden City.

Back again, three weeks on, and the pavement outside the Gate of Heavenly Peace was a little quieter; most of the early tour groups had already made their way inside, I guessed and later risers had not yet arrived. The morning air was heavy and thick. The flags on top of the tower draped limply against the flagpole, and the stillness of the air exacerbated the early heat and gave the broad expanse of concrete and granite a perverse feeling of claustrophobia. I had woken early and set out in a hazy sodium half-light. From the buildings I passed on my way to the station only a few dull lights stood out: stuck pixels on the widescreen of the city.

The subway was packed, though. I jostled elbows with commuters absorbed by their smartphone screens, and exited the station amongst a crowd of out-of-towners who paused at every decision, unsure of how to get through and out of the station and, as they emerged into the milky light onto an anonymous stretch of pavement, of where the palace and square they had come so far to see actually stood.

Along the stretch of pavement outside the Forbidden City, young guards from the People's Armed Police stood under square green parasols which matched their uniform; resting on the hedge behind each of them were a fire-extinguisher and a plastic shield. On the lamp posts outside the Gate of Heavenly Peace I counted six video cameras trained on different parts of the road and pavement: against the base of one leaned a man wearing a hat made of colourful balloon animals. A steady stream of people continued to filter across the bridges, being swallowed one by one into the dark tunnels of the Gate of Heavenly Peace. I joined them.

Beyond the tunnels underneath the exterior gates, you find yourself birthed into a broad enclosed space, almost a city square in itself, filled with chaotic lines of people extending from the ticket booths on its left-hand side. I joined a line somewhat reluctantly; my plan was to move quickly through the palace, avoiding the crowds, and thence to circle back and rejoin Long Peace Street. Today's walk, from Tiananmen to the subway station at Sihui, was only six miles as the crow flies, but one can easily lose a few hours in the nested courtyards of the Forbidden City, and even the queue looked daunting.

If Tiananmen Square has been refined and shaped to tell of the glory of New China, the meaning of the Forbidden City cannot be shifted. Completed in 1420, it was the seat of both the Ming and Qing dynasties: twenty-four emperors called it home. Its endless courtyards and halls unambiguously embody all the ceremony and majesty of the imperial age – and also tell something of its quiet coda. The crowds move along the north-south axis of the palace, drawn to the centre of power as it once was and enlivened by the thrill of trespass.

Looking around and beyond the queueing tourists and the hawkers selling maps, I was reminded of a sepia photograph of this same approach to the Forbidden City taken in the aftermath of the Boxer Rebellion of summer 1900. The image shows the soldiers of the 9th US Infantry standing to attention along either side of the pathway which runs along the middle of this courtyard to the Meridian Gate – the main front gate of the palace. Parading towards it are the American Minister to China, Edwin Conger, and his family: he bowler-hatted and purposeful; the ladies of the group in bonnets and long heavy dresses. This was one of the number of parades held in the Forbidden City after the victory of the Eight Nation Alliance over the Boxers,[1] a group of Chinese rebels who, for fifty-five days, laid siege to the diplomats of the Legation Quarter. The Boxers United in Righteousness, to give them their full title, were a motley band of mostly young rural peasants attired in colourful turbans and practicing syncretic forms of martial art and folk religion. Their slogan, 'Revive the Qing, destroy the foreign', set out their aims unambiguously, however. In the early summer of 1900, they forced the foreign diplomatic corps to retreat into their legations; the stand-off lasted for almost two months, through the fierce heat of the Beijing summer, until the Eight Nation Alliance managed to enter the city and liberate the legations.

Along each side of the courtyard through which the Congers walk, the white cloth triangles of the tents are pitched, neat and orderly like the soldiers themselves. There is obvious damage to the roof-line of the gate; in the latter days of the conflict, the foreign forces flung shells towards the Forbidden City; some of those who had been caught up in the siege questioned whether it might have been better if the soldiers had burned down the place altogether.

As the foreign troops arrived in August, the Empress Dowager, who had ruled the country from behind a screen for much of the second half of the nineteenth century, fled with her court to Xi'an, leaving the palace empty. During their absence, the foreign diplomatic corps and the soldiers who had saved them took the opportunity to explore the Great Within. Some were not above stealing the valuables left behind in the court's hurry to escape, as the writer Henry Savage Landor reported:

> At the sides were a number of lacquered cases with the Imperial dragon in gold, and handsome ivory tablets for the keys. These coffers contained magnificent gold embroideries, official insignia, jade Imperial seals, amber necklaces, decorations, and other such articles.
>
> Much to the evident annoyance of General Linievitch, a number of officers of the Allies made direct for these coffers, smashed them open, and filled their pockets with what they could get, regardless of the feelings of the spectators, who stood aghast.[2]

They were not the first foreigners to step over the threshold of the Forbidden City – missionaries, traders and diplomats from the West had all seen the inside of the Outer Court in prior centuries – though accounts from the time tend to emphasise the notion that theirs was an original experience. Alicia Little, for example, asserted that 'Through the Forbidden City no man of European race is believed ever to have freely walked until now'.[3] Certainly the freedom with which they were able to wander *was* unprecedented; they roamed the place in the spirit of the conquerors of old, laying claim to a rightful territory.

There was something undeniably symbolic about this transgression. There are countless moments in the latter decades of China's last imperial dynasty which could be said to mark an irreversible shift in the Qing's fortunes; they do not come much more dramatic than the court's abandonment of the Forbidden City and their capital, or more humiliating than the image of hundreds of foreign soldiers rooting around in their personal living quarters. It was a moment of financial, political and military disgrace. The Chinese had been unable to defend their own capital – a problem which would recur in the 1930s when the Japanese rolled in – and the deal the Empress Dowager ultimately signed in order to protect her rule included a sizable payment to the Western powers, as well as an agreement which considerably strengthened the rights of those living in the Legation Quarter. But it was more than that; it was also a moment where the curtain was drawn back, and the mystery around the court, its rituals and its material splendour suddenly evaporated.

The ticket queue moved glacially. In front of me, a young couple shared a sun parasol, she leaning her head tiredly against his shoulder. In front of the couple was a single middle-aged women in colourful outdoor gear; each time the queue moved forward in front of her, she would wait to close the gap until perhaps a few metres had opened between her and the person ahead. Each time, the young romantics would look at her, and turn around to look at me in amused confusion, yet they seemed unwilling to speak to her directly. Occasionally, someone would try to exploit the gap and and join the queue in front of the woman; each time, she managed to ward them off with a machine-gun phrase: *pai dui ne* – 'get in line'.

Eventually I reached the matter-of-fact ticket vendor who checked my passport and sold me a ticket. I set off towards the Meridian Gate, which extends out long arms on either side of the approach, beckoning you in. Another queue; another security check; and another dark cool tunnel, from which one emerges into the Forbidden City.

15

Four days in the Forbidden City

7 January 1902

It was just after noon when the steam train bearing the Empress Dowager and the thirty-year-old Guangxu Emperor pulled into the train station in Beijing. It had been nearly a year and a half since either of them had seen their capital, and they were greeted by a biting January wind, carrying in it dust and sand from the desert to the city's north. The Empress Dowager had fled Beijing in a mule cart, over roads quagmired by the summer rains, but arrived back to the city in state: yellow silk dragons hung from the engine car and that of the Emperor, and yellow sand had been scattered along the streets. The imperial buildings had been repainted, and those damaged in the fighting at the end of the Boxer siege either rebuilt or hidden behind screens.

Most of the foreign diplomatic corps in Beijing had pointedly stayed away from this pageant, concerned that their appearance might be understood to mark a form of homage to the court, but many of their wives turned up, along with journalists and curious officers and soldiers from the European forces. A special building was made available from which the Western onlookers could regard the ceremonious return, which the correspondent for the *New York Times* characterised as 'a bewildering and barbaric exhibition of Oriental tinseled splendour', though he conceded that it also marked a new openness on the part of the court, remarking that the opportunities given to the foreign community to spectate were greater than those which would have been offered in the courts of Europe.[1] Tensions still ran high, however, and the Chinese officials requested that the guards protecting the foreign legations be restricted to their quarters to avoid the possibility of a clash.[2]

After descending from the train, the Emperor and Empress Dowagers stopped and offered thanks at the Temples of the God of War and the Goddess of Mercy respectively – and mercy was one of the themes of the day, for, despite the punitive agreement she had been forced by the foreign powers to sign, the Qing still ruled, and the Forbidden City still stood. They proceeded together through the Front Gate, and then the Great Qing Gate. This was a route tradition-ally reserved for the Emperor alone, but many rules were being bent or broken on this day. Beijingers had been told to keep to their houses, but flouted the instruction, emerging to try and catch a glimpse of the Emperor and Empress Dowager. She even condescended to acknowl-edge the presence of the foreign spectators, waving and bowing in their direction in a spirit of seeming penitence and friendship. A few weeks later, she would tell Sarah Conger – wife of the American Minister, who had walked alongside her husband on the day of the military parade – of her regret over the 'late troubles' of the Boxer rebels. 'It was a grave mistake, and China will hereafter be a friend to foreigners', she would say. 'No such affair will again happen. China will protect the foreigner, and we hope to be friends in the future.'[3]

When she reached the Forbidden City, the Empress Dowager stopped short of entering via the Meridian Gate, through which hoards of foreigners had so recently poured; even in these strange new times, this particular protocol applied, and she was instead carried around to a side entrance. After her return, those in the imperial household came in turn to offer their respects – and the accounting of just what had been lost could truly begin.

5 November 1924

'The plot thickens in this city of dreadful uncertainty', wrote a Western journalist at the end of 5 November 1924 in an article headlined 'A Peking Coup'.[4] Reginald Johnston, the Emperor's tutor, would later wonder whether – just as their British counterparts 'remember, remember the fifth of November' for the machinations of Guy Fawkes and his fellow Catholics in the Gunpowder Plot – this date might be recalled by Chinese schoolchildren as a day of national repentance and humiliation.

In the Forbidden City, the day had begun normally enough – or as normally as it could begin, given the former Emperor Puyi's odd state of limbo, stuck in a monument to his faded dynasty.

It had been more than twelve years since his rule had ended, and sixteen since he had first entered the Forbidden City. In 1908, he had been picked by the dying Empress Dowager to rule after the death of her nephew, and had been just shy of three years old when he had taken nominal charge of the empire; his rule lasted until just after his sixth birthday. He had been shorn of his title even before he properly understood it, and came to manhood trapped in the vacuum of the Forbidden City; the 'tiny world' in which he spent 'the most absurd childhood possible',[5] as he later wrote.

Chapter 15

As he grew older, the last Emperor attempted to enforce a degree of control over his existence within the confines of his section of the palace, confined as he was in an imperial palace without imperial power. He dismissed the eunuchs who, for generations, had made themselves such an integral part of the bureaucracy of the Forbidden City, and introduced modernisations inspired by his affection for Western thinking and technology. He had even had the wooden thresholds of the doors in the palace sawn off so he could more easily ride the bicycle given to him by the man he called 'Johnston'.

On the morning of 5 November, he was eating an apple in his wife's quarters, when officials rushed in, telling him that soldiers loyal to a warlord who had just taken control of Beijing had arrived with a message which gave the Emperor and his court an ultimatum: they had just three hours to pack up and leave the Forbidden City. The legal agreement which guaranteed his residence in the palace, and ensured the payment of a sizeable stipend towards the upkeep of his court each year, had been annulled. If he did not leave within three hours, the men sent to deliver the message explained that they would not answer for the consequences.[6]

The military leader who had taken control of Beijing was Feng Yuxiang, known as the Christian General; a rumour, likely apocryphal, had him baptising his troops with a fire hose. His ousting of Puyi was a shock to the Beijing political class, and many of the Manchu elite sought shelter in the protected square mile of the Legation Quarter that afternoon; stories rumbled around amongst those sequestered there that the Emperor and his wife had been murdered, and that relations of the ruling family were next on the list.

Inside the Forbidden City, Puyi began to prepare his departure, with only a couple of servants to organise and carry his belongings. His father arrived at the palace in a state of emotional distress. Upon hearing earlier that his son had agreed to the new terms laid out for him and was going to leave the palace, he had removed his formal hat, decorated with a peacock feather, and thrown it to the ground, crying 'It's all over, it's all over'.[7]

As the deadline approached, Feng's officers began to threaten Puyi that the massed soldiers assembled on the hill just behind the Forbidden City would open fire with their artillery if they lingered longer. Together, the Emperor and his wife walked out through the Imperial Garden at the north of the palace, and were bundled into one of the five cars sent to collect them. For the first time, Puyi passed through one of the side arches of the Imperial City's gate towers, rather than through the central opening reserved for the Emperor. 'Evidently', wrote Reginald Johnston, who had been purposefully kept out of the palace all that day, '"Mr Puyi" was to be taught without delay that there was nothing to differentiate him from his fellow-citizens – except perhaps certain regrettable limitations on his personal freedom'.[8]

Puyi was taken to the house of his father, a stately mansion on the banks of Houhai, or Rear Lake, where he had been born. When he arrived, he was asked whether he intended to try to become emperor again, or whether he was content to be an ordinary citizen. Puyi, who had been looking for a way out of the strictures of the Forbidden City for some time, replied 'From today onwards I want to be an ordinary citizen'.[9]

He would shortly move from his father's house to the relative safety of the Japanese Legation. From there, he would indulge himself in night time bicycle rides, savouring the anonymity of the dark. One night he rode as far as the moat around the Forbidden City. Looking at the quiet silhouettes of the gate towers and high walls, a closed world filled with a settling darkness, now deepening into night, he resolved that one day he would return, a conquering king once more. 'Muttering an ambiguous goodbye', he would later write, 'I remounted my bicycle and rode away at high speed'.[10]

18 August 1966

In his autobiography, Puyi had written of the odd acoustic effect that meant that, even deep in the Forbidden City, the sounds of early morning Beijing could be heard: 'You could make out the cries of pedlars quite distinctly, as well as the rumbling of the wooden wheels of heavy carts and, at times, sounds of soldiers singing', he wrote. 'The eunuchs used to call this phenomenon the "city of sounds".'[11] On 18 August 1966 the overheated, still air in the abandoned halls of the Forbidden City reverberated with the distant songs and shouts of the more than a million students who had amassed on Tiananmen Square in the pre-dawn light.

Jiang Qing and her Cultural Revolution Group had organised the rally, and Red Guards had been arriving since midnight in the hope of catching a glimpse of Chairman Mao. The Great Helmsman deigned to meet the students in person during this, the first of many rallies at Tiananmen in the early months of the Cultural Revolution. Lin Biao gave a speech in which he cited Chairman Mao as the 'greatest genius' of the age and encouraged the Red Guards to destroy the four olds: the ideas, cultures, customs and habits of the past.[12] The students, in dull, quasi-military garb, enlivened by a smear of red around the arm marked with the yellow characters 'Mao Zedong Thought', and below 'Red Guard', danced and sang songs which extolled the value of loyalty and the wonder of the Great Helmsman; 1,500 of them were invited onto the rostrum of the Gate of Heavenly Peace itself to observe the rally. In a gesture of support, Mao accepted a Red Guard armband from one of them, a young female student named Song Binbin, and encouraged her to change her gentle sounding name, Binbin, to 'Yaowu', meaning 'Willing Fighter'.

The centre of Beijing was so busy that to get to Tiananmen was an achievement in itself: one disappointed student stuck in the west of the city recalls that the flow of people from east to west along Long Peace Street was impossible to fight against.[13] The rally marked the beginning of the worst excesses of 'Bloody August' in Beijing – in which even the smallest transgressions were enough to get you beaten or killed by wandering bands of Red Guards. There would be more rallies on the square; Mao would witness 10 million students prostrate themselves before him over the course of the coming months.

The Gate of Heavenly Peace, which the Red Guards faced, had been linked with Mao and the revolution since his declaration of the founding of the People's Republic of China in 1949 from its balcony. The Forbidden City hidden behind it, however, was the embodiment of the 'four olds', of course, and all the iniquities of the past. The rallying students began to agitate to get inside the palace, bent on visiting physical destruction on it similar to that being exacted on other sites in the city.

Premier Zhou Enlai, hearing of the threat to the palace, issued a directive closing the Forbidden City that night and setting guards around it. On returning to find the heavy wooden gates of the palace shut, the Red Guards put up a plaque marked with the characters 'Xuelei Gong' – 'Palace of Blood and Tears'. They continued their graffiti with other slogans: 'Burn the Forbidden City to the ground' and 'Trample the old palace'.[14]

Zhou kept the Forbidden City closed for the next five years; in the end, he would dispatch a garrison of soldiers to live there, such were the constant threats.[15] Long grass grew up in the courtyards, and apart from the soldiers and a skeleton staff, the palace sat empty.

In 1970, Zhou ordered that it be prepared for reopening. In April of the following year, the Chinese authorities would extend a surprising invitation to the US Table Tennis team, who were on a tour of Japan. They were the first invited American visitors to China since the cessation of diplomatic and economic ties in 1949; their journey behind the bamboo curtain gave rise to the term 'Ping-Pong Diplomacy', and laid the foundations for the visit, the following year, of Secretary of State Henry Kissinger. In what would become a familiar tour for those who arrived on official business in the coming years, the Chinese authorities guided the American team along the crenellated dragon's back of the Great Wall and through the empty courtyards of the Forbidden City, showing off its seemingly timeless splendours to an audience who had no idea how close it had come to destruction.

4 August 2016

It is with repetition that the Forbidden City asserts its grandeur, rather than through scale or ornament. It has these as well, but it is the endless reiteration of the same, symmetrical spaces and the same visual motifs that one remembers. The effect can be taken in at a glance from Scenery Hill behind the palace; line after line of dull gold rooflines subdivide the rectangular compound: all uniform; all perpendicular, enclosing courtyards ranging from the miniature to the vast.

On the ground, however, you experience each space distinctly, passing across those courtyards to funnel through narrow apertures. In the expansive enclosures at the front of the palace, the visitors who move across it are made small and static, like the precise, minute figures of a Chinese scroll painting. Bustling across these empty spaces, footsteps echoing on the stone floor, courtiers had ample time to reflect on the appropriate sense of obeisance they should carry in to their meeting with the occupant of the Dragon Throne.

The Forbidden City is not history as narrative. Try as you might, it is hard to access the countless stories which harbour themselves here; the signs dotted around the place restrict themselves to the recitation of a litany of dates and names, and there are no helpful guides standing ready with an explanation. Instead, this is history as experience, in which simply being here must suffice. In particular, and ever increasingly, this means photographed experience.

'Excuse me, photograph?' a trio of school children queried as I stood looking out over a broad courtyard, the bulky foreigner blocking a stairwell. They took a few angled selfies, shouting '*Qiezi*' – 'Aubergine!' – with each snap, fingers spread in the ubiquitous V-sign. Everywhere around me, people were organising themselves for their own photographs: families of grandparents, parents and children; young couples; groups of coach-party tourists. The devices brandished ranged from cheap Chinese-brand smartphones to heavy, long-lensed Japanese cameras. The reason for this fervour of documentation was the large double-roofed building behind us: the Hall of Supreme Harmony, the coronation hall of all twenty-four emperors of the Ming and Qing who ruled from the Forbidden City. Up the steps and inside the hall, crowds of people pressed to get a look at the south-facing sandalwood throne. A golden ball, orbited by six smaller spheres, hangs from the intricately patterned roof above it; legend said these would fall on anyone who attempted to ascend to the throne unrightfully.

Symbolism abounds throughout the palace. The colours, the decorations, the layout and orientation of the buildings: they hum with associations beyond the literal. Swathes of lacquered golden ceramic; blood-coloured walls; bronze dragons, phoenixes, tortoises and herons: that nothing of the design and decoration is the result of chance is obvious, even if the meaning is not always clear to the uninitiated. The challenge of deciphering the symbolism of the palace was beyond one English visitor who, delighted by gaining a glimpse inside the palace after the Empress Dowager's departure in 1900, wrote of the pattern of curious curves and loops which decorate the gable ends of the Forbidden City's roofs: 'as if it had been dashed off by a master pen writing in pure gold'.[16] In fact, despite the elegance of her interpretation, she had failed to notice that the curves and loops are in fact a queue of small ceramic animals who line up along the pointed eave corners. Each of the animals is weighted with distinct symbolic meaning: the dragon standing for the emperor and the power invested in him; the phoenix signifying virtue; the seahorse bringing good fortune.

Chapter 15

And, for all the drama and upheaval that had afflicted it, good fortune had blessed the Forbidden City. It was remarkable, I thought, as I wandered away from the photographing crowds to walk northward through the palace edges, that the compound had remained intact after all the tumult of China's recent past. There had been so many moments when conflict had created the conditions for its destruction – and its destruction would not have been a difficult thing as, like most traditional Chinese buildings, it is built primarily from wood. Indeed, many of its buildings had, at one time or another, suffered damage from fire; the court officials were so conscious of the threat that they kept large bronze vats filled with water close to the buildings. It had been disfigured by conflict more than once; shelled and bombed during the darker days of the twentieth century. What had been destroyed had almost always been rebuilt, however – indeed, as with most historical sites in China, it is best not to concern oneself too much with the originality of what presents itself.

Today, the Forbidden City has a sense of permanence at the centre of the city, bequeathed by its status as a UNESCO World Heritage Site and one of the world's most visited museums: in 2016, I was one of 16 million people who passed through the palace gates. The ever-changing dramas and mysteries of its past have been replaced by the comparably mundane and predictable daily procession of streams of tourists from across China, and around the world, passing in an endless procession from south to north.

In the former capital Nanjing – a city which places great value on its long history – I saw what the Forbidden City might have become. An imperial palace of similar style and age had once stood there, built by the first ruler of the Ming dynasty, Zhu Yuanzhang, who rose from an upbringing in a peasant family to become, in 1368, Emperor of China. Nanjing was the site Zhu chose for his capital and he built a palace of courtyards and grand halls on the outskirts of the city that became the centre of imperial power in China. It was next to this palace, in fact, that the first Chang'an Jie had run; the Ming's reign was, they hoped, to be both long and peaceful. In 1402, however, and after a four-year civil war, Zhu Yuanzhang's grandson, the Jianwen Emperor, was forcefully usurped from the throne.[17] His Nanjing palace was set alight, with the Emperor apparently still inside – though some stories claim that he had fled in disguise before the attack – and its halls were left badly damaged by the fire. A further series of blazes over the following decades meant that the palace gradually fell into ruin. What remained was cannibalised for use elsewhere, including another grand palace of sweeping yellow roofs constructed by the Taiping, a group of Christian rebels who threatened Qing rule in the mid-nineteenth century and established their capital at Nanjing: this too would subsequently be razed to the ground by fire.

Today, the site of the Ming dynasty's first Forbidden City is a public park. I visited on a sweltering August day. Nanjing is notorious for its summer heat, but even the locals kept mentioning that it was *tebie re* – 'especially hot': the hottest for twenty years, so the local TV news said.

Yet the park, a much smaller proposition than the plot housing Beijing's Forbidden City, was far from empty, despite the heat. At picnic tables in the shade, local retirees played cards, umbrellas hanging from tree branches above to provide extra protection from the afternoon sun. An old man and his young disciple practised the diabolo, tossing and catching its whirling body on a string. Across the shaded courtyard came a younger man holding something large and round under his t-shirt: '*Xigua! Xigua!*' – Watermelon! Watermelon! – he cried excitedly as he approached the card players; they looked up in smiling welcome. The shaded pavilions which had once stood here, sheltering concubines from the afternoon heat as they composed a poem or practised their calligraphy, were evidenced only by a few scattered stone pedestals and column bases, and the grey brick of gate platforms; the grand wooden towers which once stood atop them

Chapter 15

now distant memories. Low bridges arched over still, jade-coloured water. The glories of the Emperor: the colour and decoration, the bronze animals, the symmetrical grandeur, were gone.

In the cool tunnels of one of the ivy-covered gates, a woman silently practised the slow movements of *taijiquan*, her figure precisely silhouetted by the dimming late afternoon light. The park echoed suddenly with the laughter of the card players – someone had won. They gathered up the cards and dealt them out once more.

16

Out of the Forbidden City – scholar trees – dislocation – destruction – impressions of Beijing – going native – Legation Street today – fireworks over Tiananmen

Passing along the quiet corridors of the western edge of the palace, and having paused to rest in a cypress-shaded courtyard – empty save for me and a young security guard who followed me like a shadow – I eventually and inevitably rejoined the crowds in the Imperial Garden at the northern tip of the palace. Here, outcrops of pitted limestone mimic mountains, set amongst high-reaching pines, junipers and cypresses and pavilions of red and gold, offering a landscape in miniature for a ruler to take refuge in. The tranquillity, which this area was built to preserve for the Emperor, was hard to perceive today amongst the dense, slow-moving crowds who shuffled along the narrow pavements and bobbed in and out of the gift shops around the courtyard's perimeter.

Chapter 16

No matter the idiosyncrasies of the route you choose through the palace, all eventually pass through here, and then funnel out of the northernmost gate to find themselves once more in modern China: a busy many-laned avenue ahead; the sound of wheezing diesel engines; the shouts and cries of hawkers; and the deepening realisation that, in a triumph of urban planning, the only viable option to return you to the point where you entered the palace is to walk the long way around its perimeter. Despite the tens of thousands of tourists who emerge here each day, there is as yet no subway stop, only crowded bus lines, and I passed these by to join the convoy of people walking back towards their starting point, passing along the northern stretch of the palace moat and then down the crowded narrow road running south to Long Peace Street. Along the street middle-aged men ride tired-looking tourist rickshaws and shout out their few words of English – 'Hello! Rickshaw!' when they see a foreign face. The convoy of walkers was so large, and the pavements so narrow, that a majority-rule approach developed, and we filled the right-hand lane, leaving the traffic to fight its way past.

I reached Long Peace Street once again and then ducked below it through one of the broad hot underpasses that allows you to cross underneath its many unnavigable lanes from the Gate of Heavenly Peace to Tiananmen Square. Emerging into the light, and passing the austere columns of the National Museum, I took a left into what used to be the diplomatic centre of China: Beijing's Legation Quarter.

The quiet shaded street was a relief after the hot open courtyards of the Forbidden City and the crowded streets I had just trudged along. What is left of the Legation Quarter is set along a narrow ribbon of road, little more than an alleyway, hidden up a few steps on the eastern side of Tiananmen Square and running parallel to Long Peace Street. It is unmarked, and largely unremarked upon, by the tourists who wander past, distracted as they are by the expansive square, the grandiose architecture of the National Museum and the shops selling communist kitsch where, behind plate glass windows, the smiling visages of Xi Jinping and Mao Zedong stare back from decorative plates, mugs and plaques.

Though so close to Tiananmen Square, the street never seems busy or hurried; Japanese pagoda trees dapple the pavement and grey walls with a soft confetti-like brightness, and the noise of the city is no more than a distant hum at the edge of your consciousness.

The pagoda tree, also known as the scholar tree, is the official tree of Beijing; they are ubiquitous in the city's older neighbourhoods, providing a gentle and distinctive shade and 'sedate old-world enjoyment' for the earlier occupants of the Quarter.[1] Despite its official name, *sophora japonica*, the tree is not native to Japan, and has a long association in China with imperial and religious sites; the most famous scholar tree in Beijing is that in the park behind the Forbidden City from which, the story goes, the last Ming Emperor hung himself in 1644, after he realised that his capital and his dynasty were about to fall. The tree is known as *zuihuai*, or the guilty pagoda.

The Legation Quarter was a place crafted to conjure a sense of dislocation. Diplomatic compounds everywhere are, of course, founded on the perverse idea that they are not where they are; the abstractions of politics rendering the square footage of an embassy or legation protected space, outside the bounds of many of the rules which apply to the land, and the people, which surround it. The legations at Beijing were even more emphatically dislocated, with clear distinctions, delineated more robustly over time, between the foreign world they represented and the China outside their walls. As such, they became symbols not of reciprocal and respectful diplomacy, but rather of the dysfunctional nature of the relationship between China and the rest of the world in the late nineteenth and early twentieth century, echoing the extraterritoriality that the foreigners had carved out in cities around the nation – places like Guangzhou, Qingdao and Shanghai, which had been handed over to foreign powers for them to trade from, and in some cases entirely run, in a series of bad deals which would linger long in the minds of the Chinese.

The agreement allowing diplomats to take residence in Beijing dates to 1860 when, after many years of trying, the British and French finally managed to secure permission to establish legations in the capital. The Chinese acquiescence was not the result of considered negotiations, but rather had been brought about by brute force when, in the last act of the Second Opium War, the British and French stormed in from the east towards Beijing. In retribution for the torture and killing of their intermediaries, the British troops burnt down the old Summer Palace, a vast and beautiful pleasure ground for the Emperor to the west of Beijing – an undertaking which took several thousand troops several days to accomplish.

The image of the burning palace, known in Chinese as *Yuanmingyuan*, or the Garden of Perfect Brightness, and all the innumerable treasures it contained, seared itself on the memories of those responsible. Robert McGhee, chaplain to the British soldiers, arrived on the second day of the burning; despite the justice it was intended to exact, McGhee, a man used to considering his experience in terms of the divine, could not but feel that there was something almost sacrilegious in its destruction:

> Soon the wreath becomes a volume, a great black mass, out burst a hundred flames, the smoke obscures the sun, and temple, palace, buildings and all, hallowed by age, if age can hallow, and by beauty, if it can make sacred, are swept to destruction, with all their contents, monuments of imperial taste and luxury. A pang of sorrow seizes upon you, you cannot help it, no eye will ever again gaze upon those buildings which have been doubtless the admiration of ages, records of by-gone skill and taste, of which the world contains not the like. You have seen them once and for ever, they are dead and gone, man cannot reproduce them.[2]

The Emperor had already escaped to the north, and it was left to his brother to smooth things over as the ruins of the palace smouldered. He had little option but to ratify a treaty already agreed in principle two years earlier which allowed foreign diplomats to take residence in Peking; some new punitive clauses were also added by the Western powers for good measure. These two agreements[3] are numbered amongst those many bad deals forced upon China in the nineteenth and early twentieth centuries: together, they are known, quite accurately, as the Unequal Treaties. The violence and destruction which birthed the Beijing legations would not be forgotten by China, and the Quarter became a symbol of the iniquities of the relationship between China and the world's powers, and a natural focal point for the expression of popular discontent with foreign imposition.

The Boxer Siege of 1900 was the most dramatic example of anti-foreign feeling directed at the legations. Ironically, however, the misjudged support of the Boxers by the Empress Dowager after they laid siege to the Legation Quarter ensured that the foreign community established themselves there even more permanently and separately. In the aftermath of the siege, the Legation Quarter was altered and reorganised – this time, behind a high stone wall bordered by broad grassy embankments which marked more clearly the distinction between the Chinese and foreign sections of the city. After this time, no Chinese were allowed to live within the walls, and a close watch was kept on those who visited or passed through.

The Westerners who made their home in the legations in Beijing worked hard to render their protected space as comfortable and familiar as possible, desiring generally to shut out the realities of the country which surrounded them. They lived, in the words of Edgar Snow, in 'their own little never-never land'.[4] '[I]n the middle of the Chinese capital', wrote a Russian diplomat upon his arrival in 1908, the foreigners 'had arranged a purely European mode of living'.[5] Shopping was done at stores filled with imported Western goods; garden parties were held on shaded lawns with musicians trained to play in the foreign style; summer afternoons carried the gentle sounds of leather on willow, or the metronomic rhythm of a tennis match.

And what did those who lived sequestered in this fantastical world make of the city outside their high walls?

Chapter 16

Most spent the early days of their residence struggling to acclimatise. Their accounts tend to single out that notorious Peking dust, mentioned almost invariably by visitors to the city, which Ellen La Motte went so far as to take for the title of a memoir of her time in the city.[6] Alicia Little refers to 'that plague of Peking, the dust of the Mongolian plateau',[7] whilst B.L. Putnam Weale felt that Beijing's dust was unique, 'distinguished among all the dusts of the earth for its blackness, its disagreeable insistence in sticking to one's clothes, one's hair, one's very eyebrows, until a grey-brown coating is visible to every eye'.[8]

One of the chief contributors to the dust – the heat – also took some getting used to. During the broiling months of the summer, residents would decamp *en masse* to the Western Hills, where they could seek respite from sweltering Beijing in the temples dotted on their shaded slopes, whilst looking down, both literally and metaphorically, on the city some fifteen miles distant. Between the Western Hills and the city were villages and flat green fields punctuated by the grave mounds of locals from both within and without the city.

Another favoured retreat during the summer months was a seaside resort two hundred miles or so to the east of Beijing named Beidaihe. In her novel, *Four Part Setting*, set in the 1920s, Ann Bridge catches something of the hazy summer charm of the place, describing: 'villas standing among trees, or in something approaching to real gardens – in between, all the way along the top of the bluffs which fringe the shore, lie bungalows of a medium sort, half hidden in the native growth of bushes and small trees, mimosas and thorns – their own small sandy paths lead from them down the bluffs to the shore'.[9] In more recent times, the resort has become a haven for China's Communist Party elite; they export the political machinations of the capital there each summer, as they have for decades now, turning it into a sort of Zhongnanhai-on-Sea.

Beyond first trips further afield to the Great Wall, and the Imperial Tombs just outside Beijing, the other diversions outside the Legation

Quarter tended to be limited to perusing the antique shops of the Chinese City, or perhaps taking a stroll on the wall. This latter activity was of particular appeal due to the fact that the Chinese themselves were generally not allowed to take their leisure there; as Sarah Conger wrote to her sister: 'The city wall is a quiet, clean walking place; Chinese are seldom allowed upon the wall, and you feel safe and free'.[10]

As Conger's letter implies, the attitude of many of the Legation Quarter's inhabitants towards the people of Beijing, and of China more generally, was one of distrust. Their prejudices were exacerbated, of course, by the events of the Boxer Rebellion, but Western views of the Chinese in the late nineteenth and early twentieth century were commonly, though not universally, deeply suspicious of the so-called 'Yellow Peril' they represented – a suspicion recounted with a remarkable certainty. Henry Savage Landor, for instance, speculated on the imperial court's excitement at the news of the increasing hostility of the Boxers, and their belief

> that the moment had come when the Chinese could at last either kill or drive into the sea every foreign devil. It must ever be borne in mind that this notion is and will always be firmly rooted in every Chinaman's mind. The higher he is in official position the deeper is his feeling of contempt and hatred for foreigners.[11]

The Legation Quarter is distrust writ large in architecture, with the different nationalities walled off from each other and from the outside – the vast, frightening outside, which stretched so endlessly, so unreadably, so threateningly around them.

To live outside the perceived safety of the Quarter was regarded as something of an eccentric's pursuit. The American George Kates moved to Beiping, as it was known when he arrived, on a twist of fate and impulse in 1933. He elected to live outside the Legation Quarter; a decision which prompted dire warnings from the diplomatic contingent, particularly regarding the unsanitary conditions he would face

– a constant source of anxiety amongst foreigners – as he recounted in his memoir, *The Years That Were Fat*:

> Wiseacres of long residence, generally established foreign style in the Legation Quarter, and the diplomatic corps generally, called this 'going native.' The words were supposed of themselves to be sufficient admonition to deter one from such an awful course. [...] Other ruddy faced Europeans [...] declared that they seriously feared for my health if I actually planned to live in a completely unimproved Chinese house.[12]

Kates, along with a handful of others, remained the exception in choosing to live outside the comforting gates and walls of the Legation Quarter. And the reality was that Beijing in the early decades of the twentieth century was a place in which the practical ability to close the door to the outside world must have been a welcome reassurance. Whispers of conflict and fresh upheaval would regularly pass around the ballrooms and dining tables of the Quarter – some founded in fact, some in paranoia. But the realities needed little embellishment. In the twenty-five years after the Boxer Rebellion, the legations would stand witness to the end of the Qing dynasty; the imperial pretensions of a new president; the arrival of a carousel of various warlords; the mass protests of the May Fourth Movement; and the evacuation of the last emperor from the Forbidden City – who would find refuge in the Japanese Legation for a time. For much of this period and beyond, it was unclear who, if anyone, was in charge of the vast nation which extended all around them, and at times the Legation Quarter must have felt very small indeed.

In the Legation Quarter, my sense that I was in fact walking through two cities – one old and one new; one made of concrete and steel, and another of memory and imagination – was particularly vivid, for there are few parts of China that have been more closely documented by outsiders than its modest rectangular plot. By virtue both of the era in which it existed, when letter- and diary-writing was approached as a daily obligation, the function it served as a diplomatic outpost, and the desire back home for first-hand tales of the Middle Kingdom – especially after the Boxer Rebellion, which was front page news across the world – accounts of life in the compounds of the Legation Quarter abound, particularly from the early years of the twentieth century. 'When I went to China I had a great ambition', wrote the Reverend E.J. Hardy just after 1900. 'It was to gain the distinction of not writing a book on that country.'[13]

The accounts from the legation years, both published and archival, offer a vivid portrait of those who lived there and of the place itself, which was a distinctive mix of architectural styles, with each nation trying to preserve something of their national character in the legations they constructed. Like pavilions for some Great Exhibition, they were embellished with flourishes designed to hint to one of home, to conjure just for a moment that reassuring sense of familiarity; to remind those living here that, no matter the dusty plains and thousands of miles that separated them from a culture, a people, a nation, they carried the important things with them.

Today, one must work hard to glimpse the place as it used to be. Some of the buildings remain, but unlike Shanghai's famous riverfront Bund, where the grand piles constructed by the foreign trading companies and banks have been given over to expensive bars, restaurants and boutiques, what does remain has a slightly sad, forgotten look to it. The former American Embassy, which had, until recently, been the site of a French restaurant of some refinement, was now empty, the reverberations of jackhammers and drills ringing out from behind the dark open windows: another part of Beijing busy becoming something else.

I walked along the quiet street slowly. On each visit I inevitably found that some new detail or hidden architectural motif revealed itself to me: a pair of dull gold Lions Rampart on a crest above a disused gateway; a faded street sign still bearing the old Western name; a European roofline falling and rising like a line-graph behind a high wall. I knew also that, as with the American Embassy, each stroll through the Quarter tended to reveal further change; piece by piece, and building by building, this reminder of a fraught period of Chinese history was being quietly erased.

Along the first stretch of what was once Legation Street, amongst the most obvious relics remaining from the old days are a former bank, now repurposed as Beijing's Police Museum, which channels Wall Street with its grand Ionic columns, and, opposite, the three-arched entrance gates of the old Russian Legation, which now guard the glossy mirrored-glass Supreme People's Court. This has been the site of protests and petitions against injustice in recent years, and is now not even to be looked at, let alone photographed: the young guard, true to expectation, quickly held out a hand and shouted 'No!' when I slowed my pace to look more closely at the gateway and the stone lions which sit either side of it.

At the next junction, where I turned north to cut back towards Long Peace Street, the old Yokohama Specie Bank building still stands, with its bright red cupola; beyond it are the twin neo-gothic spires of St Michael's church, hidden amongst reaching branches heavy with leaves, in a street scene which would not seem out of place in a provincial French town.

The esplanade that I followed north, running in a cool, verdant band back towards Long Peace Street, had buried beneath it, like a sublimated memory, an old drainage ditch which had carried water away from the Imperial City and, providing an even greater service to the diplomats, had allowed in the men of the Eight Nation Alliance who had come to liberate those besieged in the legations during the Boxer Rebellion; on the afternoon of 14 August 1900 they had entered at the gate in the city wall where the canal flowed out of the city, to the cheers of the foreign residents.

On the southern corner where I had turned had once been the Hotel Wagons-Lits. It was the centre of the quarter's social swirl; in the large, gaudy lounge one could often also spot members of the city's Chinese elite, who would retreat there at times of threat or upheaval. In Ann Bridge's novel *Peking Picnic*, the beautiful Lilah looks around at these people – refugees from their own city – and observes: 'How nice for them to have a Legation Quarter to come to!'[14]

The end for the Legation Quarter, and all but a handful of its inhabitants, came in 1949, with the founding of the People's Republic. Really, though, the place had never been the same after the capital was officially moved from Beijing to Nanjing by the Nationalists in 1928 – a move that was a calamity for the city in general. Most stayed put, but the diplomatic contingent were forced to regularly slog south to the new capital.

Then, in 1937, the Japanese arrived. They initially left the foreigners in peace, but the material change happening all around the Legation Quarter was impossible to ignore. Preparing to leave in 1940, George Kates compared the mood amongst the legation residents to that of a man suffering from a fatal illness who, though perfectly comfortable at present, knows implicitly of the illness 'clawing … in the dark at his vitals'.[15] This foreboding was proved prescient: in 1941, the day after the Japanese bombed Pearl Harbour, their troops marched into the Legation Quarter and took charge. It would get worse: in early 1943, those allied foreigners left in the city received a letter requesting that they assemble with their belongings at the American Embassy compound. They were to be transferred to an internment camp in Shandong province, and would remain there until the Second World War came to an end in 1945. After their release, some would shuffle back to Beijing and try to piece together their former life; many would cut their losses and leave.

Those who came back and held out would see the PLA troops roll into the city in January 1949 and then, in October, hear the echoing shouts of the massed crowds in Tiananmen Square, as Mao Zedong declared the founding of New China from the Gate of Heavenly Peace, just a few hundred yards from the legations. 'The people throughout China have been plunged into bitter suffering and tribulations since the [...] Kuomintang reactionary government betrayed the fatherland, colluded with imperialists and launched the counter-revolutionary war', he declared. His new administration was 'willing to establish diplomatic relations with any foreign government that is prepared to observe the principles of equality, mutual benefit, and mutual respect of territorial integrity and sovereignty', he said, but outside China's communist fellow-travellers, those governments would be few, at least initially.[16]

From the square, the cries of '*Mao zhuxi wan sui*' – 'Long live Chairman Mao!' carried on the autumn air, drifting over the walls and through the quiet gardens of the legations, illuminated in the twilight by the fireworks exploding in the sky above Long Peace Street and Tiananmen. Their noise and light commemorated a new beginning for China and, for the last diplomats and expatriates of old Beijing, marked the end of an era.

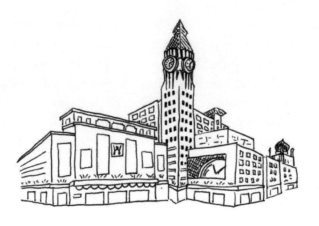

17

The man who died twice – Wangfujing – a literary traveller – the end of the Qing – Morrison and Yuan Shikai – a sad coda – Palm Sunday in Sidmouth

On 17 July 1900, *The Times* of London published an obituary of one of its own; a victim, they wrote, of 'Chinese treachery and ferocity' during the siege of the Legation Quarter by the Boxers, which by then had been going on for nearly a month. The obituary went on to say that, in the long list of those whose deaths they were reporting that day, 'not many names … will evoke more widespread sympathy than that of our devoted Correspondent at Peking'.[1]

The correspondent was George Ernest Morrison, and, amongst other distinctions, he had given his name to the broad busy avenue on which I now found myself, running north from Long Peace Street just past the expansive frontage of the Beijing Hotel a little east of the Legation Quarter. It had been named 'Morrison Street' in

174

recognition of George Ernest's service to China's president, Yuan Shikai, and for the fact that Morrison had been a high-profile resident of the street, living from 1902 in a grand courtyard house with an extensive and scrupulously organised library.

'It was always a grateful, sharp change to step from the confusion, dust and noise of the crowded street across the threshold into Morrison's peaceful, sunny court, as clean as a hospital, and bright with flowers',[2] wrote a correspondent in *Harper's Weekly* of the dwelling on Morrison Street. The house was on the east side of the street, about two hundred yards north of the junction with Long Peace Street, its entrance guarded by a red gate flanked by twin lions, and marked by a plate announcing that this was the home of 'Dr Mo'.

His service to China's president, and his residency from 1902 in this clean, bright courtyard house on Morrison Street, would seem material impossibilities, of course, given his death in 1900, when, as his somewhat melodramatic obituarist phrased it, the 'last heroic remnants of Western civilization in the doomed city were engulfed beneath the overwhelming flood of Asiatic barbarism' – but for the fact that on 17 July 1900, George Ernest Morrison was not actually dead.

Nor indeed were Sir Claude MacDonald, the British Minister, or Sir Robert Hart, Inspector General of China's Imperial Maritime Custom Service, both of whom were eulogised at length on the same page of that day's paper, apparent victims of the 'appalling catastrophe'. *The Times* was reporting erroneous information given to another British newspaper, and though Morrison had been slightly injured in the fighting, Claude Macdonald seemed not just alive but in the rudest of health when, just under a month later, he greeted the soldiers who had brought the siege to an end – clad in pristine tennis whites.

There is no marker of this street's former name, nor is there any remnant of Morrison's house, the last vestiges of which were torn down to make way for new shops in the run-up to the 2008 Olympic

Games.[3] It was a name used mainly by the foreign community of Beijing in any case; though the title was transliterated into Chinese as *Molixun* Street, the thoroughfare had for centuries been known to Beijingers as *Wangfujing* or 'The Well of the Princely Mansions', which hints at the stately residences which once spread along the streets and hutong of this area. They, like Morrison's house, and almost every other remnant of old Beijing, are entirely absent along a broad thoroughfare now best known for its malls and hotels.

Wangfujing is version 1.0 of Western commercialism in China, all fake pink marble, mirrored glass and primary-colour advertising hoardings. It now looks a dated relic compared to the slick new malls further east, clad in their smooth metallic gloss, but its legacy of being first has ensured that it retains a primacy in guides to the city, and the whole street is now filled with visitors, Chinese and foreign, all seemingly experiencing a simultaneous sense of tourist's remorse: 'Is this it?' they ponder. I watched one family, newly arrived, looking around at the toy-town architecture with camera in hand, forced to scoot quickly sideways as a white plastic tourist train motored determinedly towards them, its trebly loudspeaker narration cutting sharply through the hum of the crowds.

After the occasion of Morrison's actual death in 1920, one obituary noted that the career of this Australian from the port town of Geelong near Melbourne 'read like a romance'. His young life had been punctuated by a series of improbable journeys, including one in which he reversed the ill-starred expedition of the explorers Burke and Wills, travelling alone on foot across Australia from north to south – a journey of over 2,000 miles. His trip coincided with early rains, and for portions of it he was obliged to contend with swirling floodwaters up to his chest, carrying in them insects and snakes. A few months on from his successful completion of this journey, he set out again, this time to penetrate the little-known interior of New Guinea. After being ambushed by hostile islanders, he would be invalided back home still bodily carrying a memento of his time in New Guinea – a large fragment of the spear with which he had been pierced. It was later removed by a surgeon in Scotland.

His studied nonchalance regarding these journeys, and his belief in the power and purpose of walking for its own sake, had long endeared him to me. Morrison was, to my mind, a forgotten member of that eclectic club of literary travellers, of Victorian sensibility if not birth, whose simple need to shake off the strictures of modern society led them to embark on self-propelled journeys of adventure and escape. Patrick Leigh Fermor, who in the early 1930s walked from the Hook of Holland to Istanbul as twilight settled on old Europe; Wilfred Thesiger, conqueror of the vast desert of Arabia's 'Empty Quarter'; Robert Louis Stevenson, an inveterate walker who, in his essay 'Walking Tours', wrote of the need to travel always alone, 'because freedom is of the essence. [...] You should be as a pipe for any wind to play upon' – these are all his kin. 'I am as free as a lark', Morrison wrote to his mother on his Australian odyssey: 'I camp as soon as hungry and live as happy as the day is long'.[4]

Morrison would make his name, of course, as the pre-eminent correspondent of China's tumultuous early twentieth century, and not as a literary traveller. However, his initial encounters with the country were on foot; after a first visit in 1893, he decided whilst in Japan the following year to travel up the Yangtze River by boat from Shanghai to Chongqing, and then across land by foot into Burma – a trip of around 3000 miles. The account he wrote after the conclusion of this expedition is a masterpiece of Victorian understatement:

> The journey was, of course, in no sense one of exploration; it consisted simply of a voyage of 1500 miles up the Yangtse River, followed by a quiet, though extended, excursion of another 1500 miles along the great overland highway into Burma, taken by one who spoke no Chinese, who had no interpreter or companion, who was unarmed, but who trusted implicitly in the good faith of the Chinese.[5]

He had begun in China, he acknowledged, with a prejudice common to his fellow Westerners, but this was overturned by his time on foot in China's south-west; he crossed the mountains and valleys of Sichuan and Yunnan province without any significant difficulties, and felt that the locals had treated him in accordance with their precept: 'deal gently with strangers from afar'. The published account of his journey – *An Australian in China* – was enough to secure him the offer of a job as Peking correspondent for *The Times*. Despite his lack of written or spoken Chinese, which he did little to rectify, he spent the next fifteen years in the job, gaining a reputation along the way as a perceptive and sympathetic interpreter of the complex political situation in China.

During his stint as a correspondent, Morrison was a witness to the conflict and existential uncertainty which characterised China in the early twentieth century, filing reports on the Boxer Rebellion, the attempted Qing reform movement, the Russo-Japanese War of 1904–5, fought on Chinese soil – and, most significantly, the revolution of 1911, which led to the end of the Qing dynasty, and was also to mark a turning point in Morrison's life.

On Thursday 12 October 1911, *The Times* carried a story from their correspondent in Peking of a 'Serious Rising at Wuchang', a city to the south in Hubei province: 'Peking is thoroughly alarmed by the news of a revolutionary outbreak and mutiny of troops at Wuchang', Morrison wrote. The short final act of China's long imperial drama had begun.

Three days earlier on 9 October, an explosion had been reported in the Russian quarter of Hankou, a port city on the opposite bank of the Yangtze River from Wuchang. A bomb built by anti-Qing revolutionaries had been accidentally detonated and, in the ensuing investigation, police discovered a document listing those involved in the plotting.

The rebels quickly came to a realisation: after all the months of planning, it was now or never; they could either act, or be arrested. Mutinies were launched in the next-door cities of Hanyang and Wuchang – the latter that reported on by Morrison – and from there the anti-Qing uprising escalated, gathering irreversible momentum as it spread from province to province. Those who followed the revolutionary call were not united by a desire for a republic, but were, in the main, simply fed up with the rule of the Manchu Qing dynasty.

On 19 January 1912, a little over three months later, subscribers to *The Times* would read a story by Morrison headlined: 'The Abdication of the Manchus – Yuan Shih-Kai to be President'. China's grand imperial tradition was ending with a whimper, and Yuan had been nominated to take charge of the new republic.

Below the main article in *The Times*, a three-line addendum noted that 'three men who attempted to assassinate Yuan Shih-kai were strangled this morning by the executioner'. George Morrison could offer a first-hand account of this attempt on Yuan's life: from the gate of his house on Wangfujing – it was not yet known as Morrison Street – he had watched the General's carriage pass by alongside his secretary, and then heard an explosion, after which 'the sky darkened',[6] he wrote. Yuan was unhurt, and Morrison was impressed at the efficiency with which the perpetrators were dealt. It was a signal, however, of just how fraught this transition from empire to republic promised to be.

On 12 February 1912, the boy-Emperor Puyi would abdicate, officially inaugurating China's new era, as well as a new era for Morrison. In recent years, Morrison had grown disillusioned with his job as Peking correspondent for *The Times*, and was dogged by concerns over both his ill-health and financial situation. His motivation in taking a job with China's new president, who had a reputation for violence which Morrison did his best to overlook, was thus partly personal: the salary was generous, and the position provided a practical way to remain living in the city he loved. It was also, of course, a high-profile appointment, complete with an office in Zhongnanhai overlooking the lake and its wild ducks. Reading through his letters, however, it is clear that Morrison was also motivated by a sincere desire to assist China as it embarked on this great experiment in democratic rule.

The reality of the job did not, however, match his expectation. Morrison was one of a number of foreign advisors, some more qualified than others, whom President Yuan enlisted – and then generally ignored. Another was an American named Frank Goodnow, who was employed to help to draft China's new constitution. Goodnow ended up convinced that the country could only be ruled by a monarch – he was one of those who supported Yuan's ill-fated attempt to become China's next emperor. These advisors were given few meaningful responsibilities, and, from week to week, often had little real work to do. When he did see Yuan, Morrison tended to find the President startlingly ill-informed on the realities of the country he ruled, filled with misinformation by sycophantic advisors.

These were times, and Yuan Shikai a man, too intractable for the forthright, clear-eyed Morrison to master. When Yuan died in 1916, he was let off the hook, somewhat, but the job was left undone, with all the attendant dissatisfaction that entailed. He had achieved little of concrete significance in his position as Yuan's advisor, and for a man of determination like Morrison, who measured himself and others by their tangible achievements, this must have been profoundly frustrating. He would write self-critically of his 'vain delusion': 'I was the greatest failure of all, for my hopes were higher than those of others. I honestly believed in the greatness of China's future, and I was anxious to be associated with her rise to power'.[7]

The last phase of Morrison's life reads as something of a sad coda. Ill-health continued to afflict him. He returned to Australia for the first time in many years, only to find he had been away too long; his fellow countrymen struck him as unrefined and indolent. He sold his magnificent library of 20,000 books, assembled over the previous two decades, to the Japanese for £35,000; after his years of diligent care in the library of his courtyard house on Morrison Street, they were damaged by flood almost as soon as they were brought ashore in Tokyo.

Becoming seriously unwell during a trip to Europe in 1919, in which he represented China at the disastrous Versailles conference which would lead to the protests of the May Fourth Movement, he consulted a long list of doctors in Britain, none of whom seemed able to arrest his dramatic weight loss and general decline. He remained desperate to return to Beijing, but practicalities prevented him from travelling, and instead he retired to convalesce by the English seaside, in the genteel town of Sidmouth on the Devon coast, suffering from chronic pancreatitis.

It was here that he died at the end of May 1920. In a letter to Morrison's mother, his wife would write of their hopes of returning to his 'beloved' Peking so that he could die in his old Beijing courtyard house on Morrison Street, 'amid the old surroundings and friends that he had so loved. But Fate decreed otherwise'.[8]

Palm Sunday. Along the esplanade at Sidmouth, day-trippers mill about in the first spring sun, lounging on walls and benches to eat their ice-cream and fish and chips and warding off the over-familiar seagulls. Behind them the dark windows of a long row of whitewashed Georgian villas look out across the slate water of the English channel. The shingle grinds as the paper curl waves roll in. The world and his wife has emerged at the hint of a cold winter finally turning, and the narrow streets of this British seaside town are filled with noise and bustle.

A little walk up the hill, and Sidmouth Cemetery is a study in contrasts. Save for a pensioner who has taken up a sunny corner spot on a bench with his dog, the graveyard is empty and silent.

Morrison's final resting place is not hard to find, up on a stepped bank behind the small Victorian red-brick chapel where his funeral service was held. It is the largest tomb, a stone box of low walls, with a balustrade running around on all four sides. Along the front wall of the tomb, almost illegible now, runs the inscription: 'George Ernest Morrison of Peking'. Below it, added three years later, is the dedication to his wife. On either side are plaques commemorating his children, including Ian his son, who would become a *Times* correspondent himself and die in the Korean war in 1950, and Hedda Morrison, who would marry another son, Alastair, and who became a photographer famed for her documentary photographs of northern China.

From the earth held within the tomb, a straggly buddleia, limp-leaved after the rigours of the winter, moves in the sea breeze, its branches caught amongst the coiling arms of a bramble. A few bright celandines poke out from beneath, little saucers of gold heralding that spring really is on its way. But their brightness cannot disguise the sad, untended air of the grave, and I wish I had more time and some means to restore it to order. The house sparrows chatter on the breeze and, looking out across the banked rows of gravestones and the orderly rooflines of the town, the green fields beyond climbing to the wooded crest of Salcombe Hill, I feel a long way from the crowds and noise of Morrison Street, Peking.

18

Oriental Plaza – walking in cities – the Imperial Observatory – origins of the Chinese calendar – the Jesuits – the Republican calendar – time in modern China

Does a surplus of history cultivate an indifference towards it? To the casual wanderer of China's streets today, it might well seem that way. In the early years of Mao's New China, the country's abundant past was precisely what the Communists were rebelling against, and remnants of the old world were enthusiastically torn down in order to physically erase a culture in the process of being replaced. Today, practicality and profit are the twin enemies of the old; what is left of China's architectural heritage must compete with an instinct to consider what sits on a given square-footage of soil in terms of whether something bigger, newer and more lucrative could replace it.

That soil is a more diligent protector of China's history, however, offering a passive and preserving indifference to the relics of the past.

In the process of all this endless destruction and rebuilding, new archaeological sites of interest are regularly turned up; the problem being, of course, that what is found below the surface in China's towns and cities can be a bigger inconvenience to this pursuit of practicality and profit than what previously stood on top of it.

The silver-glass mall which sweeps around the eastern corner of Morrison Street and Long Peace Street is part of a complex named 'Oriental Plaza', which looks not even vaguely oriental, and has no plaza, if one takes the notion of a plaza to mean an open space to be enjoyed by the public. There were plenty of objectionable new buildings which had sprung up in the square miles of the old city in the last few decades, but Oriental Plaza had attracted particular attention in the 1990s both for its flouting of planning guidelines regarding height and scale, and the forced delay to its construction resulting from the discovery of Paleolithic remains, dating back around 25,000 years, whilst initial excavations were taking place.

The discovery did not delay the developers for long. Some of what was uncovered – stone tools, fossils – was buried again down in a tiny museum in the basement of the mall: the architectural definition of an afterthought. A plaque outside the museum told of how the findings proved 'the existence of a long and stretched cultural course in a continuous line up to now on the beautiful land of Beijing, which at the same time confirms that the Wangfujing area in Beijing is a suitable home for human beings'. Today, the museum was closed, a tattered sheet of A4 stuck to the Perspex ticket booth explaining that it was undergoing renovation, and would open its doors again in June. It was now early August and there was no sign of light or life behind the metal shutters.

I had slunk guiltily into the mall in search of some cool and caffeine, and sat for a quiet twenty minutes in a coffee shop watching the people come and go. At a table behind me, a young Austrian visiting the city struck up a conversation with a local girl, and offered his first impressions on the place: 'It's so... big', he said. I could not help but silently concur. Most cities, he said, seemed big compared to the small towns of Austria, but Beijing was something else.

I eventually forced myself from the air-conditioned sanctuary of the mall back out onto the overheated pavement of Long Peace Street, and then slid along the inscrutable frontage of Oriental Plaza, which extended along the entire block.

The streets around here were centre-city busy, full of shoppers and purposeful, smartly dressed office workers on a lunch break. Here, in the thick of the city, everybody walked with direction, on their way somewhere. Nobody lingered. I felt like the only pedestrian without real motive; I had nowhere to be by any particular time. Nothing insisted that I carried on to the arbitrary goal of my journey; that I did not simply descend the long escalator down to the subway and head back for a quiet afternoon in the cool and dark of an air-conditioned room. A breeze was blowing from the east like a damp hairdryer, and my skin and clothes had a cold clammy feel after my diversion through the crisp-aired chambers of the mall. I was about five and a half miles from my destination at Sihui East subway station; I had started counting carefully.

To what extent, I could not help but wonder, was this fondness for walking through cities an acquired characteristic; an affectation of sorts? Certainly it seemed, at times, to defy rational explanation, for cities are not places which generally reward the walker in any straightforward way.

Cities exist in indifference to your individual presence within them. The forces which shape cities are collective, rather than singular; they are machines built for the masses. Even on its best days, the city is a friend manifesting a benevolent disinterest in you; hopefully it does not get in your way too much, but neither is it there to make life too easy. On foot in the city, you are always subject to the forces of the majority; there is no real possibility of striking off the beaten path as you might on a country jaunt, because you will doubtless find your way obstructed by a building or a barrier. You must follow the routes that have been carved out for you, in between and underneath these obstructions, built for those with practical requirements of their day: getting to work; getting home; moving people and goods. Henry David Thoreau, whose passion for walking was very particularly a passion for walking in nature, observed that 'Roads are made for horses and men of business. I do not travel in them much, comparatively, because I am not in a hurry to get to any tavern or grocery or livery-stable or depot to which they lead'.[1]

The city lacks other obvious rewards of the countryside: clean air; the curve and fretwork of hill and wood, and of course, the absence of others: that precious solitude which tends to lead one away from the village, the town, the city.

However, there are some for whom the crowd is the thing. When one thinks of the tradition of the city stroller, one tends to call to mind the *flâneur*, the gentleman observer of the Parisian streets made famous in the writing of the nineteenth-century French poet Charles Baudelaire. The flâneur finds joy in distanced observation of the life of the street – moving as part of the crowd but feeling separate from it. The individual enters the crowd, in Baudelaire's definition, 'as though into an enormous reservoir of electricity'.[2] The crackle and spark of this is inspiration; to walk on the busy city streets is to discover a mental stimulation akin to, but importantly different, from that quiet, sensuous introspection encouraged by nature.

Others assert the aesthetic appeal of city walking. Some cities are indisputably beautiful, of course; Baudelaire's Paris, even after the changes of the mid-nineteenth century, when roads were widened and the city ordered and organised, is an urban landscape which visually rewards the walker. Or, if there is not beauty, the grittier realities of the city offer interest, founded in a form of voyeurism, to those passing through on foot – the marketplace or bazaar; the narrow alleys or crowded homes giving a sense of a differently real mode of living.

For me, it was the inexhaustibility of cities that I took pleasure

Chapter 18

from; their capacity to cram into square miles of what would otherwise be simple, expansive fields of wheat or sorghum or millet, complex networks of interconnecting spaces and ways through and between them: too many to travel and be one traveller; all of them dense with stories and histories. The boundaries of the city as actually lived rings in a limited circumference the streets around which we live and work: the rest retains that capacity to surprise us with novelty. I enjoyed the feeling that comfort and familiarity could be overturned by simply taking a turning I had not taken before, and that in doing so I would encounter a new story, or a defining image, or a lost piece of history. The streets of China's cities seemed to particularly encourage this sense of inexhaustibility, vast as they are, reshaped by change, and always offering a particular form of newness to me, a trespasser here.

Today, however, few of these rewards seemed evident on this arm of Long Peace Street, which parallels the western inner-city stretch: hotels and office blocks rising broad and tall along either side of the road's busy tarmac. The crowd grew thinner as I walked away from the corner of Morrison Street; the buildings here were brutally blocky, and any stories the street might have told concerned the beautiful and interesting that had been lost in reshaping the winding alleys of the old city which once ran to north and south of the road.

I was, however, heading towards an exception in this wing of modern Beijing, and a place which inevitably raised my spirits: a hidden lone fragment of that old China, and almost the definition of an anomaly amongst the concrete, steel and glass that surrounds it. For, a little further along the road, sited high on a solitary outcrop of crenellated grey-stone city wall, stands China's Imperial Observatory – a collection of the bronze astronomical instruments with which the officials of the Qing dynasty tracked the movement of the heavenly bodies.

Despite the absence of the rest of the old city wall to north and south of the Observatory, the name of the adjacent intersection and subway stop nods to the past. Known as *Jianguomen* or the Gate of National Construction, this was one of the gates punched through the old wall by the Japanese during their occupation of the city in the late 1930s. The gate met its end, as did much along this axis of the city, in the drive to build Beijing's new subway during the 1960s; as it is on the western section of the street, the absence of the wall and gate is marked by the ribboned arms of the same incomplete, neon-lit rainbow reaching across the carriageways. The Observatory itself would have been destroyed as well, were it not for the intervention of Premier Zhou Enlai, who again insisted that it be preserved as construction continued on the subway in 1968.

You access the Observatory platform, having paid a modest fee, via a steep set of stone steps. As I climbed them, an American family were returning the other way, clad in brightly coloured, matching polo shirts. I earwigged on their conversation, an overtone of disappointment in their bearing as they descended. 'You'd have thought there might be a film, or something!' the father said. Tucked away in a courtyard below, there was a brief exhibition, but I didn't recall any informative videos, and it was admittedly easy to miss altogether. 'You remember the planetarium in Chicago?' the mum chimed in, and the dad nodded silently at the memory of it.

The bronze instruments of the Observatory sit elevated on plinths on top of the fourteen-metre-high platform, tightly packed together, and fenced off from the curious. Their bases and stands are densely, ornately cast with swirls and scales and dragons' heads, and their dull green patina, combined with the dense patterning, makes them seem almost as if they have grown organically from their marble plinths. 'Beautiful as works of art',[3] A.B. Freeman-Mitford commented of them, and he was right; that these were primarily practical tools for measuring the skies seems hard to believe. Though there are brief informative plaques, I sympathised with the American visitors: how one worked these mechanical giants, and what one hoped to measure with them, is far from obvious to the non-specialist.

Chapter 18

The site of the Observatory, here at the south-eastern edge of the Tartar city, was chosen according to the belief that the sun was at its most supreme at that geographical point. It dates back to 1442, more than a century before the invention of the telescope, though an earlier observatory existed on a site nearby from 1279 and Chinese astronomers have been formally measuring the movement of the celestial bodies, with differing degrees of accuracy, for at least as long as records exist.

Understanding the heavenly bodies was deeply important for China's rulers. The emperor was, after all, the Son of Heaven, the physical connection between the human order and the natural order, and thus a crucial responsibility was in telling his subjects in advance what the heavens would be doing – something his court achieved by devising an official calendar to be distributed through China's vast bureaucracy. The emperor needed to pay close attention to the accuracy of this calendar; if unexpected heavenly events transpired, this could be a warning that he was mismanaging his country, or a portent that something undesirable was about to happen, and that he might be imminently to lose the Mandate of Heaven – his right to rule.

For most, the systems of dividing and ordering time in the Gregorian calendar used today by most nations will rarely give pause for thought: a day is a day; January is January; and a year is 365 days (except when, occasionally, it isn't). A study of the traditional Chinese approach to systematising the passage of time offers a correction to any complacency with regard to this matter, however, confronting us with a method of recording the repetitive cycles of the moon and the sun which functions quite differently from that used today in most of the world.

The means of measuring the passage of time which emerges in early Chinese history is referred to as lunisolar: as the name implies, this means it looks to the movement of both the moon and sun in its estimations. Cycles of the moon offer an obvious division of time, of course. One can trace the days from full moon to full moon, or from new moon to new moon for that matter, without any equipment: all you need to do is watch the sky – and count the days. In 28 days, the moon will be back in the state it was when you first began watching.

If you begin your count in spring, you will find that, in roughly twelve moons time, you will find yourself back in the same season – which might lead you to think that these twelve moons match a full cycle of the seasons. However, if you repeat this approach, and count another twelve moons, you will find that you are now out of sync with the seasons, and it will likely still be a little more wintery than you were anticipating: for the cycle of twelve moons is about 11 days *shorter* than the time it takes for the sun to return to the same position in the cycle of seasons. What lunisolar calendars do to correct this is periodi-cally throw in a 'leap month' to catch the sun up, as it were. If you keep records for a couple of decades, the pattern becomes clear: every nineteen years you are required to add in seven extra leap months to keep in step with the seasons.

Many ancient calendars around the world were lunisolar, and records suggest that a form of this system goes back to the second millennium BCE in China. In naming specific dates, the Chinese method adds in another element: reign titles – names given to either all or part of an emperor's period on the throne. In older times, these would change if something particularly auspicious or significant hap-pened; so, when in 116 BCE the Emperor Wu dug up an ancient bronze tripod with a mysterious inscription, that year became known as the first year of the 'Epochal Tripod' era. Ming and Qing emper-ors would take reign titles which lasted for the entire period of their rule, and hence adopted what were essentially new names when they ascended to the throne.

In addition, there was a naming system for days which used paired characters, and which meant that days repeated on a sixty-day cycle; it is from these names, later also applied to years, that we get the name of the *Xinhai* revolution, which overthrew the Qing in 1911.

Putting all of this together, we might get a date such as Epochal Tripod fifth year, fourth month, *dingchou* (the fourteenth day of the sixty-day cycle), which corresponds to our 18 June 112 BCE.

In the autumn of 1900, Sarah Conger, wife of the American Minister, visited the Imperial Observatory in Beijing and, considering the instruments ranged around her on the platform, was struck by their remarkable resistance to the passage of the years: 'These fine old instruments, standing above and below, show no wear of time, although centuries have passed over them', she wrote in a letter to her sister. 'They are like China herself.'[4]

She was right that they had stood thus for many centuries, but in truth her conception of the instruments on the platform as synonymous with an ancient, unchanging China ignored an important point: they had not been designed by Chinese astronomers. In fact, the story they tell is one of an early period of cultural exchange between the Middle Kingdom and Europe which seems incredible to anyone familiar with China's troubled relationship with the West in the nineteenth and twentieth centuries.

Just under 240 years before the First Opium War between Britain and China began in 1839 – a conflict considered the opening act in the so-called 'century of humiliation' of China by foreign powers – an Italian man named Matteo Ricci arrived in Beijing. Ricci was a Jesuit missionary, who had already lived in China for the best part of twenty years by the time of his entrance to the capital. The Jesuits were roving Catholic proselytisers, known as 'God's Marines' for their hardihood and their willingness to travel anywhere the Pope commanded. They spread themselves across the globe in the sixteenth and seventeenth centuries and, as well as conveying with them the Word of God, they also disseminated the West's intellectual knowledge during their travels. Amongst other evidence of European understanding, Ricci had brought with him two mechanical clocks as tribute, and, though he never met the Wanli Emperor, these fascinated the Son of Heaven.

Ricci gradually managed to convince him that the spiritual and cultural traditions which he represented offered expertise beyond that of his courtiers in certain respects.

In particular, Ricci came to realise that assisting with the accuracy of the Chinese calendar, which was notably unreliable at this point, would be a powerful means of attracting positive press for the Jesuits. Early during his time in the city, he wrote back to Italy requesting another missionary with a specialism in astronomy be sent out to help revise the calendar:

> If a mathematician came here, as I ask, we could turn our [astronomical] tables into Chinese characters, which I can do very easily, and undertake the task of amending the year, which would give us a great reputation, expand our foothold in China, and allow us greater stability and freedom.[5]

The request was not met in Ricci's lifetime, though he had his own influence on China's scientific understanding, translating a number of key mathematical texts into Chinese – a formidable task which required him to invent numerous new terms in the language. Ricci died at a relatively early age, worn out by the rigours of his life's work.

In the decades after his death, Ricci's successors would build on the foundations that he had established. Ultimately, a Flemish missionary named Ferdinand Verbiest would, in the later seventeenth century, be handed the responsibility of re-equipping the Observatory with more modern and accurate instruments than those which had previously graced the platform. He was appointed as Director of the Beijing Observatory, having convinced the Kangxi Emperor of his own scientific prowess. Verbiest had taken part in a head-to-head astronomical competition with the Chinese head of the Bureau of Astronomy, Yang Guangxian, to establish who was the most reliable expert in matters of the sky. It was a three-part challenge, which included the correct prediction of a solar eclipse, a tricky task that had confounded the Chinese astronomers on a regular basis. Verbiest got it right, and was duly appointed to the prestigious post; Yang was sent into exile in his home province, and died in the course of his journey there.

It was a remarkable outcome for the missionary; just a little while earlier, under the reign of a different emperor, both Verbiest and his predecessor in the job as Director, Johan Adam Schall von Bell, had been thrown into prison, and were facing down a sentence of death by being cut into small pieces: inauspicious natural disasters meant that, thankfully, the sentence was not carried out. The older instruments at the Observatory were kept for posterity, but Verbiest had six new devices cast by Chinese craftsmen, and it is these that sit, dull with the patina of years, atop the platform here at Jianguomen.

If I had felt inclined, I could have descended the stone steps and caught a subway train half a loop around Line Two to emerge within strolling distance of the quiet graveyard in north-west Beijing where the tombs of Ricci, Schall and Verbiest still lie. Ricci had expressed an especial desire to be interred in Chinese soil – he had spent so long away from Italy that, when required to speak Italian, it came far more haltingly than his Chinese – and, though there was no precedent for such a thing, the emperor acceded to the request and granted a plot of land for Ricci's burial, where Schall and Verbiest would join him in later years.

Like the Observatory, it has seen its share of conflict. During the Boxer Rebellion, the missionary remains there had been excavated and scattered. And in August 1966, when the Red Guards arrived at the cemetery in those mad first days of the Cultural Revolution, the principal of the Communist Party college in the grounds of which the memorials lay had the foresight to bury the tombstones underground for safekeeping; they would later be excavated and reset in the earth. They stand thus to this day, memorialising a group of remarkable men – inured by faith to the hardships which were the inevitable accompaniment to their sacred missionary duty, and infused with the resolve of the zealot in overcoming challenges of culture, language and bureaucracy. That Schall and Verbiest were both appointed to positions overseeing the emperor's astronomical bureaucracy is so outlandish, given the importance placed on the movement of the heavens in the Middle Kingdom, that it is hard to find an apt analogy: perhaps the nearest comparison would be the arrival in London of some intelligent life form from outer space – to whom, due to their proficiency in maths, we hand over control of the Bank of England.

In the same letter to her sister, Sarah Conger would go on to write that if left alone, the instruments of the Observatory would 'stand upon their dragon thrones for centuries to come'. Here too, she was wrong. A few months after Conger had penned her missive, the platform would be stripped of the instruments by the German and French troops of the Eight Nation Alliance, the force who had arrived in Beijing to save the foreign population of the city from the siege of the Boxers. Those taken by French soldiers would be returned the following year, but the other plinths would sit empty for some time. The five taken by the Germans to be displayed in Potsdam would not be sent back to China until 1921,[6] by which time the Qing empire, and China's imperial tradition, were nearly a decade in the past – as was the lunisolar calendar, at least nominally.

On 1 January 1912, to mark the beginning of a new, modern phase of Chinese history, it was declared that the Republic of China would adopt a solar calendar, like that used in the West, with the idiosyncratic twist that, rather than declaring the year as 1912, it would instead begin at the year 1, to mark the rebirth of the Chinese nation. In such a calendar, for example, the Japanese invasion of China would not be said to have happened in 1937, but in 26.

The change was, however, too much, too soon. Most people in the countryside were only vaguely aware of the tectonic shifts of power happening in Beijing, and the populace tended to continue as they were, observing the Lunar New Year that year as usual.

The confusion was characteristic of these early months of Republican China – a country stuck, in manifest different ways both practical and philosophical, between the old and the new. And, as with the issue of who would lead China, the uncertainty and conflict around the new calendar would rumble on for some decades. Compromises were made, and in the subsequent years the country would effectively run on two systems, the new Republican calendar used officially and by adherents to the cause, and the old Chinese calendar by everyone else. In the late 1920s, the Nationalist government would again attempt to impose the Gregorian system, labelling the old system optimistically as the 'abolished calendar'. The Nationalists also did their best to clamp down on the traditional and superstitious beliefs associated with the phases of the year, limiting the production of traditional almanacs, which had for centuries helped to guide the populace in the progress of the seasons and the most right and proper time to undertake a whole range of different activities: when to marry; when to travel; when to begin building; when to open a business. All this paraphernalia of the moon year was part of what had held China back, it was thought, and was another element of the old order which needed to be discarded.

Today, the noise of the second ring road which rumbles on below the Observatory, its orbit around the city now completed from where I had last crossed its path, is a persistent percussive reminder of the anomaly the Observatory represents in this modern metropolis. Yet, like the bronze instruments designed by Verbiest, the influence of the ancient preoccupation of China's rulers with the heavenly spheres has sustained in modern China. After the Nationalists, Mao and the Chinese Communist Party also endeavoured to rid the country of the old calendar and its superstitions; as they prepared to take power in late September 1949, they decided their new version of New China would adopt, without any tacked-on idiosyncrasies, the Gregorian calendar. Yet, observance of the old moon year and its festivals would, even through the repressive days of the Cultural Revolution, continue.

Its influence today is testified to by the continued importance of almanacs for deciding auspicious days, in the central significance and observance of annual lunar festivals in Chinese culture, and in the renewed popular affection for the 24 *jie qi* or solar terms which break the years up with seasonal markers. These periods of roughly fifteen days capture the subtle seasonal shifts which, ringing as clearly as a bell for those who lived on the land, broke up the rural year. They label the meteorological and agricultural conditions with precision and brevity: *Clear Brightness*, for example, or *Frost's Descent*. (That I was walking during *Major Heat* I did not need an almanac to divine, however.)

These ways of marking the changes between light and darkness, between winter and summer, between the old and the new year, sustain, it seems, not through any artificial means, but because over generations they have layered incrementally into an accretion of collective memory which is hard to simply sand-blast away. It is also the case, of course, that in the times of greatest uncertainty and reform, such traditions are consolations to be returned to, offering reassurance that even as the world changes, much still remains unchangeable.

I walked across to each of the cardinal points and looked out from the Observatory platform. The afternoon smog had settled heavily on the city, and I could make out little beyond a few blocks – the sky, buildings and street merging into one grey blur. I imagined the view that had greeted the visitor in the days of old Beijing, when this modest elevation and the clearer air – save for those days when the dust storms descended – permitted the eye to run out over the low roofs of the city in all directions. From here, one of the most prominent neighbouring sites to distract the eye would have been the Imperial Examination Halls – ranks of long, slant-roofed narrow sheds divided into cubicles in which, every three years, the most promising of the nation's students would take three-day long exams; at night, after the rigours of a day of scholarship, the cubicles would be refashioned into a place to sleep.

Chapter 18

In the late 1910s, Juliet Bredon, who had herself been so fascinated by the cycles of the Chinese calendar that she wrote an entire volume, *The Moon Year*, which traced its changes, had looked out from here to the west, along the line of the road I had followed across the city. 'The day is ending in a serenity of exquisite brilliance', she wrote:

> The violet masses of the hills, which form so conspicuous a background in all views of Peking that they soon assume the aspect of loved and familiar friends, stand out sharply against the fiery sky. As the light fades, their outlines soften. They seem to withdraw little by little, almost regretfully, into the shadows. Gradually one by one the monuments of the city, the palaces, the Coal Hill, the temples, follow their example fading away in a soft glow of light until, last of all, the gate-towers and the walls themselves dissolve into greyness and – it is dark.[7]

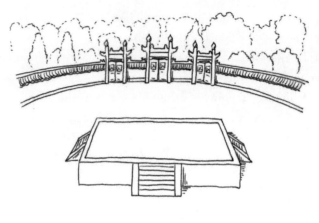

19

Outside the wall – the Grand Canal and the eastern suburbs – 22 August 1967 – 'All Palaces are Temporary Palaces' – *Forsan et haec olim* – red

Given a second chance at siting the foreign community in Beijing, the authorities chose to place them determinedly *outside* the wall. The compounds of most of today's embassies – concrete villas built in the late 1950s and early 1960s – are set out along a quiet grid of streets abutting Chang'an Jie to the east of the old city and the Observatory.

Beijing's eastern side had long been a place associated with out-of-towners. The Imperial Examination Halls had drawn in students from across the country to sit the highest tier of exams here. It was also from the east that the links to the Grand Canal, which brought goods and grain to the city, entered Beijing. The Grand Canal stretched all the way to Hangzhou, along a route 1,100 miles long, and for much of its history, Beijing was reliant on this trade route to bring in food supplies from the more fertile, rice-rich south. Had it not been for this vast feat of engineering, less visually impressive than the Great Wall perhaps, but indisputably more important functionally, Beijing would likely not be China's capital.

During the Yuan dynasty of the Mongols, the Grand Canal had entered the city, linking the markets in the north-west of Beijing and the town of Tongzhou, 18 miles or so away. Later, this section of the waterway became impassable, and goods would either travel overland or to the edge of the eastern city wall by boat.

By Qing times, the road between Tongzhou and Beijing had become a major thoroughfare: broad, paved and lined with shops and inns.[1] As well as goods, this road conveyed travellers into the city: for visitors from the south and those from outside the Middle Kingdom, it was the main route into town. David Field Rennie, a military surgeon, who was part of the party which travelled to establish the first legation in Beijing in 1861, recorded his impressions as he arrived:

> The whole line of road was thickly populated by poor people; their habitations here and there clustered together, forming small villages. In many of them were little inns, with open-air restaurants in front, where carters and the poorer class of travellers were sitting at their meals. Our general impressions, as we approached the capital, were not favourable, further than as regards the quiet and respectful bearing of the poor population that we passed through.[2]

The road followed a similar line to today's Long Peace Street, whilst the canal, concrete lined and notably lacking in romance these days, runs just a little to the south of this section of Long Peace Street. Once willow-lined, it had been a favoured picnic and boating spot for the bored diplomats of the Legation Quarter.

Where in Mongol times it wound through the hutong of the old city, flowing from here into the market, the canal has today been cleaned up and prettified, lined either side with *faux*-Qing dynasty courtyard houses, and crossed by picturesque bridges on which newly-weds come to pose for their official pictures – though large swathes of it as yet lie with only a few festering pools along the bed. An explanatory plaque next to it explains that the canal had been hidden underground in the decade after the Communist takeover, but now 480 metres of it are to be 'unfolded before people's eyes'.

These eastern suburbs sat in contrast to the mystery and history of those to the west of the city, with their mountains and temples, which drew pilgrims and travellers of a different sort. By the 1950s, however, and with the link to the Grand Canal no longer as important as it had once been, the east had become sparsely populated agricultural land. 'Blank, ugly, virtually treeless',[3] is how one British diplomat described their new place of residence when they made the move from the Legation Quarter. Out of sight of the central organs of power, confined by its isolation and notably lacking in charm and the comforts of home, it must have seemed a perfect place to put Beijing's foreign diplomats.

In the hierarchy of great British comedies of the 1960s, the film *The Wrong Arm of the Law* does not figure particularly highly. It tells the quaint story of cockney crime boss 'Pearly Gates', played by Peter Sellers, who joins forces with Scotland Yard to track down a gang of Australian criminals masquerading as police officers. The reviewer of *The New York Times* called it 'strictly lightweight clowning, longer on plot than on wit … the enterprise stands by the stiffening of Mr Sellers's cunning roguishness'.[4] There is no record, however, of what those who watched it on the overheated evening of 22 August 1967 in the British diplomatic quarters in Beijing made of the film.[5] Looking back on that night, a year into the tumult of the Cultural Revolution, they had memories of drama which far exceeded that of *The Wrong Arm of the Law*.

The trouble for the twenty-three British subjects inside the embassy had started when the authorities in Hong Kong arrested Chinese communist journalists for instigating riots and demonstrations. An ultimatum was given to the British by the Chinese, with the threat that 'dreadful things would follow' if they did not release the journalists. The British, conscious that justice must not be interfered with, refused to give way to the Chinese requests, and the day before the deadline, set for 22 August 1967, Red Guards began to mass menacingly around the gated compound of the British diplomatic buildings.

By the night of the 22nd, thousands of protestors had assembled outside, and the diplomats, having eaten a makeshift dinner and watched *The Wrong Arm of the Law* in a somewhat half-interested manner, awaited the next stage in proceedings.

Tension had been building for some time in the grid of streets housing the Beijing diplomatic corps, with other embassies and personnel having come under attack on a relatively regular basis since the opening phases of the Cultural Revolution and the horror of Bloody August one year before. The Mongolian ambassador's car had been set alight. The Indonesian Embassy had been completely razed; in order to keep in touch with the outside world, the diplomats were forced to try to reconstruct a working telephone from the broken fragments remaining combined with bits of an old teapot. The inhabitants of the embassy area were unfortunately high-profile in a China where outsiders were few, the drawbridge to the country having very definitely been drawn up to all but a handful of diplomats, journalists, teachers and communist fellow-travellers during the Mao era.

Though the authorities ultimately knew that, whilst the internal chaos was permitted, the foreign residents did have to be spared the worst of the Red Guard behaviour, the Cultural Revolution shock-troops did their best to make life extremely unpleasant. As well as the targeted violence, they employed tactics designed to cause maximum inconvenience and disruption. Earlier in the year, Red Guards had installed loudspeakers around the grounds of some embassies, chanting Cultural Revolution slogans through them around the clock to prevent the occupants from getting any sleep.

The protests were often whipped up by perceived slights against

China, but from the earliest days of the Cultural Revolution, anything foreign had been singled out for attack: haircuts that looked
too much like those popular in Hong Kong; shops which sold goods
from abroad; restaurants which served dishes in a bourgeois or international style. Christian churches had been ransacked, with painted
scenes from the Bible brought into the street and crossed through
with black paint. The name of the main road running through the
old Legation Quarter next to Tiananmen Square had been changed,
becoming 'Anti-Imperialism Street' (that on which the new British
embassy was set became 'Support Vietnam Street': the Vietnamese
embassy was a little further along it).

The mood music was not promising, then. And as the clamour
from outside grew that evening, and the realisation struck that things
could well turn nasty, those inside the British Embassy on Support
Vietnam Street retreated to what, it would soon become evident, was
not the secure room they thought.[6] At 10.45pm, the deadline for the
journalists' release expired, and the embassy buildings were almost
simultaneously set upon. Hearing the crowd advance, those inside
the embassy sent a last, desperate message back to London through
the wireless: 'They're coming in'.

Walking through the streets crisscrossing between the embassies, I
was almost alone, a hot weekday afternoon keeping nearly everyone
inside. The official buildings are plain and boxy, pebble dash brown,
white, pastel pink and yellow with few of the architectural flourishes which distinguished the old legation buildings a few miles west.
Neither, however, is there any vaguely Chinese element to their
design; they look much like what they are – guesses by the Chinese
Communist Party at what generic Western architecture looked like.
Their nationalities are signalled by plaques outside, and the occasional
tourist poster with slogans selling their homeland: 'Slovakia: Friends
Forever' or 'Egypt: Les monuments et aussi...' – followed by a check-
erboard montage of faded pictures of people enjoying themselves on

Chapter 19

Egyptian beaches. The game of guessing each embassy's nationality is encouraged by these posters. Bison; snowy branches; baby deer; a blond child holding a bunch of daisies: it must be Belarus.

At the centre of the grid of streets is Ritan Park – the park of the Altar of the Sun: a neatly tended square of green which holds one of four related altars in the city: of the Moon, the Sun, the Earth and Heaven. It was here that the emperor would give offerings at day break on the Spring Equinox, and in its form it complements the Altar of the Moon in the city's west, the *Yang* and *Yin* of the two indicated by their physical shape: where the Altar of the Sun is raised, that of the Moon is hollowed out.[7]

This too had been targeted in the Cultural Revolution. All of these altars were redolent of the imperial preoccupation with the heavens and its influence on Beijing's design as the spiritual, as well as the political, centre of the nation, with large swathes of the city, fenced off from the populace, given over to them. They were an easy target in the Cultural Revolution, literal embodiments of the superstition and old customs it was designed to sweep away. Today, the Altar is again locked away behind a bolted fence, and can easily be missed; the park's appeal was now recreational, attracting joggers and grand-parents on child-minding duty.

Occasionally, the quiet heat of the streets was disturbed by the rasping exhaust of one of the high-powered luxury cars that become a more regular sight in these parts of Beijing. I saw one young man nearly mown down by a blacked-out Range Rover as he crossed the street; on his t-shirt ran a slogan reading 'All Palaces are Temporary Palaces'. A crowd of migrant workers, starting a shift, filtered back into the courtyard of one of the unfinished new developments adjacent to the main road.

I walked to the British Embassy building to poke my nose in at the gate. Outside, a guard in peaked cap and heavy olive-green uniform stood stoically in the heat, ready to dissuade any would-be photo-takers. He had an air-conditioned glass box next to him but had not yet retreated to it. The air was still, the cicadas buzzed violently in the trees, and I wondered how many hours of guarding he still had in front of him.

I was the only person on the street, and he looked at me curiously as I stood gazing at the pale yellow villa of the embassy.[8] 'I'm English', I said, by way of explanation. 'You can't take a picture', he replied abruptly, then added in English and more sympathetically, 'Sorry'.

I tried to imagine the scenes here on that dark, hot night in 1967; the air still and carrying the cries of the Red Guards, who chanted '*Sha! Sha!*' – Kill! Kill! as they entered the compound. Through the windows of the registry to which the British had retreated flames flickered. Liquid was poured through the window – was it petrol or water? Water. As the smoke got thicker, and realising they needed to get out, the British left through the back door and were absorbed by the crowd, who rained blows on their heads and shoulders. Some of the women were groped. Having escaped the crowd and taken shelter, one of the diplomats, Percy Cradock, recalled the lines from Virgil's *Aeneid* taught to him by a Classics master at school: *Forsan et haec olim meminisse juvabit*: 'Perhaps even these things it will one day be a joy to recall'.

Jean Vincent, the correspondent for Agence France-Presse, who had watched on from outside as the embassy was overrun wrote a blow-by-blow commentary on events. 'Dawn will soon cast its rays over the golden tiles of the roofs of the old "forbidden city"', he wrote early in the morning of 23 August. 'But in the homes of the foreigners, diplomats or journalists, no one has slept tonight and no one will sleep tonight.'[9]

It seemed, however, that the PLA had instructions to protect the embassy staff from the worst of the violence, and, cuts and bruises aside, no one was seriously injured after they evacuated. Bricks and mortar were fair game, however: the main building was burnt to the ground, and the Chargé D'Affaires' house was ransacked, with his furniture pulled out on to the lawn and set alight.

Chapter 19

The controversy over the imprisoned journalists in Hong Kong would rumble on after the summer of 1967. British Reuters correspondent Anthony Grey had been arrested in July, and would be held in solitary confinement for two years and two months; he had his cat, Ming Ming, hanged in front of him by zealous Red Guards.

The British diplomats who had escaped the embassy were prevented from leaving the country, and they would doggedly continue their work from a makeshift office. The torched embassy building would eventually be rebuilt in 1972; the Chinese paid. A portrait of the Queen was rescued from the charred remains of the building, and now hangs on the wall of the Foreign Office's China section.

Reaching Long Peace Street again after my wanderings through the embassy area, I set off eastwards, tall buildings along either flank. Here, amongst all this corporatised and commercialised square footage, individual enterprise was still in evidence. A mother and daughter tended a cart selling freshly squeezed orange juice, the daughter cutting the fruit into halves, and the mother levering the heavy metal handle of the squeezing machine, which left deep circular indentations, like welts, on the discarded peel. Further on, the sticky-sweet, daiquiri smell of pineapple carried on the wind from another makeshift stall. Outside an old orange-painted housing compound, now a relic in these parts, a knife sharpener squatted in the shade, carefully and slowly guiding a blade against the sharpening stone, his customer watching on silently. From the bins, a leather-faced man with patchy short hair and a dirty polo shirt picked out plastic bottles to add to his pile; when his collecting was finished, they would be carted along to a recycling yard for the recompense of a few Yuan: individual industry doing the job of the state.

I halted every so often at the pedestrian crossings which seemed to get slower to change each time. Waiting, the crowd around you grows: people on foot; on bicycles; on electric scooters; on two-stroke tricycles, their put-putting engines filling the air with the scent of petrol: all moving slowly but insistently forward until the moment when the walk light changes to green. This part of town was as busy as any I had passed through; I was getting towards the time of day when people were thinking about heading home. The traffic was backing up too, ten lanes insufficient to cope with the sheer volume of cars. When you talk to Beijingers about the traffic, they generally have the same response: *ren tai duo le* – there are too many people. The city had introduced initiatives to try to ease the problem: license plate lotteries; restrictions on the days you can drive; a ban on bigger vehicles from the centre during the working day; but nothing seemed to make any discernible difference. Traffic like Beijing's changes the way you experience a city; when once you might have hopped a taxi across town, knowing the journey of a few miles might take twenty minutes, now you baulk at the prospect of being stuck on a ring road for forty minutes trying to make a junction. The city shrinks to the neighbourhood around you. It was one of the more prosaic reasons I had for preferring to navigate the city on foot.

As I waited at one broad crossroads, watching the traffic back up and the banks of lights across the gantry change from red to green, red to green, I thought of the suggestion made, at the height of the Cultural Revolution, that the rules of the road be altered so that it was red – the colour of progress – which signalled go.

The self-evidently absurd suggestion was never taken up, but red remains hard to escape in China. It has long been a colour weighted with symbolic meaning. In the traditional Chinese notion of *wu xing* or Five Agents, primary colours are linked to different elements, each freighted with interconnected meaning: Wood (木 mù), Fire (火 huǒ), Earth (土 tǔ), Metal (金 jīn), and Water (水 shuǐ). Red is associated with fire, and thus summer; heat; passion; and the south. It came to symbolise joy and good luck; red is the colour of Chinese New Year, when many will paste *duilian*, paired vertical poems written on red paper, on either side of their front door – itself likely red – and will give each other gifts of money contained within red envelopes or *hongbao*. In wedding ceremonies too, red is the predominant colour; white traditionally being reserved for funerals.

The modern connotations of red in China are, of course, bound up with the colour's significance within communist symbolism. Derived initially from its association with the French Revolution, the radical connotations of the colour were confirmed by the Redshirts of Garibaldi in Italy, the revolutionaries of the Paris Commune and the Bolsheviks in Russia in 1917. Red would become the colour of communism, transmuting in the process to be deployed as a noun; in America, to be 'a red' was bad news.

On 1 October 1949, during the ceremony commemorating the founding of the People's Republic of China, Mao raised the new flag of the country for the first time: a bright red field with five golden stars. The large star represented the Party; the four smaller those classes which would make up the New China: peasants, workers, the national and the petty bourgeoisie. It had been chosen in a national competition which attracted around 3,000 entries; one of the four rules for entry was that dictating the predominant colour. Fluttering atop a flagpole that day in Tiananmen Square, it was echoed by the plain red banners waved fervently by the crowds who had assembled to commemorate the founding of the People's Republic.

It was during the Cultural Revolution, however, that red reached its zenith in China. The suggestion of reversing the traffic signals was just the sort of absurd inversion of meaning that characterised political discourse in those days. Seemingly everything that was good was red: the Red Guards (who took their name from their Russian equivalents earlier in the century); Mao's Little Red Book; the song *The East is Red*, which became the *de facto* national anthem during the years of the Cultural Revolution. Even Chang'an Jie would not escape: in another suggested change of street names, 'Long Peace Street' became 'East is Red Avenue'.

That the Altar of the Sun, nestled at the heart of the enclave of embassies, should be targeted during the Cultural Revolution seems apposite, given that in these years, the only celestial figure to be worshipped was Mao himself. *The East is Red* plays on the symbolism of the rising sun: 'The east is red, the sun is rising/From China arises Mao Zedong'. Mao would come to be referred to as the 'red, red sun' in the hearts of the Red Guards. He had not replaced the emperor; he had replaced that which the emperor worshipped.

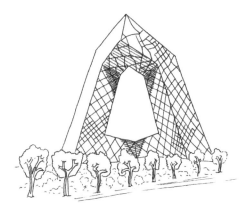

20

One city – the east is rich – weird architecture – mall life – underground

Behind the red gates of the rich wine and meat goes bad,
Out on the road are the bones of those who have frozen to death.
A foot from prosperity is decay,
Sadness stops me from saying more.

(Du Fu, 'Going from the Capital to Fengxian', 755 AD, author's translation).

There is not just one city. It reconfigures itself around you in response to material circumstance. Like its tier-one counterparts, Beijing is awash with new money, and though it might not match Shanghai for neon glamour, or Shenzhen for bleeding-edge modernity, there is no lack of wealth and conspicuous consumption in evidence.

Day two: Tiananmen to Sihui Dong subway station

Early evening in the old town and the xenon lights of a customised BMW warn you to the side of a hutong, prowling back slowly to a remodelled courtyard home: Qing dynasty on the outside, but with LEDs splashing soft light up the courtyard perimeter; air filters and double glazing to keep out the harmful particulates; a sauna and hot tub tucked away in one of its corners.

Meanwhile, behind the open doors of the unrestored siheyuan it rumbles past, three or four families crowd into the separate wings around the courtyard, sharing one or two rooms each and relying on the communal toilet across the alleyway. On the main road at the end of the alley, outside the prefabricated two-storey dormitories – nine beds to a room – tired men from distant provinces squat on stools eating bowls of cold noodles after a day building an office block. Across the corner of road and alley the fluorescent lights from the hole-in-the-wall where they bought them shine out; later, the husband and wife owner will move the tables and chairs and make their bed against the back wall.

Some of those who live here will set out next morning on their electric delivery bikes to the metal gates of housing compounds on the edge of town: clusters of new, vaguely neo-classical villas. Their invented names – La Grande Villa; Merlin Champagne Town; Grand Hills – suggest Western luxury, while their generic architectural style falls in unsatisfying compromise between Orange County and the hills of Tuscany.

Nowhere, however, is the new wealth of Beijing more evident than here in its eastern reaches. 'The east is rich and the west is aristocratic; the south is humble and the north is poor', went one Beijing saying; its first claim at least remains true today.[1] Outside its high-end hotels, Range Rovers with blacked-out windows idle in the heat, awaiting direction with the cabin cool. In the bar sixty storeys above, young couples sit in mutual silence, absorbed by supersized iPhone screens as the ice in their cocktails melts. In late afternoon, sharp-suited office workers spill onto busy pavements from the lobbies of razor-edged towers, the cost of floor space within rivalling that of London and Hong Kong.

This part of the city is the new spirit of Beijing – the new spirit of the Chinese city, one might say – rendered into architecture: ostentatious, superficial and expensive.

In the later twentieth century, the east of Beijing had become industrialised; maps from the 1980s show little beyond the embassy area apart from factories: a Lathe Plant; a Tyre Plant; a Metal Fabrication Plant; a Chemical Industry Machinery Plant. The Red Star distillery along Chang'an Jie produced industrial quantities of the Chinese spirit baijiu here, the intoxicating fumes perfuming the streets nearby with its distinctive aroma: flowers and rubber.

Over the twenty years or so since the start of the twenty-first century, however, Beijing's commercial centre of gravity has been pulled here, to ring the north and east of the embassy district. From this stretch of Long Peace Street, you can see up close the skyscrapers that have emerged to frame the Beijing sky. A new city, vertical and modern, has been assembled in this part of town, with all the haste and illogicality which characterises China's explosion of urban regeneration. As with all such sites here, it is hard to imagine it as it was before. The latest confection to join the skyline is referred to as the Zun, a gleaming, pinch-waisted tower, which looms over even the tallest of its neighbours, but there are plenty of glossy, high-profile new buildings being thrown up around the Central Business District. Cranes and fenced-off construction sites are everywhere, as Beijing's army of migrant construction workers bolt together the steel frames and slot in the mirrored glass panels of the city's next high-end hotel, mall or office block.

These projects have defined a new skyline for Beijing, and pulled in companies and conglomerations from across the globe. It is hard, walking the grid of streets through the Central Business District, to find many physical reminders of the old. A few of the worker housing compounds from the 1950s and 1960s remain, orange painted brick and rusting window cages, but on the whole what is here is new, and ostentatiously so. Thus far, I had walked amongst China's communist past, its imperial past – now I was to stroll through its future.

The most famous symbol of Beijing's rebirth as a commercial metropolis is the so-called 'Big Pants' building housing China's state broadcaster, the aptly named CCTV. Looking perhaps more like a pair of ungainly robotic legs, it bestrides this part of town – a path-finder for those ambitious developments which would follow. The CCTV headquarters was also one of the projects Xi Jinping had in mind, it seems, when in 2014 he gave a speech criticising the prolif-eration of what he called 'weird' architecture in China.

Travelling around, it is not hard to find evidence of what the President had in mind. China's cities are studded with experiments, designed by architects – often from abroad – who have come to view them as something of a playground. Nor is it a phenomenon confined to the big cities with vast sums of cash for development; some of the oddest buildings have emerged in lower-league cities, eager to attract atten-tion: little else can explain the design of the tourist information centre in Wuxi, for example, which mimics the form of a traditional teapot in bronze cladding and glass, and is capable of rotating 360 degrees.

Alongside the 'Big Pants', one can stumble across a number of unlikely shapes and forms in and around this part of the city: a collec-tion of ribbed white eggs along the second ring road; a cross-hatched steel donut; soft mountains, as if from a scroll painting, rendered in polished glass. These are merely the most high-profile of Beijing's architectural experiments, but the eastern stretches of the city show-case a number of similarly esoteric examples.

However, in 2016, China's State Council announced, following President Xi's directive, that it was outlawing 'weird architecture that is not economical, functional, aesthetically pleasing or environmen-tally friendly', and hence it seems for now, the city as architectural playground is closed for business.

The concern around the shape and form of the new Beijing was reminiscent of those rumbling disagreements which characterised the first decade or so of the Mao era, when nobody seemed to be able to reach a satisfactory decision about what the new Communist capital should look like. Was the use of native architectural flourishes, like those big sweeping roofs, wasteful? Was it patriotic? Too redolent of the despised imperial past? Should simple functionality be the priority? The bland, Soviet-tinged buildings which resulted reeked of compromise and indecision.

The question now is, if Xi does not want weird buildings, what does he want? In the same speech, he suggested that, more broadly, art should 'disseminate contemporary Chinese values, embody traditional Chinese culture and reflect Chinese people's aesthetic pursuit', which chimes with his brand of muscular nationalism. What this means for Beijing's architecture will become materially evident soon enough. What no one can doubt, though, is that building will continue apace here in the east of the city.

I paused at a gateway at the edge of a building site and peaked through the blue metal panels. Through the gap, I watched the ink lines of countless cranes pirouetting above more new shadows in the Beijing smog.

Banks of Tesla electric cars sit outside a dealership, tethered to charging points and radiating heat from their gloss black curves. In the air-conditioned, white-marbled concourse of the mall attached to it, the only thing disturbing the quiet is the echoing piped music. There is an inevitability to the brand names: Chanel, Dior, Gucci, Louis Vuitton, Burberry. The air carries on it the scent of perfume. There are few shoppers, but when a single Gucci handbag might set you back 30,000 Yuan, the bored clerks need only to clear a couple of sales each day.

If the mood takes after shopping here, you can move next door to enjoy a meal at Beijing's branch of the high-end Japanese restaurant Nobu, or take a room at the JW Marriott for another few thousand

Yuan a night. These air-conditioned, vacuum-sealed chambers of recreation and commerce are retreats from the life of the street, with its noise, heat and people. There are malls like this all over this part of Beijing, symbols of new money, of ambitious developers, of consumer desire in a section of town which was once fields, factories and small villages.

Today, not far beyond the mall, the path along Long Peace Street heads underground. You walk first through a grove of willows which runs alongside a polluted ditch, behind which rise promotional billboards of blue skies and synthetically green grass, screening the towers of an electricity plant: one of the last relics of this area's industrial past. 'Promote the coordinated development of Beijing, Tianjin and Hebei', reads one. Long Peace Street briefly becomes an overpass, and you head down into the shadows of a concrete pedestrian subway which runs for six or seven hundred metres.

Taxis park all along the side of the underpass, doors open and a lolling limb of afternoon nappers protruding here and there: some of Beijing's army of taxi drivers seeking refuge and respite from the city. Pools of stagnant water stand around from the last of the summer rainfall. On the level above, the fenced compound of a scooter workshop is crammed with bikes and discarded metal parts. A man kneels next to a rusting chassis, illuminating the grey concrete with flashes of blue-white from his acetylene welder.

Meanwhile, on the low walls and scrubby gravel to either side of the path lie the sleeping bodies of a few of Beijing's homeless population; generally unseen or ignored when above ground, they have found a quiet and dry shelter here below Long Peace Street. From above comes the drone of car tires. The air is heavy, hot and thick down here, a mix of diesel fumes and humidity. I quicken my pace.

There is not just one city.

21

G103 – the story of a nation – the end

I was approaching the end of Long Peace Street, or at least that section of it conducive to navigation on foot. Beyond Sihui East station, the road finally begins to free itself from its straightness, and turns into the motorway it has been longing to become for so much of its route through the centre of Beijing. It wavers east, and then turns south through the towns and fields of the North China Plain, more or less following the arc of the Grand Canal to Tianjin, where it eventually peters out in the confusion of roads around that city.

Emerging from the underpass to walk alongside the road once again, feeling the sweep of hot air and blinking in the hazy light, it seemed as though I was striding out into China more broadly. Out here, Long Peace Street had inevitably changed name once again, now becoming the unromantically titled G103, but it seemed I had merely looped back to the beginning of my walk, and was once more in amorphous suburbia: old apartment buildings, quiet pavements, long landscaped borders of shrubs and mown grass. From here, if I wished, I could have carried on by car to Tianjin amongst similar sprawl and the flat farm land of the North China Plain which showed Beijing to be the outlier, the exception, the privileged.

For of course Beijing is not China, just as London is not England, nor New York America. Its enormous population makes up just 1.6 per cent of China's total. Its sprawling municipal area makes up less than a quarter of a per cent of China's total land mass. Even a place as vast as Beijing is dwarfed by the scale of the nation which surrounds it.

Yet the story of Beijing tells much of that nation. 'There is scarcely a building of any age in this great city that cannot make its contribution towards the history of the country'[1], one guide to the city wrote in the 1930s; an observation still true today, despite the destruction. And what a history it was: whilst my route through it had been straightforward, the tale itself was anything but; filled rather with diversions, twists and turns, ups and downs, with subplots, what-ifs and might-have-beens. It was a story of invasion and conquest, and the ever-present fear of the same. It was the story of imperial power rendered into architectural majesty and bureaucratic control, the like of which the world had never seen. It was the story of the impositions of outside powers, and a slow unfastening of the ties that bound the nation together. It was the story of conflict and uncertainty and shifts of authority. It told of history dynamited and bulldozered away in the name of a bold socialist future. It was a story of the ebb and flow of protest and repression. It was a story, which like Long Peace Street, had brought me to the here and now.

And here, today, at the end of my short walk, what could I truly say with any certainty about this place? Modern Beijing is a mess, a glorious mess. Noisy, endlessly sprawling, confounding to navigate, and echoing with the muffled shouts of those who chafed against its impositions: physical, spiritual, political. Rather than hearing those voices, the city seemed instead to rouse itself now only for the promise of more change; change without considered thought, without anything but a call to action, a picking-up of hammers and pickaxes and drills, and *bang* another new building *bang* another new road *bang* another lost hutong *bang* another accreted layer of concrete and steel ringing around it.

But, as I watched the city around me, I thought about the people who had lived on this flat plain, all the way back to the first conurbation built on this land, *Ji*, which stood here about 1,000 years before Christ; all those tens of millions of people who, either by birth or by choice or by force, came to settle in this place and identify as part of it. It was they who had made the city; its story was their story. And today it seemed that these people, their history, their culture, somehow kept it still from spinning away from itself in this continuous revolution, away from some undefined and endearing centre which we define as: *what?* Character? Identity? Place?

Or perhaps that was merely the wishful thinking of a romantic outsider, and in fact, like Theseus's boat, Beijing today had been remade into something entirely new: a suitable capital for a country in which the past has become a police state. And maybe that did not matter: maybe this new capital of New China suited a new world. The more I considered the question, the less sure I was.

The long low building of the subway station ran alongside the street here, filled with the noise of the subway trains finally emerging from the sooty darkness of Line One, which I had traced all the way from the far west of the city to terminate at this station. It seemed as good a place as any to stop. At the foot of the stairs up to the station was a small restaurant and shop, the woman inside busy cleavering meat to fill the pork sandwiches, *rou jia mo*, which resemble a sort of Chinese hamburger. I bought a drink and sat on a wobbly stool outside, not quite ready for the long, dark subway ride back west.

Day two: Tiananmen to Sihui Dong subway station

Opposite me, a salt-and-pepper haired security guard wandered around at the foot of the steps up into the subway station, shirt untucked. He held a folding beach chair with a stuck mechanism: again and again he swung it against the floor in an attempt to free the rusted metal and open it. The noise echoing off the building, he finally managed to shift its hinge, and, setting it carefully to face the hazy sun now creeping towards the horizon of rooflines back to the west along Long Peace Street, placed his flask of tea on the ground next to him, reclined contentedly – and promptly went to sleep.

Epilogue

The dust rose in waves, great heavy clouds spilling off the open ground and obscuring everything: the road, the hills, the buildings. The spring wind had cleared Beijing of its pollution, but out here, back at the old Shougang factory nearly two years after my cross-town amble, it whipped up the dry soil and rained it down like a judgement. To the north and east, the land had been cleared, razed, all the way to the hills where the concrete outlines of old high-rise buildings came in and out of view as the dust thickened and then dissipated on the vacillations of the wind's mood. Studded across this blanked-out landscape, yellow cranes swayed in the brute power of the current running in from the west. Away in the distance still stood the hulking industrial buildings of the Shougang factory, diminished slightly in number, rusting and cracked, but stubbornly, defiantly there.

Back here at my starting point, and having the same conversation at the same checkpoint, now rendered more solidly in steel. 'It's residents only beyond here', the policeman told me, as if reading from a script. Behind him, maybe a mile down the broad road, what looked like a large white platform was being layered together by more cranes. Long Peace Street was being made even longer: this was the beginnings of a new bridge, he told me, which would help carry the road another four miles westward.

As with all that I had passed through, I had built this place in my mind in the months after my walk: orienting buildings; shifting fence-panel walls into place; judging the ochre tone of rusting furnaces. Coming back, I had expected to be confronted by unrecognisable modernity, to have my mental image razed and replaced. In this story of the new Beijing, that was what this revisiting had promised. But, beyond the bridge and the now-blank landscape to the east, little had really changed.

Adjacent to the barrier, two broad billboards illustrated the next new future for the old plant. Computer-generated figures milled around a plaza, whilst behind them, angular new architecture rose up, including a striped blue and purple tower of uncertain purpose. The billboard was emblazoned with a logo hovering above an image of the Olympic rings: Beijing 2022. The slogan read: 'Make the Beijing Winter Olympics a wonderful and extraordinary Olympic Games'. The plant's fate was now bound up with the new and unlikely sequel to Beijing's original Olympic story, in which the summer heat of 2008 is swapped for the dry cold of winter 2022. The billboard captured my expectations, but this was just a piece of laminated board rocking steadily in the dust-laden wind.

'There's another gate around the corner; they might let you in there', he shouted above the breeze as I gazed. I wandered away in the direction of his pointed finger, along the road running north from

Epilogue

Long Peace Street, into the dust storm. The pavement was empty, and even the road carried only the occasional city bus. High fence panels stood along either side of the carriageway. A little further up, a gate stood open; behind it ran ranks of construction workers' temporary housing. A dirty brown mongrel jogged cheerfully over to say hello; behind him followed one of the workers, more stern in demeanour. 'But there's nothing to see here', he said in response to my request to have a look around. Or rather, he said, 'There's nothing *good* to see here'.

They were in charge of the new apartment buildings being constructed across the street, and had little interest in what was happening to the old Shougang plant. This was where, two years earlier, low rows of shops, houses and workshops had run, where I had stopped for a bottle of water: the girl and her fellow inhabitants were long gone and I wondered whether they had left the city altogether, or simply moved on to another point on its periphery. The razed, empty land left behind from where their houses used to stand was the source of all this dust. 'The Olympic section is further out to the west', he said, pointing down the road again. 'They might let you in there.' I wrapped my scarf around my face and headed on down the long straight road once more.

Left at a junction and further down another empty pavement along a highway, and there it was: confirmation in brick and steel of Shougang's new life. Behind a metal accordion barrier, a handful of new industrial-chic office buildings stood, angular constructions of plate glass and rusted metal, with an official sign outside: 'Beijing Organising Committee for the 2022 Olympic and Paralympic Winter Games'. There was little else to show, but the overall plans for the site were ambitious, I read later: as well as the headquarters, Shougang's square miles were to host a snowboarding ramp, a village for Olympic athletes, training facilities and assorted new hotels and offices. The watchword of the project was 'sustainability' – a radical notion in a place where the blank landscape trailing a demolition crew was the preferred canvas of city planners. Rather than tearing down and rebuilding, what was already here was to be reused, as far as possible. The offices are repurposed iron ore silos; offices and worker housing will become athlete accommodation; the snowboard ramp is to hang from the rim of a cooling tower; towers and furnaces will be made structurally sound and left in place. Heritage will be highlighted, rather than destroyed.[1]

As I stood at the entrance, a blacked-out Audi swung into the drive and the security guard scrambled to open the gate. I tried to follow it in to sneak a look, but came up against the intransigence of the gateman once more. So I walked back along the highway, towards the nearest subway station, the western terminus of Line One, *Pingguoyuan*: 'Apple Orchard'. The bucolic rural scene conjured by its name is not matched by the place itself: a scrubby, pot-holed high street lined with blue monolithic hangars shielding the engineering works for the new subway line which will reach out here. The new scourge of the Beijing pavements, rental bikes, were piled in mounds alongside the metal fence next to the roadway. Diesel buses ran up and down the street, their gouts of exhaust adding to the clouded air.

As I joined the procession to enter the subway station, zig-zagging through the metal fences, I looked back across to the towers of the Shougang factory, standing proud before the saw-teeth of the Western Hills. As I turned to go in, the dust descended once more, and they faded like a mirage.

Sources and notes

Jonathan Spence's *The Search for Modern China* is rightly considered an indispensable resource for those looking to make sense of the country's recent past; it was a regular point of reference during the course of my writing. *China: A Cultural and Historical Dictionary*, edited by Michael Dillon, *The Cambridge Encyclopedia of China*, *The Oxford Illustrated History of Modern China*, and Endymion Wilkinson's exhaustive *Chinese History: A New Manual* were also kept close at hand to assist with general queries.

Introduction

1 Jie 街 is often also translated as 'avenue'.
2 At the historical moments when Beijing was replaced as the capital, it was renamed 'Beiping' or 'Northern Peace'.
3 Edgar Snow, *Red Star Over China* (London: Grove Press, 2018), 151. Mao was, however, impressed by the beauty of the city: 'In the parks and the old palace grounds I saw the early northern spring, I saw the white plum blossoms flower while the ice still held solid over the North Sea. I saw the willows over Pei Hai [Bei Hai] with the ice crystals hanging from them and remembered the description of the scene by the T'ang poet Chen Chang, who wrote about Pei Hai's winter-jeweled trees, looking "like ten thousand peach trees blossoming." The innumerable trees of Peking aroused my wonder and admiration'. Snow, *Red Star*, 152.
4 See Shuishan Yu, *Chang'an Avenue and the Modernization of Chinese Architecture* (Seattle: University of Washington Press, 2012) for more on this idea. Professor Yu's volume on the relationship between ideology and architecture on Chang'an Jie is comprehensive and fascinating.
5 M.A. Aldrich, *The Search for a Vanishing Beijing: A Guide to China's Capital Through the Ages* (Hong Kong: Hong Kong University Press, 2006), 70.

6   Quoted in Jasper Becker, *City of Heavenly Tranquillity: Beijing in the History of China* (Oxford: Oxford University Press, 2008), 39.

7   Alexander Michie, *The Siberian Overland Route from Peking to Petersburg* (London: John Murray, 1864), 32.

8   David Strand, *Rickshaw Beijing: City People and Politics in the 1920s* (Berkeley and Los Angeles: University of California Press, 1989), 21.

9   Ellen La Motte, *Peking Dust* (New York: The Century Co., 1919), 17.

10 Simone de Beauvoir, *The Long March: An Account of Modern China*, trans. Austryn Wainhouse (London: Phoenix Press, 2001), 15–16.

1

1   'Shougang Transforms Caofeidian', *China.org.cn*, July 2007, www.china.org.cn/english/China/216873.htm. Accessed 4 January 2019.

2   'Big Beijing Steel Maker Cuts Production to Help Reduce Pollution for Olympics', *New York Times*, 14 July 2008, www.nytimes.com/2008/07/14/business/worldbusiness/14iht-shougang.1.14477923.html. Accessed 4 January 2019.

3   Wang Jun, *Beijing Record: A Physical and Political History of Planning Modern Beijing* (Singapore: World Scientific Publishing Company, 2011), 85 & 88.

4   Wang Yi, *A Century of Change: Beijing's Urban Structure in the 20th Century* (Berlin: Springer, 2016), 34.

5   Frank Dikötter, *Mao's Great Famine: The History of China's Most Devastating Catastrophe, 1958–62* (London: Bloomsbury, 2010), 57.

6   Zhou Xun, *Forgotten Voices of Mao's Great Famine, 1958–1962: An Oral History* (New Haven: Yale University Press, 2013), 109.

7   Zhou, *Forgotten Voices*, 110.

8   Zhou, *Forgotten Voices*, 110–111.

9   Percy Cradock, 'Interview with Sir Percy Cradock', interview by Malcolm McBain, 1997, Churchill Archives Centre, British Diplomatic Oral History Programme, DOHP.

10 Zhou, *Forgotten Voices*, 114.

11 '首钢工人用镜头记录激情燃烧的钢铁年代', *People.com.cn*, September 11, 2011, http://history.people.com.cn/GB/198819/217098/16183095.html. Accessed 4 January 2019.

12 '首钢正式完成搬迁治理 有90年历史的'钢城'光荣退役', *China.com.cn*, 13 January 2011, www.china.com.cn/economic/txt/2011-01/13/content_21733279.htm. Accessed 4 January 2019.

13 Jonathan Watts, 'Beijing Goes for Green with Olympic Clean-Up', *The Guardian*, 19 July 2008, https://www.theguardian.com/environment/2008/jul/19/pollution.china. Accessed 4 January 2019.

14 David Stanway, Stian Reklev and Kathy Chen, 'Beijing Govt, Shougang to Set up Fund to Redevelop Old Steel Mill Site', *Thomson Reuters Foundation*,

Sources and notes

26 September 2014, http://news.trust.org/item/20140926090707-rlxg9/. Accessed 4 January 2019.

2

1 Lewis Mumford, *The City in History: Its Origins, Its Transformations, and Its Prospects* (New York: Penguin, 1961), 553.
2 Mumford, *The City in History*, 581.
3 Quoted in Rusty Monhollon, ed. *Baby Boom: People and Perspectives* (Santa Barbara: ABC-CLIO, 2010), 160.
4 World Bank, *East Asia's Changing Urban Landscape: Measuring a Decade of Spatial Growth* (Washington D.C.: World Bank, 2015), 53.
5 See the *IBM Global Commuter Pain Survey*, 2011 and 'Commuting Time in Capital Averages 97 Minutes', *China Daily*, 24 November 2014, www.chinadaily.com.cn/china/2014-11/24/content_18967891.htm. Accessed 4 January 2019. Beijing's local government responded to this report by promising to reduce the average length of commutes within the Fifth Ring Road, which orbits the city's periphery and cuts through the heart of Shijingshan, to sixty minutes by 2020.
6 '城市异化排行榜', *New Weekly*, 22 August 2013, www.neweekly.com.cn/article/103107. Accessed 4 January 2019.
7 Zhang Wumao, 'Beijing Has 20 Million People Pretending to Live Here', *Whatsonweibo.com, trans. Manya Koetse, July 26 2017, https://www.whatsonweibo.com/beijing-20-million-people-pretending-live-full-translation. Accessed 4 January 2019.*
8 Tom Miller, *China's Urban Billion: The Story behind the Biggest Migration in Human History* (London: Zed Books, 2012), Kindle edition, location 1655.
9 David Kidd, *Peking Story* (London: Eland, 1988), 37.
10 Wang, *Beijing Record*, 15.
11 'Beijing Park Underscores Piracy Battle, Analysts Say', *CNN*, 24 May 2007, https://web.archive.org/web/20070524234252/http://edition.cnn.com/2007/BUSINESS/05/10/china.copying.ap/. Accessed 4 January 2019.

4

For biographical detail, this chapter draws particularly on Jürgen Domes, *Peng Te-Huai: The Man and the Image.*
1 See Chang-Tai Hung, *Mao's New World: Political Culture in the Early People's Republic* (Ithaca: Cornell University Press, 2011), 224–232.
2 The ashes of the last Qing Emperor, Puyi, had also been interred at Babaoshan after his death in 1967; they were moved to a new cemetery near the Western Qing tombs in 1995, following a deal made with Puyi's widow.
3 Snow, *Red Star*, 265.
4 Domes, *Peng Te-Huai*, 44.

Sources and notes

5 Frederick C. Teiwes, 'Peng Dehuai and Mao Zedong', *The Australian Journal of Chinese Affairs*, no. 16 (1986): 81–98.

6 Jung Chang and Jon Halliday, *Mao: The Unknown Story* (London: Vintage, 2007), 144.

7 Alexander V. Pantsov and Steven I. Levine, *Mao: The Real Story* (New York: Simon and Schuster, 2012), Kindle edition, location 8899.

8 Christopher Howe and Kenneth R. Walker, eds. *The Foundations of the Chinese Planned Economy: A Documentary Survey, 1953–65* (London: Macmillan, 1989), 88.

9 Domes, *Peng Te-Huai*, 83.

10 Domes, *Peng Te-Huai*, 94.

11 Roderick MacFarquhar, ed. *The Politics of China: The Eras of Mao and Deng* (Cambridge: Cambridge University Press, 1997), 104–106.

12 Yan Jiaqi and Gao Gao, *Turbulent Decade: A History of the Cultural Revolution*, trans. D.W.Y. Kwok (Honolulu: University of Hawai'i Press, 1996), 214.

13 Jung Chang, *Wild Swans: Three Daughters of China* (London: HarperCollins, 2003), Kindle edition, location 7522.

14 Domes, *Peng Te-Huai*, 124.

15 Domes, *Peng Te-Huai*, 126.

16 Domes, *Peng Te-Huai*, 127.

5

1 See Yu, *Chang'an Avenue*, 13–34.

2 They also obstructed the free and safe flow of traffic. See Wang, *Beijing Record*, 241–242.

3 Peng Dehuai who, until that summer and the Lushan Conference, had been in charge of the armed forces and thus would have ordinarily overseen the parade, had been replaced by Lin Biao.

4 Yu, *Chang'an Avenue*, 23.

5 Jacques Marcuse, *The Peking Papers: Leaves from the Notebook of a China Correspondent* (London: Arthur Baker, 1967).

6 Alexander C. Cook, *The Cultural Revolution on Trial: Mao and the Gang of Four* (Cambridge: Cambridge University Press, 2016), 16.

6

1 This site is, according to sources on the Chinese internet, the People's Liberation Army Logistics Command College.

2 Kidd, *Peking Story*, 37.

3 Stephen G. Haw, *Beijing: A Concise History* (Abingdon: Routledge, 2007), 111.

4 Wang, *Beijing Record*, 114.

5 Yu, *Chang'an Avenue*, 81.

Sources and notes

7

1 In 2018, the North Korean leader Kim Jong-un would stay at Diaoyutai – the latest historic visitor to the guesthouse.
2 Henry Kissinger, *On China* (New York: Penguin, 2011), 255.
3 Ross Terrill, *The White-Boned Demon: A Biography of Madame Mao Zedong* (New York: William Morrow, 1984), 385.
4 Cook, *The Cultural Revolution on Trial*, 74.
5 Frank Dikötter, *The Cultural Revolution: A People's History, 1962–1976* (London: Bloomsbury, 2016), 56.
6 Dikötter, *The Cultural Revolution*, 74.
7 Kidd, *Peking Story*, 196. The crematorium was that at Babaoshan.
8 Geremie R. Barmé, 'Beijing's Bloody August', *Danwei*, www.danwei.org/Beijings%20Bloody%20August.pdf. Accessed 4 January 2019.
9 Terrill, *The White-Boned Demon*, 375.
10 Fox Butterfield, 'Revenge Seems to Outweigh Justice at Chinese Trial', *New York Times*, 5 December, 1980.

8

Stephen G. Haw's *Beijing: A Concise History* is, as its title suggests, a good, brief introduction to the city's development. Becker's *City of Heavenly Tranquillity*, Jaivin's *Beijing* and Aldrich's *The Search for a Vanishing Beijing* all delve more deeply into the history of the city.

1 The dawuding style never entirely disappeared however; a particularly startling modern example can be seen at the city's West Railway Station, which looks as though a tiered temple roof was one day simply craned on to the top of its bland modern towers.
2 John Man, *The Mongol Empire: Genghis Khan, His Heirs and the Founding of Modern China* (London: Corgi, 2015), 63.
3 Though Beijing's name translates as 'Northern Capital', the Khitans, another nomadic group from the north – demonstrating that geography is always relative – referred to the city as their 'Southern Capital', as it sat to the south of the lands they dominated.
4 Though the city would continue as co-capital of the nation for a number of years afterwards, until in 1441 Beijing became the undisputed capital.
5 Jonathan D. Spence, *The Gate of Heavenly Peace: The Chinese and Their Revolution, 1895–1980* (Harmondsworth: Penguin, 1982), 37.
6 Later the same figures would argue that perhaps Shanghai was the preferable choice.
7 Derk Bodde, *Peking Diary: A Year of Revolution* (New York: Henry Schuman, 1950), 9.

Sources and notes

9

For a broad understanding of the revolutionary history of modern China before the establishment of the People's Republic, James Sheridan's *China in Disintegration* is a lucid and readable account of the first half of the twentieth century. In addition to those other texts cited below, see Craig Calhoun, *Neither Gods nor Emperors: Students and the Struggle for Democracy in China*; Louisa Lim, *The People's Republic of Amnesia*; and the 1995 documentary film, *The Gate of Heavenly Peace*, which offers an excellent, visual introduction to the events of June 1989.

1 Quoted in Spence, *The Gate of Heavenly Peace*, 171–172.
2 For more on the complexities of this term, see: Tianjian Shi, *The Cultural Logic of Politics in Mainland China and Taiwan* (Cambridge: Cambridge University Press, 2015), 201; Joseph W. Esherick and Jeffrey N. Wasserstrom, 'Acting Out Democracy: Political Theater in Modern China', *The Journal of Asian Studies* 49, no. 4 (1990): 835–865, https://doi.org/10.2307/2058238.
3 From 'To a Certain Woman'. David S.G. Goodman, *Beijing Street Voices: The Poetry and Politics of China's Democracy Movement* (London: Marion Boyars, 1981), 32.
4 Goodman, *Beijing Street Voices*, 67. The Four Modernisations were originally formulated by Zhou Enlai, but had been openly adopted by Deng Xiaoping in 1978. The areas to be modernised were: agriculture, industry, science and technology, and defence.
5 Quoted in Spence, *The Gate of Heavenly Peace*, 409.
6 MacFarquhar, *The Politics of China*, 323.
7 Timothy Brook, *Quelling the People: The Military Suppression of the Beijing Democracy Movement* (California: Stanford University Press, 1998), 48.
8 Bodde, *Peking Diary*, 101.
9 John Pomfret, 'It's "Live Fire! Live Fire!" in Muxidi Battle', *Los Angeles Times*, 5 June 1989.
10 Orville Schell, *Mandate of Heaven: The Legacy of Tiananmen Square and the Next Generation of China's Leaders* (New York: Touchstone, 1995), 142.

10

Invaluable guides to the history of Beijing's walls can be found in: Madeleine Yue Dong's *Republican Beijing: The City and its Histories*; Wang Jun's *Beijing Record*; and Susan Naquin's *Peking Temples and City Life, 1400–1900*, as well as Osvald Sirén's detailed account referenced below.

1 The main island had been in British hands since 1842, after the First Opium War; in 1898, the Chinese signed a deal leasing the rest of the surrounding lands to Britain.
2 Osvald Sirén, *The Walls and Gates of Peking* (London: The Bodley Head, 1924), 1.
3 La Motte, *Peking Dust*, 15.

Sources and notes

4   La Motte, *Peking Dust*, 16.
5   Long before, the city had been known as Chang'an, and was the capital city of more than ten imperial dynasties. During the rule of the Tang, one of China's most revered dynasties, it had been ringed by an even longer wall than that which stands today.
6   Kidd, *Peking Story*, 191.
7   'Xinhua Insight: What Does China-Style Democracy Matter to Its People?', *Xinhua*, 10 March 2017, http://news.xinhuanet.com/english/2017-03/10/c_136118749.htm. Accessed 5 January 2019.

11

1   De Beauvoir, *The Long March*, 14.
2   Yu, *Chang'an Avenue*, 266.
3   David Kestembaum and Jacob Goldstein, 'The Secret Document That Transformed China', *NPR*, 20 January 2012, https://www.npr.org/sections/money/2012/01/20/145360447/the-secret-document-that-transformed-china. Accessed 4 January 2019.
4   SASAC was established in 2003. In Chinese the name is even more exhausting, at fourteen characters long: in Pinyin, it is the Guówùyuàn Guóyǒu Zīchǎn Jiāndū Guǎnlǐ Wěiyuánhuì.
5   For a cogent account of China's modern economy, see Arthur Kroeber, *China's Economy: What Everyone Needs to Know* (Oxford: Oxford University Press, 2016).
6   Mary Hooker, *Behind the Scenes in Peking* (London: John Murray, 1911), 91.

12

1   Revolutionary leader Sun Yat-sen had briefly held the post before Yuan.
2   Reginald Fleming Johnston, *Twilight in the Forbidden City* (Vancouver: Soul Care Publishing, 2009), Kindle edition, location 3224.
3   Feng Youlan, *The Hall of Three Pines: An Account of My Life* (Honolulu: University of Hawai'i Press, 2000), 47.
4   Lao She, *Camel Xiangzi*, trans. Shi Xiaojing (Hong Kong: Chinese University Press, 2004), 250.
5   Lao She, *Camel Xiangzi*, 448.
6   Sima Qian, *Records of the Grand Historian*, trans. Burton Watson (New York: Columbia University Press, 1993), 65.
7   Snow, *Red Star*, 92–93.
8   Chang and Halliday, *Mao: The Unknown Story*, 406–407.
9   Li Zhisui, *The Private Life of Chairman Mao: The Inside Story of the Man Who Made Modern China* (London: Chatto & Windus, 1994), 94.
10 See the first chapter of Li Zhisui, *The Private Life of Chairman Mao*.

Sources and notes

13

On the history of Tiananmen Square, see Chang-Tai Hung's *Mao's New World: Political Culture in the Early People's Republic*; Wu Hung's *Remaking Beijing: Tiananmen Square and the Creation of a Political Space*; Wang Jun's *Beijing Record* and Shuishan Yu's *Chang'an Avenue*.

1 Marcuse, *The Peking Papers*, 21.
2 Yu, *Chang'an Avenue*, 84.
3 Ian Johnson, 'At China's New Museum, History Toes Party Line', *New York Times*, 3 April 2011, www.nytimes.com/2011/04/04/world/asia/04museum. html?pagewanted=all. Accessed 4 January 2019.
4 Hung, *Mao's New World*, 122.
5 'Communists: The Body Snatchers', *Time*, 11 October 1961.

14

On the Boxers, *History in Three Keys: The Boxers as Event, Experience, and Myth* by Paul Cohen offers a helpful overview of the rebellion and its influence.

1 The Alliance was made up of soldiers from the United States, Great Britain, Germany, France, Austro-Hungary, Italy, Russia and Japan. A good proportion of the British troops were in fact from India.
2 Arnold Henry Savage Landor, *China and the Allies*, vol. 2 (London: Heinemann, 1901), 379.
3 Mrs Archibald Little, *Round About My Peking Garden* (London: T. Fisher Unwin, 1905), 15.

15

For more on the palace's history, see Geremie R. Barmé's *The Forbidden City* and Frances Wood's *Forbidden City*.

1 'The Court Back in Peking', *New York Times*, 8 January 1902.
2 'The Court's Return', *The Times*, 7 January 1902.
3 Sarah Pike Conger, *Letters from China* (Chicago: A.C. McClurg & Co., 1909), 220.
4 *The Times*, 5 November 1925.
5 Aisin-Gioro Pu Yi, *From Emperor to Citizen: The Autobiography of Aisin-Gioro Pu Yi*, trans. W.J.F. Jenner (Oxford: Oxford University Press, 1987), 38.
6 Johnston, *Twilight in the Forbidden City*, 382.
7 Aisin-Gioro, *From Emperor to Citizen*, 148.
8 Johnston, *Twilight in the Forbidden City*, 384.
9 Aisin-Gioro, *From Emperor to Citizen*, 148.
10 Aisin-Gioro, *From Emperor to Citizen*, 167. Though his wish would not be fulfilled, he did become puppet emperor of the Japanese-controlled state of

Sources and notes

Manchukuo in China's north-east between 1934 and 1945. Arrested by the Russians at the end of the war, he was subsequently returned to China and kept in a prison camp in Liaoning province. When eventually pardoned by Mao in 1959, he returned to Beijing. Soon after his arrival, he took a tour of his former palace residence. In *From Emperor to Citizen*, which was shaped by its ghostwriter to demonstrate that Puyi had been successfully reformed by the CCP, he observes that, in this new Communist era, it seemed the sun was shining on the Forbidden City more brightly than it ever had before.

11 Aisin-Gioro, *From Emperor to Citizen*, 77.
12 Dikötter, *The Cultural Revolution*, 74.
13 Barmé, 'Beijing's Bloody August'.
14 'The Intelligence, Blood and Sweat of the Labouring Masses: The Palace Museum in the Cultural Revolution', *China Heritage Quarterly*, December 2005, www.chinaheritagequarterly.org/. Accessed 4 January 2019.
15 See Barmé, *The Forbidden City*, 18–22.
16 Little, *Round About My Peking Garden*, 16.
17 The capital was then returned back to Beijing by the Yongle Emperor, who centred his city around a new palace: the Forbidden City.

16

Those wishing to learn more of the history of the Legation Quarter will find particularly illuminating: Julia Boyd's *A Dance with the Dragon: The Vanished World of Peking's Foreign Colony*, and *Foreigners Within the Gates: The Legations at Peking* by Michael J. Moser and Yeone Wei-Chih Moser. Paul French's *Midnight in Peking* also offers a vivid portrait of the Legation Quarter in the 1930s. Robert Bickers has written extensively on Western involvement in China: see *The Scramble for China: Foreign Devils in the Qing Empire, 1832–1914* and *Out of China: How the Chinese Ended the Era of Western Domination*.

1 Little, *Round About My Peking Garden*, 46.
2 Robert McGhee, *How We Got to Pekin: A Narrative of the Campaign in China of 1860* (London: Richard Bentley, 1862), 287.
3 The Treaty of Tientsin and the Convention of Peking.
4 Snow, *Red Star*, 40.
5 D.I. Abrikosov, *Revelations of a Russian Diplomat* (Seattle: University of Washington Press, 1964), 163.
6 Peking Dust is also the name given to a dessert of ground chestnuts with whipped cream.
7 Little, *Round About My Peking Garden*, 34.
8 Bertram Lenox Putnam Weale, *Indiscreet Letters From Peking* (Shanghai: Kelly and Walsh, 1922), 31.
9 Ann Bridge, *Four-Part Setting* (London: Bloomsbury, 2014), Kindle edition, location 107.

Sources and notes

10 Conger, *Letters from China*, 68.

11 Landor, *China and the Allies*, vol. 1, 61–62.

12 George Kates, *The Years That Were Fat: Peking 1933–1940* (New York: Harper & Brothers, 1952), 12–13.

13 E.J. Hardy, *John Chinaman at Home* (New York: Charles Scribner's Sons, 1905), 9.

14 Ann Bridge, *Peking Picnic* (London: Capuchin Classics, 2010), 58.

15 Kates, *The Years That Were Fat*, 258.

16 The vacated legation buildings would handed over to allies like East Germany, Hungary and Burma, or converted for government use.

17

For more on Morrison, see his collected two-volume correspondence, Lo Hui-Min, ed. *The Correspondence of G.E. Morrison*; Cyril Pearl's *Morrison of Peking*; and Lien-Teh Wu's 'Reminiscences of George E. Morrison; and Chinese Abroad'.

1 'Dr G.E. Morrison', *The Times*, 17 July 1900.

2 Quoted in Cyril Pearl, *Morrison of Peking* (Sydney: Angus & Robertson, 1967), 272.

3 Claire Roberts, 'George E. Morrison's Studio and Library', *China Heritage Quarterly*, March 2008, www.chinaheritagequarterly.org/features.php?searchterm=013_morrison.inc&issue=013. Accessed 4 January 2019.

4 Quoted in Pearl, *Morrison of Peking*, 30.

5 George Ernest Morrison, *An Australian in China: Being the Narrative of a Quiet Journey across China to Burma* (London: Horace Cox, 1902), 1.

6 Lo Hui-Min, ed. *The Correspondence of G.E. Morrison 1895–1912, Volume One* (Cambridge: Cambridge University Press, 2013), 708.

7 Quoted in Pearl, *Morrison of Peking*, 325.

8 Lo Hui-Min, ed. *The Correspondence of G.E. Morrison 1912–1920, Volume Two*, 964.

18

For a detailed explanation of the origins of the imperial calendrical systems, see Christopher Cullen's *Heavenly Numbers: Astronomy and Authority in Early Imperial China*. For more on the Republican calendar, beyond the details offered by more general histories, David Strand's *An Unfinished Republic: Leading by Word and Deed in Modern China* is helpful. Juliet Bredon and Igor Mitrophanow's *The Moon Year* is a remarkable and detailed record of the traditions of the lunar calendar. Ian Johnson's *The Souls of China: The Return of Religion After Mao* offers fascinating insight into the recent return to older ways of thinking in China.

1 Henry David Thoreau, *Excursions* (Boston: Hougton, Mifflin and Company, 1863), 172.

Sources and notes

2 Charles Baudelaire, *The Painter of Modern Life* (London: Penguin, 2010), 9.
3 A.B. Freeman-Mitford, *The Attaché at Peking* (London: Macmillan, 1900), xxviii.
4 Conger, *Letters from China*, 172–173.
5 Quoted in Michaela Fontana, *Matteo Ricci: A Jesuit in the Ming Court* (Lanham: Rowman and Littlefield, 2011), 238.
6 In the 1930s, they would be removed again and taken for safe keeping to Nanjing.
7 Juliet Bredon, *Peking: A Historical and Intimate Description of Its Chief Places of Interest* (Shanghai: Kelly and Walsh, 1920), 35.

19

In researching the Grand Canal, *China's Imperial Way* by Kevin Bishop was a helpful guide. For those interested in the stories of the British embassies in China, see also: J.E. Hoare, *Embassies in the East: The Story of the British and Their Embassies in China, Japan and Korea from 1859 to the Present*, and M.D. Kandiah, ed. *Witness Seminar: The Role and Functions of the British Embassy in Beijing*.
1 Susan Naquin, *Peking Temples and City Life, 1400–1900* (Berkeley and Los Angeles: University of California Press, 2000), 432 and Nicholas Dennys, *Notes for Tourists in the North of China* (Hong Kong: A. Shortrede & Co., 1866), 18.
2 D.F. Rennie, *Peking and the Pekingese: During the First Year of the British Embassy at Peking* (London: John Murray, 1865), 22–23.
3 Percy Cradock, *Experiences of China* (London: John Murray, 1999), 22.
4 3 April 1963.
5 Interestingly, and testifying to the fickleness of memory, some accounts assert that the diplomats watched a different film, also starring Peter Sellers as a criminal: *Two Way Stretch*.
6 Percy Cradock, 'Interview with Sir Percy Cradock', interview by Malcolm McBain.
7 Juliet Bredon and Igor Mitrophanow, *The Moon Year: A Record of Chinese Customs and Festivals* (Shanghai: Kelly and Walsh, 1927), 65.
8 It had been painted since the photos I had searched out before I visited had been taken, having previously been a dull pink. One of the images showed the pavements outside the embassy covered in debris, evidence of a later tumult on these streets, when in 1999 protestors gathered outside the nearby American Embassy to demonstrate against the NATO bombing of the Chinese Embassy in Belgrade; an accident, but one which was treated as a hostile act by the powers in Beijing. The US ambassador was confined to the embassy, and in the southern city of Chengdu the residence of the US consul was set alight.

Sources and notes

9 Jean Vincent, 'Red Guard Attack as Ultimatum Expires', *The Times*, 23 August 1967.

20

1 Yu, *Chang'an Avenue*, 17.

21

1 L.C. Arlington and William Lewisohn. *In Search of Old Peking* (Peking: Henri Vetch, 1935), 1.

Epilogue

1 'Beijing's former industrial complex Shougang district sees sustainable urban regeneration push', *Olympic.org*, 20 August 2018, https://www.olympic.org/news/beijing-s-former-industrial-complex-shougang-district-sees-sustainable-urban-regeneration-push. Accessed 4 January 2019.

Select bibliography

Abrikosov, D.I. *Revelations of a Russian Diplomat*. Seattle: University of Washington Press, 1964.

Aisin-Gioro Pu Yi. *From Emperor to Citizen: The Autobiography of Aisin-Gioro Pu Yi*. Translated by W.J.F. Jenner. Oxford: Oxford University Press, 1987.

Aldrich, M.A. *The Search for a Vanishing Beijing: A Guide to China's Capital Through the Ages*. Hong Kong: Hong Kong University Press, 2006.

Arlington, L.C. and William Lewisohn. *In Search of Old Peking*. Peking: Henri Vetch, 1935.

Barmé, Geremie R. *The Forbidden City*. London: Profile, 2008.

Baudelaire, Charles. *The Painter of Modern Life*. London: Penguin, 2010.

Beauvoir, Simone de. *The Long March: An Account of Modern China*. Translated by Austryn Wainhouse. London: Phoenix Press, 2001.

Becker, Jasper. *City of Heavenly Tranquillity: Beijing in the History of China*. Oxford: Oxford University Press, 2008.

Bickers, Robert. *Out of China: How the Chinese Ended the Era of Western Domination*. London: Penguin, 2017.

———. *The Scramble for China: Foreign Devils in the Qing Empire, 1832–1914*. London: Penguin, 2012.

Bishop, Kevin. *China's Imperial Way*. Hong Kong: Odyssey, 1997.

Bodde, Derk. *Peking Diary: A Year of Revolution*. New York: Henry Schuman, 1950.

Boyd, Julia. *A Dance with the Dragon: The Vanished World of Peking's Foreign Colony*. London: I.B. Tauris & Co. Ltd, 2012.

Bredon, Juliet. *Peking: A Historical and Intimate Description of Its Chief Places of Interest*. Shanghai: Kelly and Walsh, 1922.

Bredon, Juliet and Igor Mitrophanow. *The Moon Year: A Record of Chinese Customs and Festivals*. Shanghai: Kelly and Walsh, 1927.

Bridge, Ann. *Four-Part Setting*. London: Bloomsbury, 2014.

———. *Peking Picnic*. London: Capuchin Classics, 2010.

Select bibliography

Brook, Timothy. *Quelling the People: The Military Suppression of the Beijing Democracy Movement*. California: Stanford University Press, 1998.

Broudehoux, Anne-Marie. *The Making and Selling of Post-Mao Beijing*. New York: Routledge, 2004.

Calhoun, Craig. *Neither Gods nor Emperors: Students and the Struggle for Democracy in China*. Berkeley and Los Angeles: University of California Press, 1997.

Campanella, Thomas J. *The Concrete Dragon: China's Urban Revolution and What It Means for the World*. New York: Princeton Architectural Press, 2008.

Chang, Jung and Jon Halliday. *Mao: The Unknown Story*. London: Vintage, 2007.

Chang, Jung. *Wild Swans: Three Daughters of China*. London: HarperCollins, 2003.

Cohen, Paul. *History in Three Keys: The Boxers as Event, Experience, and Myth*. New York: Columbia University Press, 1997.

Conger, Sarah Pike. *Letters from China*. Chicago: A.C. McClurg & Co., 1909.

Cook, Alexander C. *The Cultural Revolution on Trial: Mao and the Gang of Four*. Cambridge: Cambridge University Press, 2016.

Cradock, Percy. *Experiences of China*. London: John Murray, 1999.

————. 'Interview with Sir Percy Cradock'. Interview by Malcolm McBain. Churchill Archives Centre, British Diplomatic Oral History Programme, DOHP, 1997.

Cullen, Christopher. *Heavenly Numbers: Astronomy and Authority in Early Imperial China*. Oxford: Oxford University Press, 2017.

Dennys, Nicholas. *Notes for Tourists in the North of China*. Hong Kong: A. Shortrede & Co., 1866.

Dikötter, Frank. *Mao's Great Famine: The History of China's Most Devastating Catastrophe, 1958–62*. London: Bloomsbury, 2010.

————. *The Cultural Revolution: A People's History, 1962–1976*. London: Bloomsbury, 2016.

————. *The Tragedy of Liberation: A History of the Chinese Revolution 1945–1957*. London: Bloomsbury, 2013.

Dillon, Michael, ed. *China: A Cultural and Historical Dictionary*. Routledge: Abingdon, 2013.

Domes, Jürgen. *Peng Te-Huai: The Man and the Image*. London: C. Hurst & Co., 1985.

Feng Youlan. *The Hall of Three Pines: An Account of My Life*. Honolulu: University of Hawai'i Press, 2000.

Fontana, Michaela. *Matteo Ricci: A Jesuit in the Ming Court*. Lanham: Rowman and Littlefield, 2011.

Freeman-Mitford, A.B. *The Attaché at Peking*. London: Macmillan, 1900.

French, Paul. *Midnight in Peking: How the Murder of a Young Englishwoman Haunted the Last Days of Old China*. London: Penguin, 2011.

Goodman, David S.G. *Beijing Street Voices: The Poetry and Politics of China's Democracy Movement*. London: Marion Boyars, 1981.

Select bibliography

Grey, Anthony. *Hostage in Peking*. London: George Weidenfeld & Nicolson Ltd, 1988.

Hardy, E.J. *John Chinaman at Home*. New York: Charles Scribner's Sons, 1905.

Haw, Stephen G. *Beijing: A Concise History*. Abingdon: Routledge, 2007.

Hoare, J.E. *Embassies in the East: The Story of the British and Their Embassies in China, Japan and Korea from 1859 to the Present*. Abingdon: Routledge, 2014.

Hook, Brian ed. consultant editor, Denis Twitchett. *The Cambridge Encyclopedia of China*. Cambridge: Cambridge University Press, 1991.

Hooker, Mary. *Behind the Scenes in Peking*. London: John Murray, 1911.

Howe, Christopher and Kenneth R. Walker, eds. *The Foundations of the Chinese Planned Economy: A Documentary Survey, 1953–65*. London: Macmillan, 1989.

Hung, Chang-Tai. *Mao's New World: Political Culture in the Early People's Republic*. Ithaca: Cornell University Press, 2011.

Jaivin, Linda. *Beijing*. London: Reaktion Books, 2014.

Johnson, Ian. *The Souls of China: The Return of Religion After Mao*. New York: Pantheon Books, 2017.

Johnston, Reginald Fleming. *Twilight in the Forbidden City*. Vancouver: Soul Care Publishing, 2009.

Kandiah, M.D., ed. *Witness Seminar: The Role and Functions of the British Embassy in Beijing*. Foreign and Commonwealth Office, 2012.

Kates, George. *The Years That Were Fat: Peking 1933–1940*. New York: Harper & Brothers, 1952.

Kidd, David. *Peking Story*. London: Eland, 1988.

Kissinger, Henry. *On China*. New York: Penguin, 2011.

Kroeber, Arthur. *China's Economy: What Everyone Needs to Know*. Oxford: Oxford University Press, 2016.

La Motte, Ellen. *Peking Dust*. New York: The Century Co., 1919.

Landor, Arnold Henry Savage. *China and the Allies*. 2 vols. London: Heinemann, 1901.

Lao She. *Camel Xiangzi*. Translated by Shi Xiaojing. Hong Kong: Chinese University Press, 2004.

Li Zhensheng. *Red-Color News Soldier: A Chinese Photographer's Odyssey Through the Cultural Revolution*. London: Phaidon, 2003.

Li Zhisui. *The Private Life of Chairman Mao: The Inside Story of the Man Who Made Modern China*. London: Chatto & Windus, 1994.

Lim, Louisa. *The People's Republic of Amnesia*. Oxford: Oxford University Press, 2014.

Little, Mrs Archibald. *Round About My Peking Garden*. London: T. Fisher Unwin, 1905.

Lo Hui-Min, ed. *The Correspondence of G.E. Morrison 1895–1912*. Volume One. Cambridge: Cambridge University Press, 2013.

———, ed. *The Correspondence of G.E. Morrison 1912–1920*. Volume Two. Cambridge: Cambridge University Press, 2013.

237

Select bibliography

MacFarquhar, Roderick. *The Politics of China: The Eras of Mao and Deng.* Cambridge: Cambridge University Press, 1997.

Man, John. *The Mongol Empire: Genghis Khan, His Heirs and the Founding of Modern China.* London: Corgi, 2015.

Marcuse, Jacques. *The Peking Papers: Leaves from the Notebook of a China Correspondent.* London: Arthur Baker, 1967.

McGhee, Robert. *How We Got to Pekin: A Narrative of the Campaign in China of 1860.* London: Richard Bentley, 1862.

Meyer, Michael. *The Last Days of Old Beijing: Life in the Vanishing Backstreets of a City Transformed.* New York: Walker and Company, 2008.

Michie, Alexander. *The Siberian Overland Route from Peking to Petersburg.* John Murray, 1864.

Miller, Tom. *China's Urban Billion: The Story Behind the Biggest Migration in Human History.* London: Zed Books, 2012.

Monhollon, Rusty, ed. *Baby Boom: People and Perspectives (Perspectives in American Social History).* Santa Barbara: ABC-CLIO, 2010.

Morrison, George Ernest. *An Australian in China: Being the Narrative of a Quiet Journey across China to Burma.* London: Horace Cox, 1902.

Moser, Michael and Yeone Wei-Chih, *Foreigners Within the Gates: The Legations at Peking.* Chicago: Serindia Publications, Inc., 2006.

Mumford, Lewis. *The City in History: Its Origins, Its Transformations, and Its Prospects.* New York: Penguin, 1961.

Naquin, Susan. *Peking Temples and City Life, 1400–1900.* Berkeley and Los Angeles: University of California Press, 2000.

Pantsov, Alexander V. and Steven I. Levine. *Mao: The Real Story.* New York: Simon and Schuster, 2012.

Pearl, Cyril. *Morrison of Peking.* Sydney: Angus & Robertson, 1967.

Poon, Shuk-wah. *Negotiating Religion in Modern China: State and Common People in Guangzhou, 1900–1937.* Hong Kong: Chinese University Press, 2011.

Putnam Weale, Bertram Lenox. *Indiscreet Letters From Peking: Being the Notes of an Eye-Witness, Which Set Forth in Some Detail, from Day to Day, the Real Story of the Siege and Sack of a Distressed Capital in 1900 – The Year of Great Tribulation.* Shanghai: Kelly and Walsh, 1922.

Quick Access to the People's Republic of China – The First Sixty Years (1949-2009). Beijing: Foreign Languages Press, 2010.

Rennie, D.F. *Peking and the Pekingese: During the First Year of the British Embassy at Peking.* London: John Murray, 1865.

Schell, Orville. *Mandate of Heaven: The Legacy of Tiananmen Square and the Next Generation of China's Leaders.* New York: Touchstone, 1995.

Schmitz, Rob. *Street of Eternal Happiness: Big City Dreams Along a Shanghai Road.* London: John Murray, 2016.

Sheridan, James E. *China in Disintegration: The Republican Era in Chinese History, 1912–1949.* New York: The Free Press, 1975.

Select bibliography

Shi, Tianjian. *The Cultural Logic of Politics in Mainland China and Taiwan*. Cambridge: Cambridge University Press, 2015.

Sima Qian. *Records of the Grand Historian*. Translated by Burton Watson. New York: Columbia University Press, 1993.

Sirén, Osvald. *The Walls and Gates of Peking*. London: The Bodley Head, 1924.

Snow, Edgar. *Red Star Over China*. London: Grove Press, 2018.

Spence, Jonathan D. *The Gate of Heavenly Peace: The Chinese and Their Revolution, 1895–1980*. Harmondsworth: Penguin, 1982.

Spence, Jonathan D. *The Search for Modern China*. New York: W.W. Norton & Company, 1990.

Strand, David. *An Unfinished Republic: Leading by Word and Deed in Modern China*. Berkeley and Los Angeles: University of California Press, 2011.

———. *Rickshaw Beijing: City People and Politics in the 1920s*. Berkeley and Los Angeles: University of California Press, 1989.

Terrill, Ross. *The White-Boned Demon: A Biography of Madame Mao Zedong*. New York: William Morrow, 1984.

Thoreau, Henry David. *Excursions*. Boston: Hougton, Mifflin and Company, 1863.

Wang Jun. *Beijing Record: A Physical and Political History of Planning Modern Beijing*. Singapore: World Scientific Publishing Company, 2011.

Wang Yi. *A Century of Change: Beijing's Urban Structure in the 20th Century*. Berlin: Springer, 2016.

Wasserstrom, Jeffrey N. ed. *The Oxford Illustrated History of Modern China*. Oxford: Oxford University Press, 2016.

Wilkinson, Endymion. *Chinese History: A New Manual*. Cambridge, Massachusetts: Harvard University Asia Center, for the Harvard-Yenching Institute, 2018.

Wood, Frances. *Forbidden City*. London: The British Museum Press, 2005.

Wu Hung. *Remaking Beijing: Tiananmen Square and the Creation of a Political Space*. Chicago: University of Chicago Press, 2005.

Wu Lien-Teh, 'Reminiscences of George E. Morrison; and Chinese Abroad', George Ernest Morrison lecture in ethnology; no. 5. Canberra: Australian Institute of Anatomy, 1935.

Yan Jiaqi, and Gao Gao. *Turbulent Decade: A History of the Cultural Revolution*. Translated by D.W.Y. Kwok. Honolulu: University of Hawai'i Press, 1996.

Yu, Shuishan. *Chang'an Avenue and the Modernization of Chinese Architecture*. Seattle: University of Washington Press, 2012.

Yue Dong, Madeleine. *Republican Beijing : The City and Its Histories*. Berkeley and Los Angeles: University of California Press, 2003.

Zhou Xun. *Forgotten Voices of Mao's Great Famine, 1958–1962: An Oral History*. New Haven: Yale University Press, 2013.

Index

Index

Index

CPSIA information can be obtained
at www.ICGtesting.com
Printed in the USA
JSHW010322240421
13915JS00024B/25

9 781526 151735